THE FREEDOM
OF
MORALITY

CONTEMPORARY GREEK THEOLOGIANS

NUMBER THREE

CHRISTOS YANNARAS

THE FREEDOM
OF
MORALITY

translated from the Greek
by
ELIZABETH BRIERE

with a foreword
by
BISHOP KALLISTOS OF DIOKLEIA

ST. VLADIMIR'S SEMINARY PRESS
CRESTWOOD, NEW YORK 10707
1984

Library of Congress Cataloging in Publication Data

Giannaras, Chrestos, 1935-
　The freedom of morality.

　Includes bibliographical references and index.
　1. Christian ethics—Orthodox Eastern authors.
2. Freedom (Theology). 3. Orthodox Eastern Church—
Doctrines I. Title.
BJ1250.G53 1984　　　241'.0419　　　84-9030
ISBN 0-88141-028-4

THE FREEDOM OF MORALITY

© Copyright 1984

by

ST. VLADIMIR'S SEMINARY PRESS

ISBN 0-88141-028-4

PRINTED IN THE UNITED STATES OF AMERICA
BY
ATHENS PRINTING COMPANY
New York, NY 10018

When you enter upon the path of righteousness, then you will cleave to freedom in everything.

St Isaac the Syrian

Virtue exists for truth; but truth does not exist for virtue.

St Maximus the Confessor

Contents

Foreword

"The most tremendous thing granted to humanity is choice, freedom": so writes Kierkegaard in his *Journal,* and such also is the central conviction that inspires this present book. Its theme is "the glorious liberty of the children of God" (Rom. 8:21)—a liberty only to be attained through asceticism. Christos Yannaras has not attempted to write a systematic treatise on ethics, for he believes that it is impossible, within a genuinely Orthodox context, to provide a "system" of moral conduct. What he offers us is something different: an inquiry into the criteria and presuppositions which enable us to confront moral problems. And the most basic criterion of all, in his eyes, is freedom. He is passionately opposed to any understanding of Christian morality that views it primarily in juridical terms, as submission to a conventional legal code. Morality, as he sees it, is concerned not with rules but with persons—with persons in their freedom, persons in their mutual relationship. At its first publication in Greece in 1970, this book had a startling and even explosive impact. It is, however, a book whose significance extends far beyond Greece, a book that speaks to all of us in the West, whether Orthodox or not.

Widely regarded as the most creative prophetic religious thinker at work in Greece today, Christos Yannaras is a lay theologian, married and with two children. Born in Athens in 1935, he undertook university studies both in Greece and abroad in Bonn and Paris. He holds doctorates from the Theological School in Thessalonike and from the *Faculté des Lettres* at the Sorbonne. He has taught at the University of Geneva, and is at present Professor of Philosophy at the

9

Panteios Institute, Athens. Unusually productive as an author, he has written some twenty books as well as countless articles, many of them contributed to leading Athenian newspapers such as *To Vima*. While several of his books have already appeared in French, German and Italian, this is the first to be published in an English translation. *The Freedom of Morality* was initially composed in French, as an Orthodox contribution to the collective volume *La loi de la liberté: Evangile et Morale* (Paris 1972). A fuller version was published in Greek at Athens in 1970, and in the second Greek edition (Athens 1979) the text was largely rewritten and greatly expanded. It is from this last that the present translation has been made.

Dr Yannaras is both theologian and philosopher, and he sees no sharp dichotomy or conflict between the two roles. His work is marked also by a sensitivity, all too rare among theologians, towards literature and art. It is his aim to build bridges. In a world whose outlook has been shaped by Marx, Freud and the "Death of God," he seeks to relate the Orthodox Patristic tradition to contemporary issues. In particular he discerns vital points of contact between the apophatic approach of the Fathers—as found, for example, in the Areopagitic writings or St Maximus the Confessor—and modern existentialist philosophy, as propounded more especially by the later Heidegger. To form a bridge between these two worlds is a demanding task, and renders his argument sometimes hard to follow for those unfamiliar with the terminology of existentialism. But any reader of the present work, daunted by the opening pages, may be reassured: the first chapter is the most difficult, and the author's viewpoint grows more and more perspicuous as the book proceeds.

What Patristic theology and existentialism share in common, so Dr Yannaras believes, is a concern above all for the *person*. In any act of human understanding, the true starting-point is not abstract essence but that which is personal and specific; being or nature is apprehended in and through the person. This theme is worked out fully in the most ambitious of his works, *To Prosopo kai o Eros* (*Person and Love:* Athens 1976).

Personhood in its turn implies *relationship.* For Dr Yannaras it is no coincidence that the Greek word for person, *prosopon,* should have the literal meaning "face": each of us is authentically a person only in so far as he or she "faces" others and relates to them in love. Thus one of his key terms is *koinonia,* which in Greek signifies equally "communion" and "society" (this double sense should be kept in mind particularly in Chapter Eleven).

Personhood also means *unity,* an integral unity of soul and body; the "image of God" involves the whole human being. The body is to be seen, not merely as a "component" of the person, but as the total person's "mode" of existence, the manifestation to the outside world of the energies of our human nature in its completeness. This sense of the body's unity with the soul enables Dr Yannaras to perceive a deeper theological meaning in church canons—often dismissed today as outdated and superstitious—concerning the body and its functions (see Chapter Ten). While insisting upon asceticism, he sees it as a struggle not against but *for* the body. Always he envisages the transfiguration of *eros* and the passions and their redirection towards the Divine, not their suppression or destruction. And, because he values the materiality of the body, he is also concerned about the Spirit-bearing potentialities of *all* material things—about the use of matter in the Eucharist, in art and in technology.

In the book's title, *The Freedom of Morality,* the Greek word translated as "morality" is *ithos,* a term signifying "ethics," but also meaning "ethos," distinctive character, the "thusness" or the "Ah!" of a person or thing. When using *ithos,* the author has in view both these senses. Morality, "ethics," is nothing more or less than the expression of the person's proper "ethos." It is not to obey external rules but to become as person that which one truly is. By the same token, sin is not the transgression of some impersonal law, "but missing the mark," the failure to become oneself. As Dr Yannaras says at the start of Chapter Two, "What we call the morality or ethos of man is the way he relates to the existential adventure of his freedom."

The *adventure of freedom:* such exactly is the master-

theme of this remarkable book. On every page Christos Yannaras shows us the true implications of St Paul's words,
"Where the Spirit of the Lord is, there is freedom" (2 Cor.
3:17).

—Bishop Kallistos of Diokleia

CHAPTER ONE

The Masks of Morality
and the Ethos of the Person

1. Authoritative ethics and conventional ethics

In the language of our culture today, "morality" has the sense of an objective yardstick for evaluating the individual character or individual behavior. It has become bound up in our thought with the social categories of good and evil, and represents the extent to which the individual in society corresponds to an objective duty, a "moral obligation" graded into particular "virtues." Each man's morality or ethos is his objective valuation based on a scale of values accepted by society as a whole.

This scale of objective virtues or values which determine the morality of the individual is the core, or the result, of a more general religious, philosophical or rationalistically "scientific" interpretation of problems to do with the behavior of the individual in society. Ethics is the name customarily given to this kind of systematic concern with the problems relating to the ethos or morality of the human being. Ethics may arise out of a philosophical interpretation of man's ethos, or it may result from a given body of religious law determining how man should behave. It can also be a science, a branch of the so-called "human sciences," which tries to find the most effective scale of values for the best organization of men's social coexistence.

Regardless of its philosophical, religious or scientific

derivation, ethics can only be turned into action, into a code of behavior for society as a whole, if it has the bases and the preconditions for objective application. It seems that there are two such preconditions for the application of ethics: authority and convention.

In the first place, it is only a supreme and infallible, and therefore divine, authority which can decide and impose a general code of human behavior beyond any possible dispute. This supreme authority can be "divine" in a religious or mythological sense: it can also be represented by a party leadership, or by the impersonal principle of state power.

If we reject authority, we are then obliged to accept the conventional character of social ethics. The rules for behavior and for the evaluation of individual character then follow from an agreement or convention, either conscious or dictated by custom. We accept, on utilitarian grounds, ideas about good and evil which may either be those put forward in each particular case, or those hallowed by experience. And we constantly seek to improve them, using philosophy or science to study the manifestations of social behavior.

2. The morality of man and the being of man

It is clear that ethics, in the form we have described up to now, separates the ethos or morality of man, his individual behavior and value as a character, from his existential truth and hypostatic identity—from what man *is*, prior to any social or objective evaluation of him. Thus ethics leaves outside its scope the *ontological* question of the truth and reality of human existence, the question of what man really *is* as distinct from what he *ought* to be and whether he corresponds to this "ought." Does human individuality have an ontological hypostasis, a hypostasis of life and freedom beyond space and time? Does it have a unique, distinctive and unrepeatable hypostatic identity which is prior to character and behavior, and which determines them? Or is it a transient by-product of biological, psychological and historical conditions by which it is necessarily determined, so that "improvement" in character and behavior is all we can achieve by resorting to a utilitarian code of law?

If we accept morality simply as man's conformity to an authoritative or conventional code of law, then ethics becomes man's alibi for his existential problem. He takes refuge in ethics, whether religious, philosophical or even political, and hides the tragedy of his mortal, biological existence behind idealized and fabulous objective aims. He wears a mask of behavior borrowed from ideological or party authorities, so as to be safe from his own self and the questions with which it confronts him.

3. The freedom of morality

In the Christian Church, and particularly in the tradition of the Orthodox East, the problem of human morality has always been identified with the existential truth of man. Morality is not an objective measure for evaluating character and behavior, but the dynamic response of personal freedom to the existential truth and authenticity of man. For freedom carries with it the ultimate possibility of taking precisely this risk: that man should deny his own existential truth and authenticity, and alienate and distort his existence, his being. The morality of man is first and foremost an existential event: the dynamic realization of the fulness of existence and life, or else failure and the distortion of his true hypostasis.

In other words, morality relates to the event of man's salvation. For man to be *saved* means that he becomes "safe and *sound*," or *whole*, and realizes to the full his potential for existence and life beyond space, time and conventional relationships: it means conquering death. The insatiable thirst common to all human existence is a thirst for this *salvation*, not for conventional improvements in character or behavior. This is why for the Church, the question of ethics takes as its starting-point the freedom of morality— freedom from any schematic valuation of utilitarian predetermination.

In the tradition of the Orthodox Church, we define
morality through studying the existential truth of man. This
means beginning with the ontological question: what is being,
and what does it mean for man to *be*? What relationship
is there between what he is as a biological entity and being
in itself, the definitive and immutable potential for existence?
Does the individual distinctiveness of each human being, the
unique, distinct and unrepeatable expression of his physical
build, his speech, his thought, his creative capacity and his
love, partake in being and have ontological substance? Or
is it simply an ephemeral and incidental biological differentiation, inexorably predetermined by the necessity of man's
"species" or "nature"?

It is clear that without answering the question about
being, about the boundless and true potential for existence,
it is impossible to approach the existential adventure of man's
freedom—the way he preserves or loses the universal potentialities for life, which is to say his morality. In the Orthodox
Church, therefore, when we are to study the truth about
man and his morality we start with the truth about being,
with its source and cause: we start from the acceptance of
God's revelation, from the truth about God.

4. The ethos of trinitarian communion

In the life of the Church, God reveals Himself as the
hypostasis of being, the personal hypostasis of eternal life.
The personal existence of God is the comprehensive and
exhaustive expression of the truth of being. It is not the
essence or the energy of God which constitutes being, but
His personal *mode* of existence: God as person is the
hypostasis of being.

In other words, the Church does not identify the truth
of being with God as an objective and abstract first cause
of existence and life: God is not a vague supreme being, an
impersonal essence which may be approached only through
the intellect or the emotions. Nor is He a "prime mover,"
a blind energy which sets in motion the mechanism of the

world; nor yet an image of man exalted into an absolute, an infinite magnification of the individual characteristics and psychological demands of the human being. The God of whom the Church has experience is the God who reveals Himself in history as personal existence, as distinctiveness and freedom. God is person, and He speaks with man "face to face, as a man speaketh unto his friend" (Ex 33:11).

It is precisely as personal existence, as distinctiveness and freedom from any predetermination by essence or nature, that God constitutes being and is the hypostasis of being. When Moses asks the identity of the God whose will he is to proclaim to the Israelites, the answer is "I am He who is" (Ex 3:14). God identifies the truth of existence, the reality of being, with His personal hypostasis. This means that the divine essence or nature is not an ontological reality prior to God's personal existence and determining it: God's being is not an ontological datum, anterior to the distinctiveness and freedom of the divine person. Rather, it is the personal hypostasis of God which is the comprehensive and exhaustive expression of His being. "And when speaking to Moses, God did not say, 'I am essence,' but, 'I am He who is'; for He who is, is not from the essence, but the essence is from Him who is. He who is has comprehended within Himself all being."[1]

The identification of being with the personal existence of God—an identification with vital consequences for the truth of man and human morality—explains the revelation of the God of the Church, who is one and at the same time trinitarian. The one God is not one divine nature or essence, but primarily one person: the person of God the Father. The personal existence of God (the Father) *constitutes* His essence or being, making it into "hypostases": freely and from love He begets the Son and causes the Holy Spirit to proceed.[2] Consequently, being stems not from the essence,

[1]Gregory Palamas, *In Defence of the Holy Hesychasts* 3, 2-12; ed. Christou vol. I (Thessaloniki, 1962), p. 666.

[2]"God the Father, moved outside time and in love, proceeded to a distinction in hypostases, remaining without division or diminution in the wholeness proper to Him, supremely unified and supremely simple": Maximus the Confessor, *Scholia on the Divine Names*, PG 4, 221A.

which would make it an ontological necessity, but from the person and the freedom of its love which "hypostasizes" being into a personal and trinitarian communion. God the Father's *mode of being* constitutes existence and life as a fact of love and personal communion.

The identification of being with the freedom of love—of that love which forms being into hypostases—reveals that the truth of the ethos or morality is equivalent to the truth of being. When we speak of the unity and communion of the three divine persons, we are referring to God's *mode of being*, which is the ethos of divine life. And the ethos of God is identical with His being. When the Christian revelation declares that "God is love" (1 Jn 4:16), it is not referring to one among many properties of God's "behavior," but to what God *is* as the fulness of trinitarian and personal communion.

Thus love is singled out as the ontological category *par excellence*, the only possibility for existence, since it is through love that God gives substance to His essence, and constitutes His being. Any other definition of God's ethos with evaluative content is ontologically unfounded: it applies *a priori* conventional predicates, taken from philosophical thought or social experience, to the mode of divine existence, which is nothing other than personal distinctiveness and the freedom of love. If we accept evaluative definitions of the Godhead, we make the personal distinctiveness of divine love subordinate to them, and consequently do away with it. Evaluative categories could refer only to nature or essence, but then personal distinctiveness would be subordinated to the necessity imposed by natural definitions, and consequently, once again, it would be non-existent or substantially curtailed. In that case, the person of God would "undergo" whatever happened to the nature. The "accidents" of the nature would be "passions" of the person—things undergone passively. This is why St Maximus the Confessor affirms of the Godhead: "It is neither beautiful nor good: for these are as it were passions, and conditions and accidents."[3]

[3]*Scholia on the Divine Names*, PG 4, 412BC. Cf. also Dionysius the Areopagite, *On Mystical Theology* 5, PG 3, 1045D-1048AB.

5. The ethos of man "in the image" of God

The reality of man's creation "in the image" of God is related to the unity of ethos or morality with being. In the light of the truth about the trinitarian hypostasis of being, the Church is enabled to shed light on the mystery of human existence, and to give an ontological foundation to human morality.

Created "in the image" of God in Trinity, man himself is *one in essence* according to his nature, and *in many hypostases* according to his persons. Each man is a unique, distinct and unrepeatable person; he is an existential distinctiveness. All men have a common nature or essence, but this has no existence except as personal distinctiveness, as freedom and transcendence of their own natural predeterminations and natural necessity. The person is the hypostasis of the human essence or nature. He sums up in his existence the universality of human nature, but at the same time surpasses it, because his *mode of existence* is freedom and distinctiveness.

This mode of existence which is personal distinctiveness forms the image of God in man, making man a partaker in being. It is not as nature that man constitutes an image of God: it is not because he has natural attributes in common with God, or analogous to His. Man constitutes an image of God as an ontological hypostasis free from space, time and natural necessity.

The reason for this is that human existence derives its ontological substance from the fact of divine love, the only love which gives substance to being. The creation of man is an act of God's love: not of His "kindly disposition," but of His love which *constitutes* being as an existential event of personal communion and relationship. Man was created to become a partaker in the personal mode of existence which is the life of God—to become a partaker in the freedom of love which is true life.

Man does not cease to be a created being. His nature is a created nature, and his natural individuality is corruptible and mortal. His existential hypostasis is not due to his nature; human nature of itself cannot form a hypostasis of life. Upon this created and mortal nature, however, God has set the imprint of His "image": He has "breathed into it the breath of life" (Gen 2:7), the possibility of true life—beyond space, time and natural necessity. This is why the existential hypostasis of each man is more than his biological individuality. What man *is* as a hypostasis of life, of life eternal, is his personal distinctiveness, which is realized and revealed in the existential fact of communion and relationship with God and with his fellow men, in the freedom of love.

Every other creature derives its ontological hypostasis from the will and energy of God, and is a dynamically effected manifestation of the creative principle of divine love. Man, however, derives his ontological hypostasis not simply from the will and energy of God, but from the *manner* in which God gives substance to being. This manner is *personal* existence, the existential potentiality for loving communion and relationship—the potentiality for true life. Man is not only a dynamic manifestation of God's word or inner principle, but a hypostasis of the principle of personal distinctiveness and love free from any predetermination. This is why man is capable of either accepting or rejecting the ontological precondition for his existence: he can refuse the freedom of love and personal communion, and say "no" to God and cut himself off from being.

The truth of the personal *relationship* with God, which may be positive or antithetical but is nevertheless always an existential relationship, is the definition of man, his *mode of being*. Man is an existential fact of relationship and communion. He is a person, πρόσωπον, which signifies, both etymologically and in practice, that he has his face (ὤψ) towards (πρός) someone or something: that he is opposite (in relation to or in connection with) someone or something.[4] In every one of its personal hypostases, the created

_____

[4] The prefix πρός with the substantive ὤψ (gen. ὠπός), meaning "look," "eye," "face" or "aspect," make up the composite notion of πρόσ-ωπον. See Dimitrakos, *Great Dictionary of the Greek Language* (in Greek) vol 9, p. 8056. John Zizioulas ("From Prosopeion to Prosopon," in *Tributes in Honour of Metropolitan Meliton of Chalcedon* [Thessaloniki,

nature of man is "opposite" God: it exists as a reference and relation to God.

Thus the person represents a mode of being which presupposes natural individuality, but is at the same time distinct from it. Each person is a sum of the characteristics common to all human nature, to mankind as a whole, and at the same time he transcends it inasmuch as he is an existential distinctiveness, a fact of existence which cannot be defined objectively. Man's nature in general—mankind as a whole, as a biological species—can be defined objectively: it possesses will, reason, intellect, etc. But each human person exercises his will and converses and thinks in a way that is unique, distinct and unrepeatable.

Consequently, the person is not an *individual*, a segment or subdivision of human nature as a whole. He represents, not the relationship of a part to the whole, but the possibility of summing up the whole in a distinctiveness of relationship, in an act of self-transcendence. The relation of a part to the whole, of the individual to the totality, is always one of analogies and comparisons, definitive and therefore constraining on the individual—there is no room for existential freedom from what nature has predetermined. On the other hand, the relationship which sums up the totality of nature

Patriarchal Institute for Patristic Studies, 1977], p. 290) denies that the term *prosopon* had an original sense "of *reference* and *relationship*, on the basis of a particular etymological analysis of it." He prefers "that the term *prosopon* should be derived from a strictly anatomical analysis: for example, the point determined by the two eyes, 'the part round the eyes' (πρὸς τοῖς ὠψί)." It is quite obvious, however, that what we have here is not merely "a particular etymological analysis" but at least the most widely accepted. Pierre Chantraine, *Dictionnaire Étymologique de la Langue Grecque* (Histoire des mots), vol. III (Paris, 1974), p. 942, and Hjalmar Frisk *Griechisches Etymologisches Wörterbuch* (Heidelberg, 1960), p. 602, and also Eduard Schwyzer, *Griechische Grammatik*, vol. II (Munich, 1950), p. 517, all accept the etymology which interprets *prosopon* as "what is opposite the eyes [of the other]," and ascribe only to Sommer (*Nominalkomposita* 115, n. 1) the interpretation "the part of the head around the eyes." Chantraine writes: "Like μέτωπον, πρόσωπον is a hypostasis [here 'hypostasis' means that a substantive is formed from a prepositional phrase] coming from the root of ὤψ by prefixing προτὶ (or πρός)—but the interpretation must be different and the word must mean 'that which is facing the eyes (of someone else)' ... The word finally could be understood as a verbal noun corresponding to προτιόσσομαι, προσόψομαι"—cf. the German *Angesicht*. Exactly the same view is expressed in Frisk and in Schwyzer.

in self-transcendence defies comparison, and is unique and distinctive. This uniqueness and distinctiveness—which has its being and is experienced only as a fact of communion and relationship—defines the personal existence of man, his mode of being.

6. Person and individual

In everyday speech, we tend to distort the meaning of the word "person." What we call "person" or "personal" designates rather more the individual. We have grown accustomed to regarding the terms "person" and "individual" as virtually synonymous, and we use the two indifferently to express the same thing. From one point of view, however, "person" and "individual" are opposite in meaning.[5] The individual is the denial or neglect of the distinctiveness of the person, the attempt to define human existence using the objective properties of man's common nature, and quantitative comparisons and analogies.

Chiefly in the field of sociology and politics, the human being is frequently identified with the idea of numerical individuality. Sometimes this rationalistic process of leveling people out is considered progress, since it helps to make the organization of society more efficient. We neutralize the human being into a social unit, bearing the characteristics, the needs and desires, which are common to all. We try to achieve some rationalistic arrangement for the "rights of the individual," or an "objective" implementation of social justice which makes all individual beings alike and denies them personal distinctiveness.

In everyday life, too, we generally distinguish persons by applying to individuals the characteristics and attributes common to human nature, with merely quantitative differentiations. When we want to designate a person, we make a collection of individual attributes and natural characteristics which are never "personal" in the sense of being

[5]See V. Lossky, *The Mystical Theology of the Eastern Church* (London, 1957), p. 121f.

unique and unrepeatable, however fine the quantitative nuances we achieve for designating individuals. We say, for instance, that so-and-so is a man of such-and-such height, with such-and-such a facial appearance, character, emotional make-up and so on. But however many detailed descriptions we give, they are bound to fit more than one person, for the existential uniqueness and distinctiveness of the personal manifestation is impossible to define objectively, in the words and formulae of our common speech.

Personal distinctiveness is revealed and known only within the framework of direct personal relationship and communion, only by participation in the principle of personal immediacy, or of the loving and creative force which distinguishes the person from the common nature. And this revelation and knowledge of personal distinctiveness becomes ever more full as the fact of communion and relationship achieves its wholeness in love. Love is the supreme road to knowledge of the person, because it is an acceptance of the other person as a whole. It does not project onto the other person individual preferences, demands or desires, but accepts him as he is, in the fulness of his personal uniqueness. This is why knowledge of the distinctiveness of the person achieves its ultimate fulness in the self-transcendence and offering of self that is sexual love, and why, in the language of the Bible, sexual intercourse is identified with *knowledge* of a person.[6]

Personal distinctiveness *forms the image* of God in man. It is the *mode of existence* shared by God and man, the *ethos* of trinitarian life imprinted upon the human being. In the Orthodox Church and its theology, we study man as an image of God, and not God as an image of man exalted into an absolute. The revelation of the personal God in history manifests to us the truth about man, his ethos and the nobility of his descent.

This does not mean that we apply some authoritatively given theoretical principle to the interpretation of human existence. In the historical revelation of God, we study true personal

---

[6]Cf. Gn 4:1, 4:17, 4:25; Mt 1:25; Lk 1:34; R. Bultmann, in *Theologisches Wörterbuch zum Neuen Testament*, ed. G. Kittel, vol. I (Bonn, 1950), p. 199.

existence free from any constraint—from the constraint imposed on man by his own nature after his fall, which was the free subjection of his personal distinctiveness to the necessities and dictates of natural individuality, as we shall see in the pages that follow.

What principally concerns us here is that the revelation of God throws light on the fact of man's personal distinctiveness and freedom, with all the tragic consequences of that freedom. The image of God in man is preserved precisely through the tragedy of his freedom, because it is identified with hypostatic realization of freedom—with the personal mode of existence which is capable of either realizing or rejecting the true life of love. What we call the *morality* of man is the way he relates to this adventure of his freedom. Morality reveals what man *is* in principle, as the image of God, but also what he *becomes* through the adventure of his freedom: a being transformed, or "in the likeness" of God.

7. Ignorance of the truth of the person and the legalistic understanding of morality

Our interpretation of the creation of man "in the image" of God has vital consequences for the definition of morality and for ethics. When Christian dogmatics fell under the sway of Western rationalism, being "in the image" was connected with the nature of man in general, as a species. Indeed, the image of God in man was interpreted exclusively with reference to one of the two "parts" of a necessarily divided nature—to the "spirit" of man.[7] Certain properties of man's "spiritual" nature, specifically rationality, free will and "dominion," are designated elements of his being "in the image."

These existential predicates were used by the Greek fathers to indicate the ontological difference between person and nature, revealing both the common potentialities of

[7]Cf. Thomas Aquinas, *Summa Theologica* I, 93, 4-8. J.-H. Nicolas, *Dieu connu comme inconnu* (Paris, Desclée de Brouwer, 1966), pp. 332, 334, 339. Ch. Androutsos, *Dogmatics* (in Greek—Athens, 1907), p. 137. Trembelas, *Dogmatics* (in Greek), vol. I (Athens, 1959), p. 487.

nature and the uniquely personal manner in which these natural potentialities are existentially realized. They were then interpreted by rationalistic theology as objective, "spiritual" properties of natural individuality.

If, however, God gives substance to life in the form of distinctive personality, love and freedom from any natural predetermination, then the image of God cannot correspond to man conceived of as an individual or to objective attributes of natural individuality, and especially not to one "part" of the individual nature. "The image is not a part of the nature," says St Gregory of Nyssa;[8] and Michael Choniates adds, "It is not the soul alone or the body alone that is called man, but both together; and it is with reference to both together that God is said to have created man in His image."[9]

Rationality, free will and dominion define the image of God in man because they relate, not to the "spiritual" nature of man, but to the ways in which the person is distinguished from the nature and constitutes in itself a hypostasis of a life unshackled by any natural predetermination.[10] Man is rational, and has free will and dominion in creation because he is a personal being, and not because he is a "spirit." We do not know these human capacities as generic, objective properties: that is simply how thought converts them into independent and discrete concepts. We know them as something absolutely different in every distinctive personality. They are, to be sure, potentialities or energies of human nature in general, and possessed by every human being; but they always reveal the uniqueness of a person. They have no

[8] *On the Formation of Man* 16, PG 44, 185.
[9] *Prosopopœiae*, PG 150, 1361C.
[10] Man partakes in true life, beyond space, time and natural predetermination, because he is a *personal* being, and not because he has a "spirit" or an "immortal soul." "If the soul is immortal by nature, then personal survival is *necessary* . . . Even God is then immortal through His nature, that is, of necessity, and man is related essentially—necessarily—to God. All this, which was so natural for the ancient Greek, who had no concept of the person, creates enormous existential problems when applied to the person. For an inescapable immortality is not conceivable for the free God and constitutes a challenge to the person. How then is the absolute and unique identity of the person ensured, seeing that the essence cannot do it?" J. Zizioulas, "From Prosopeion to Prosopon," p. 306.

existence other than as manifestations of personal distinctiveness.

This issue is of vital significance in defining human morality. If we relate the image of God to the nature and not to the personal distinctiveness of man, then morality, the truth and authenticity of existence, is something predetermined by nature and an *essential* necessity for man. In that case, ethics is understood as conformity by the individual to objective or natural requirements, and violation of these has consequences which are "destructive" to his nature: it does not simply distort the image of God imprinted on man's nature, but actually wipes it out.[11] Correspondingly, individual conformity to the objective or natural requirements of morality is certainly an achievement, a "virtue" with objective worth; but all it secures is faithfulness to nature. And nature of itself is created and mortal: it is not this that constitutes a hypostasis of eternal life.

Thus morality ceases to be related to the truth of the person, to the dynamic, existential realization of true life, of love and communion in freedom. It is related to natural individuality, in the forms of intellectual self-awareness, the psychological ego and volition put into practice—in other words, to the subjective preconditions for individual conformity with the natural requirements of "virtue."

This is the road to an understanding of ethics as individual obligation or individual achievement. Inevitably, the obligations and achievements are classified into general codes of individual behavior, and into laws which lay down the relationship between the individual's rights and his obligations. Morality is understood within the objective context of social coexistence, and constitutes an external and ultimately legal necessity.

When the truth of the person is undervalued or ignored

[11]This is the classic Protestant position on the effects of the fall on the image of God in man. See e.g. Heinrich Heppe, *Die Dogmatik der evangelisch-reformierten Kirchen* (Neukirchener Verlag, 1958), pp. 254-260. Wolfgang Trillhaas, *Dogmatik* (Berlin, 1962), pp. 207-208. See also the classic formulation in the Westminster Confession (1647), ch. 9 § 3, in Karl Müller *Die Bekenntnisschriften der reformierten Kirche* (Leipzig, 1903), p. 564.

in the realm of theology, this inevitably results in the creation of a legalistic, external system of ethics. Man's ethical problem ceases to be an existential one, a problem of how to be saved from natural necessity—from space, time, the passions, corruption and death. It becomes a pseudo-problem of objective obligations which remain devoid of existential justification. When intellectual and conventional categories replace ontological truth and revelation in Christian theology, then in the historical life of the Church, too, the problem of salvation is obscured by a shadow that torments mankind, that of a "law" which leads nowhere.

CHAPTER TWO

Sin: Existential Failure and "Missing the Mark"

1. The fall from life to survival

What we call the morality or ethos of man is the way he relates to the existential adventure of his freedom: morality manifests what man *is* in principle as an image of God—as a person—and also what he *becomes* through the adventure of his freedom—a being transformed, or "in the likeness" of God. This view of morality allows us to approach the real content which Orthodox theology has given to the truth of the fall and of sin, a content of life and existential experience.

For Orthodox theology, the fall of man takes place when he freely renounces his possibility of participating in true life, in personal relationship and loving communion—the only possibility for man to *be* as a hypostasis of personal distinctiveness.[1] The fall arises out of man's free deci-

---

[1] "Life and love are identified in the person: the person does not die only because it is loved and loves; outside the communion of love, the person loses its uniqueness and becomes a being like other beings, a "thing" without absolute "identity" and "name," without a face. Death for a person means ceasing to love and to be loved, ceasing to be unique and unrepeatable, whereas life for the person means the survival of the uniqueness of its hypostasis, which is affirmed and maintained by love": J. Zizioulas, "From Prosopeion to Prosopon," p. 307. To this outstanding formulation, it need only be added by way of further explanation that love here is taken not simply as a sentimental connection which ensures "remembrance" of a person, but as a *mode of existence* which exalts human individuality to a

sion to reject personal communion with God and restrict himself to the autonomy and self-sufficiency of his own nature.

The biblical account of the fall refers to the initial choice of natural autonomy on the part of the first-formed humans: "In the day ye eat of the fruit of the tree of the knowledge of good and evil, ye shall be as gods" (Gen 3:5). This provocation places before man the existential possibility of self-sufficiency and autonomy for his nature: the possibility for nature on its own to determine and exhaust the fact of existence.

This kind of "deification" of human nature goes against its very truth: it is an "existential lie," a fictitious possibility of life. Man's nature is created and mortal. It partakes in being, in true life, only to the extent that it transcends itself, as an existential fact of personal distinctiveness. Man has being, and constitutes a hypostasis of life and transcends the mortality of his nature, only in so far as he realizes the personal mode of existence which is God's.

This means that man derives the potential for hypostatic identity, beyond space, time and the restrictions of nature, from the personal existence of God: it is his existential answer to God's call to personal communion with Himself, the call which bestows being. From the moment when the human person rejects this call and this communion in which he himself is grounded, from the moment when he seeks natural and existential autonomy, he becomes alienated from himself. His personal existence is not destroyed, because it is precisely this that presupposes his freedom to experience existential alienation. But his personal distinctiveness ceases to sum up the possibilities of human nature in the existential fact of a relationship and communion which transcends nature and frees existence from natural necessity. Personal distinctiveness is confined within nature, as an individual au-

hypostasis of personal distinctiveness and freedom, a hypostasis of eternal life. So death for the person does not mean non-existence, but a mode of existence "contrary to existence," as St Maximus puts it: it means an existence which does not come to fruition, which shuts itself off from the "end" for which it was made—life as love and communion. See *The Person and Eros*, §§ 80, 86.

tonomy which confronts the autonomy of others, thus fragmenting nature. Human nature is fragmented into individual wills expressing the individual being's need and effort to survive in his natural self-sufficiency: existence is identified with the instinctive, natural need for independent survival. The natural needs of the individual being, such as nourishment, self-perpetuation and self-preservation, become an end in themselves: they dominate man, and end up as "passions," causes of anguish and the utmost pain, and ultimately the cause of death.

2. The perpetuation of the fall

What has been said above explains why the first fragmentation of nature is decisive. The first choice of individual autonomy has irrevocably split nature, and condemned the will of all other human persons to be merely an individual will expressing and enforcing the necessities of the fragmented nature. The natural need for individual survival runs counter to the personal freedom and distinctiveness which can be realized only as love, threatening to shackle it. The freedom of the person is not destroyed, only distorted and changed into an antithetical separation from nature, a ceaseless polarization of antithetical impulses. It is experienced as a tragic division within the human being: "I see another law in my members, warring against the law of my mind, and bringing me into captivity to the law of sin which is in my members" (Rom 7:23).

After its initial fragmentation, human nature acquires a dynamic impulse to make itself absolute as individual autonomy. For nature does not exist except as personal hypostases, and the first man identified the fact of his existence, not with the personal distinctiveness of his natural hypostasis, but with its survival and self-existence. Thus each new human person is born subject to his individual nature's need to survive as existential autonomy. He is born condemned to be the bearer of an individual or natural will subordinated to the absolute need for survival.

For this reason, the fragmentation of nature is effected incessantly and inevitably with each natural birth, since each birth means the addition of one more individual, existential self-sufficiency within the common nature. The individuality of each claims from the others the absolute right to exist of itself. It is dominated by the natural, instinctive need to survive, to perpetuate itself and to make its mark, since it is individuality that exhausts the existential possibilities of nature, and not the personal distinctiveness which unifies nature existentially in the fact of communion and relationship, in its transcendence of its own individuality.

Thus the tragic words of Sartre prove true: "My original sin is the existence of the other."[2] The "other" is always an affirmation of the inescapable fragmentation of our nature. Every "other" is an immediate, empirical testimony to the person's inability to overcome the dynamic impulse towards the fragmentation of human nature into individual, autonomous units: the "other" is my condemnation to be the bearer of an individual or natural will for survival. For this will is not the product of freedom, but an impulse, an instinct and a need: it is the subjection of personal distinctiveness to the natural demand for the survival of the species. This demand is a torment to us, since it can be fulfilled only as an antagonistic confrontation with the existential autonomy of other individuals.

This is also why "hell is other people," as again Sartre says in *In Camera*.[3] Coming from the pen of Sartre, this statement clearly means that hell for man is not an individual punishment, objectively imposed. The element of punishment in man's hell is other people. The failure of personal existence to form an ontological hypostasis, its decline into natural individuality which claims an absolute right to existence of itself, places it in opposition to the individual natures of the "others." Thus the "other" becomes the af-

---

[2]Ma chûte originelle c'est l'existence de l'autre": *L'Être et le Néant* (Paris, 1943), p. 321.

[3]*In Camera*, end of scene five: "L'enfer, c'est les autres." See also Maximus the Confessor, *Ambigua*, PG 90, 256B: "The one nature has been divided into thousands of parts; and we who are of the same nature fall prey one to another, after the fashion of reptiles."

firmation of my existential failure, my inability to transcend my natural will which has come to be identified with the self-defence of the biological and psychological ego. The "other" is hell because he torments me with the revelation that I am tragically condemned to my individual autonomy, incapable of existing free from natural predetermination, loving and loved.

Before Sartre, Dostoevsky had defined hell in the same perspective, only more fully: "Hell is the torment of not loving."[4] This definition means that other people simply provide the occasion for my own hell, while its cause is to be found in my own inability to relate, my own incarceration in the egocentric autonomy of my individuality. So hell becomes the more agonizing when the "other" is not an individual at an existential distance which nullifies the possibility of a relationship, but a Person whose loving self-transcendence and self-offering call me to existence and true life, while I cling to my individual autonomy. Hell is man's free choice; it is when he imprisons himself in an agonizing lack of life, and deliberately refuses communion with the loving goodness of God, the true life.

3. Existential "alteration" of nature

Man's insistence on individuality is an indication of his failure to realize his personal distinctiveness and freedom, of his falling away from the fulness of existence which is the life of the Trinity, personal coinherence and communion in love. This falling away is sin, ἁμαρτία, which means *missing the mark* as to existential truth and authenticity. The patristic tradition insists on this interpretation of sin as failure and "missing the mark," as the loss of that "end" or aim which for human nature is its existential self-transcendence, taking it into the limitless realm of personal distinctiveness and freedom. Characteristic are the words of St Maximus the Confessor: "Failure and weakness introduce

---

[4]*Brothers Karamazov*, I, 6, 3, From the teaching and conversations of Staretz Zosima, 9.

evil, doing what is against nature because of the lack of that which is in accordance with nature."[5] Elsewhere, commenting on the author of the Areopagitic writings, he writes: "This lack or deprivation is what he calls *sin* (ἁμαρτία), that is to say, the failure to attain and the falling away from what is fitting. By sin he means, to take a metaphor from archery, the shot that misses the mark instead of hitting the target. For when we fail to attain the good, and the movement and order which is in accordance with nature, we are carried into an irrational, all-embracing and unreal state of non-existence which is contrary to our nature."[6]

The church fathers refuse to view sin hypostatically, as a hypostasis of life different from the only form of existence that gives substance to life, the divine personal goodness. Sin is not a nature, an evil nature which exists hypostatically as the opposite pole to the divine existence and life of love. There is nothing in God's creation which is hypostatically and naturally evil, not even the devil himself. Sin is failure, a failure as to existence and life: it is the failure of persons to realize their existential "end," to confirm and conserve the uniqueness of their hypostasis through love.

This failure on the part of persons is bound to have consequences for the nature of man, since it distorts the nature and fragments it, transferring its existential possibilities from the freedom and distinctiveness of the person to the instinctive and absolute need for survival in the individual. But this existential "alteration" of nature[7] does not mean that it is changed in its essence into an evil nature. It is to preclude such an interpretation that St Maximus goes so far as to characterize the fall of nature as "blameless sin" as compared with the "blameworthy" sin of the intention. He writes: "The intention of Adam's natural reason was corrupted

[5]*Scholia on the Divine Names*, PG 4, 348C.
[6]*Ibid.*, PG 4, 305B.
[7]The term comes from St Maximus: "In condemnation of Adam's freely chosen sin, his nature became subject to passion and corruption and death. This state was not caused by God, nor was it something that man possessed in the beginning; but man himself caused it and came to know it when through his disobedience he brought into existence freely chosen sin. His condemnation to death is clearly a consequence of this": *Ambigua*, PG 90, 408C.

first, and this corrupted his nature with it, by rejecting the grace of freedom from passions, and so sin came to be. The first and culpable act was the fall of the intention from good to evil: but the second, the blameless alteration of nature from incorruption to corruption, happened because of the first. For there were two sins committed by the fore-father when he transgressed the divine commandment: the one was culpable, but the other was blameless since it had been caused by the one which was blameworthy. The one took place when the intention voluntarily set aside what is good; and the other, when the nature involuntarily laid aside immortality because of the intention."[8]

The existential "alteration" of human nature, the fall from the true existence of personal coinherence and communion in love to the corruption of autonomous but mortal individuality, is a fall from being—a kind of "non-existence," as St Maximus says in one of the passages quoted above. Sin is a mode of existence contrary to existence, and contrary to nature since it fragments and destroys nature; it means separation from being and exclusion from life.

Starting from such a concrete and existential concept of sin, the Orthodox tradition has refused to confine the whole of man's relationship with God within a juridical, legal framework; it has refused to see sin as the individual trans-gression of a given, impersonal code of behavior which simply produces psychological guilt. The God of the Church as known and proclaimed by Orthodox experience and tradi-tion has never had anything to do with the God of the Roman juridical tradition, the God of Anselm and Abelard;[9] He has never been thought of as a vengeful God who rules by fear, meting out punishments and torment for men.

---

[8]*Ambigua*, PG 90, 405C.

[9]Anselm, Archbishop of Canterbury, 1033-1109. Peter Abelard, French scholastic theologian and philosopher, 1079-1142. For further information about their juridical theological theories and the influence these had on the theological and spiritual life of the West, see J. Romanidis, *Original Sin* (in Greek—Athens, 1957), pp. 12f., 87f. See also Étienne Gilson, *La philosophie au Moyen Age* (Paris, 1962²), pp. 243f., 286f. Jean Cottiaux, "La conception de la théologie chez Abélard," *Revue d'histoire ecclésiastique* 28 (1932), pp. 247-295, 533-551, 788-828. Jean Jolivet, *Arts du langage et théologie chez Abélard* (Paris, 1969), especially p. 276ff. Karl Barth, *Fides quaerens intellectum* (Darmstadt, 1958²).

God is not the "judge" of men in the sense of a magistrate who passes sentence and imposes a punishment, testifying to the transgression. He is judge because of what He *is*: the possibility of life and true existence. When man voluntarily cuts himself off from this possibility of existence, he is automatically "judged." It is not God's sentence but His existence that judges him. God is nothing but an ontological fact of love and an outpouring of love: a fulness of good, an ecstasy of loving goodness.

God is Himself existence "in truth," the hypostasis of life, a hypostasis of personal distinctiveness and freedom; it is for this reason, and because man is created in His image, that God's presence is a *judgment* for man. As St Maximus says of the Holy Trinity, one in essence, "He is one God, by nature the Creator who manifests providence and judgment for His creatures. For as the act of creating is common to the Father, the Son and the Holy Spirit, so is judgment and the exercize of a providential care towards those They have made."[10] When he commits sin, man "is already judged": "for this is the judgment, that . . . men loved darkness rather than light."[11] Man is judged according to the measure of the life and existence from which he excludes himself. Sin is a self-inflicted condemnation and a punishment which man freely chooses when he refuses to *be* as a personal hypostasis of communion with God and prefers to "alter" and disorder his existence, fragmenting his nature into individual entities— when he prefers corruption and death.

4. "Beyond good and evil"

The concept of ethics, then, which stems from the interpretation of sin as failure and "missing the mark" does not depend on the conventional social idea of "good" and "evil," of merit or transgression; it involves the dilemma between life and death,[12] between existential truth and authenticity

[10]Maximus the Confessor, *Ambigua*, PG 90, 364B.
[11]Jn 3:18-19.
[12]"There are two roads, one of life and the other of death . . . the road

on the one side, and existential deprivation and corruption on the other. The Church's ethics are "beyond good and evil": they relate to ontological realities and not to evaluative categories. "You should know," says St Maximus, "that what is simply called evil is not altogether evil, but evil in one way and not in another. In the same way, what is simply called good is not altogether good, but is good in one way and not in another."[13]

The ethics of the Church have nothing to do with this essential indeterminacy of good and evil, whose conclusions and development cannot be other than conventional. They preclude relativity in values, and do not have reference to any convention, whether customary or consciously accepted, which would permit objective valuations and juridical calculations. The Church's ethics "judge" man by revealing the image of God in the human person, distinguishing existence and life from ephemeral survival and the illusion of self-existence.

What the Church has in view is the freedom of morality from schematic gradations and utilitarian prescriptions. It aims at the morality, the ethos of personal distinctiveness and freedom: this means not simply that individuals' characters and the *mores* of social behavior are "improved," but that man is restored to the fulness of life and existence as he transcends the corruption and death of his created nature.

This restoration can take place only if man undergoes an existential change, a change in his mode of existence; and this is the aim of the Church's ethics. Man must refuse to be wrapped up in the individuality which he as an ego sets against the individual natures of other people. He must free himself from the absolute claims of his individual nature which bind him to the impersonal survival of the species. Only through this liberation from a natural necessity that has become existentially autonomous can man *exist* as a distinctive personality, putting into effect the *life* of love.

Only by this road of freedom can man achieve his *likeness*

of life is this: first, you will love God . . . second, your neighbour as yourself": *Teaching of the Twelve Apostles*, 1, 1-2.

[13]*Ambigua*, PG 90, 413B.

to God; only thus can his own nature, too, constitute a fact of life and existential fulness, a fact of unity and communion of hypostases free from corruption and death. But this existential change in the human nature "altered" by the fall is beyond the capacities of fallen man. It is fundamentally the work of the head of a new humanity: the work of the second Adam, Christ, who in His own person summed up and recreated human nature as a whole, the mode of man's existence. It is the existential reality of the "new creation" of His body, the Church. We shall return to this "renewal" of human nature by Christ at a later stage.

5. The psychological guilt complex

At this point, let us make one supplementary observation: what a liberation it is for man, and especially for modern man in the post-Freudian era, when sin is identified not with transgression and guilt, but with failure and "missing the mark." The idea cultivated in western Christendom, which identified sin with legal transgression and salvation with individual justification and atonement, linked Christian ethics in people's minds with a host of psychological complexes offering no way of escape. The striving for individual justification and atonement leaves man still enslaved to his autonomous individuality, separated from the possibility of life and existence. Not only this, but it also frequently manifests itself as a morbid incarceration in the psychological super-ego, or as a schizophrenic splitting of the ego between the reality of life and an abstract, evaluative "ought."

Innumerable expressions of the social and individual life of modern western man—trends and movements in the fields of art, psychology, sociology and philosophy, as well as fashion and morals—appear to be an effort on man's part to throw off his enslavement to the psychological oppression of guilt complexes engendered by a legalistic concept of sin.[14]

[14]On one of these manifestations of contemporary life, the eroticism which dominates literature, Alberto Moravia writes characteristically: "Eroticism in modern literature has no resemblance to eroticism in pagan literature, nor to eroticism in the literatures that followed it, though if

What we characterize as the "moral crisis" of our day sometimes looks like modern man's desperate attempt to call into question or reject the evaluative forms of conventional ethics—an ethic unrelated to his existential problem and the tragic adventure of his freedom. It seems to be his attempt to assure himself of his own distinctiveness and freedom by transcending impersonal, legal restrictions and utilitarian canons of behavior: an attempt to face without fear the truth about his fall, and even the ultimate alienation of his person. It is, perhaps, man's attempt to free himself from the relativity of good and evil, from the false "super-ego" of social propriety, and ultimately from pseudo-Christian idealism, that false "angelism" found in the conventional forms of an ethic based on a code of values.

This quest on man's part—his effort to face up to the truth about himself whatever it may be, and his refusal to hide or gloss over the reality of his failure out of fear or legal guilt—represents an attitude of life not totally unrelated to the experience required for an understanding of the ethics of the Orthodox Church. The egocentric fear of transgression, and the tendency to gloss over sin or to reach an accommodation with it are extensions and consequences of the psychological guilt complex, and neither has any place in the spiritual climate of Orthodox ethics. On the contrary, the conscious recognition of sin can be used in the Church to lead us into recognizing our human inadequacy and seeking the grace of God—the life bestowed on man as a possibility of participation in communion and relationship with God.

In man's sin, in his failure to be what he is called to be, the Church sees an affirmation of the truth of the person:

there are any resemblances at all these are to the former rather than the latter. But there is the difference that in pagan literature eroticism has all the innocence, brutality and cohesion of a nature not yet divided and turned against itself by the Christian sense of sin, whereas eroticism in modern literature is bound to take the Christian experience into account. In other words, eroticism in modern literature derives not from a situation of nature, but from a process of liberation from pre-existent prohibitions and taboos. With the pagans, freedom was an unconscious, simple fact, whereas with the moderns it has been reclaimed, rediscovered, rewon": *Man as an End: A Defence of Humanism* (tr. Bernard Wall, London, 1965), p. 228 ("Eroticism in Literature").

personhood is affirmed even in man's capacity to say no even to life and existence itself, to say no to God, although relationship and communion with Him are all that makes existence into a hypostasis of life. In man's sin, the Church sees the tragic adventure of human freedom, which is human morality in its real, ontological truth. She sees human morality in sin (actual deviation) and in deification (the natural sequel and consequence of human morality within the Church). There are no abstract theoretical principles or conventional, legal "axioms" in the ethics of the Church, no impersonal imperatives. The foundation of this ethic is the human person; and person means constant risk, freedom from all objectification, and the dynamics of death and resurrection.

6. The dynamics of repentance

Sin is the measure of our awareness of separation from God, of separation from life—it is the measure of our conscious recognition of death. And it is only through conscious experience of death that man can approach the revelation of life, the possibility of rising with Christ. Thus sin becomes a starting-point for repentance, μετάνοια. This word in Greek means "change of mind," in other words a change in man's whole *attitude*—in his existential stance, not simply in his behavior. Repentance is the recognition that man's self-sufficiency is inadequate; it is a search for the life which is realized in personal relationship with God, a thirst for personal communion with Him.

The transformation of sin into repentance, of existential failure into fulness of life—this is the real substance of the Church's "gospel," her good news. And this news is not simply a promise, but an actual fact with historical flesh; it is the body of the Church, the body of Christ. Christ assumed human nature, the nature of corruption, sin and death, and brought it to life; He gave it once again the possibility of becoming a hypostasis of eternal life, of partaking in God's life.

Christ's assumption of human nature is the event which

brings the Church into being. What Christ has assumed is all of us who make up the body of the Church, burdened as we are with daily failure: and He shows us to be partakers in His life, in His own mode of existence. The consequences of our forefather's rebellion are undone from the moment when the nature which had become existentially autonomous was hypostatically united with God. From this point on, there is within the confines of our fragmented nature a person who constitutes a hypostasis of life, the person of Christ. And this person becomes the axis around whom "the children of God that were scattered abroad are gathered together,"[15] so that previously autonomous individuals form a unity of personal coinherence and love.

Participation in the theanthropic body of Christ, in the existential unity of the communion of saints, is not secured by individual merit or the objectively recognized "virtues" of the individual: it is secured by repentance, by the new attitude of trust in God—when, through the Church, the Christian entrusts to Christ his whole life, unsuccessful and sinful though it is. Repentance does not mean simply the "improvement" or even "perfection" of individual behavior and individual psychological feelings, or the strengthening of the individual will. All these can come about while a man still remains a prisoner in his autonomous individuality, unable to love or to participate in the communion of love which is true life. Repentance is a change in our mode of existence: man ceases to trust in his own individuality. He realizes that existing as an individual, even a virtuous individual, does not save him from corruption and death, from his agonizing existential thirst for life. This is why he takes refuge in the Church, where he *exists* as someone loving and loved. He is loved by the saints, who give him a "name" of personal distinctiveness and take him into the communion of their love despite his sinfulness; and he himself strives to love others despite their sinfulness, to live free from the necessities of his mortal nature. He struggles to overcome his individual resistances, his individual wishes and autonomous impulses, not in order to "improve himself" individ-

[15] Jn 11:52.

ually, but in order to measure up to the "frenzied love" of Christ and the saints, to the preconditions required for personal life as opposed to natural survival.

Thus the Christian does not fear sin with the psychological fear of individual guilt, the complex of depression over individual transgression which lessens the "moral worth" of his individual self. He knows that Christ, the Mother of God and the saints love him despite the fact that he is a sinner— Christ loved him in his sinfulness "unto death on a cross." He knows that in the Church his sin becomes the starting-point for him to experience the miracle of his salvation by Christ. He knows that, even in its most "virtuous" manifestations, the reality of the human state is all sin, all failure and "missing the mark," and that "Christ alone is without sin." He fears sin only as deprivation of the potentiality to respond to the love of Christ. But a "fear" such as this is already a first step toward love.

7. Studying freedom

In discussing the dynamic transformation of sin into repentance, we should call to mind the great spiritual guides of the Orthodox tradition: the wise men of the desert, with their life-long study and exploration of the depths of human sin and their striking affirmation of the truth of man, their denial of the conventional embellishments and illusions of objective "virtue."

Man's need to face up to his fall, to his existential failure, is a basic principle of Orthodox monasticism, a prerequisite for the "philosophical life" of repentance. Just as Byzantine iconographers used to spend a long period in the study of natural reality before they reached the stage of painting icons, so the monk, and indeed every Christian, ought to study his nature, the manifest and hidden resistances caused by his autonomous individuality, so as to reach the point of overcoming nature and realizing the image of God in his person. Repentance is irreconcilable with idealistic illusions and utopian embellishments. Faithfulness to what is natural is the precondition for transfiguring it.

"One who does not know evil is not pure in heart, for he is merely like a beast," says St Isaac the Syrian.[16] Knowledge of evil is knowledge of the fall of man. Any pursuit of virtue which ignores the fact of the fall ends either in falsification and perversion, or in the moral neutrality of dumb beasts—and there are many forms of unconscious and "idealistic" or "spiritualized" brutishness.

Recognition of sin is a real starting-point, from which man begins to search God's truth for living solutions and answers. "Let us who are subject to the passions beseech the Lord insistently," writes St John of the Ladder, "for all those who are free from the passions advanced to that state from subjection to the passions."[17] Subjection to the yoke of the passions does not preclude repentance. On the contrary, the taste of passionateness or even enslavement to his nature's susceptibility to passion gives man a chance to become aware of the tragedy of his personal alienation, aware of the various forms of tyranny exercised by his natural will. When this true knowledge and study of nature in its rebellion leads to repentance, it is transfigured into a rich knowledge of humanity, a discernment which finds its true value in the service of love. St John of the Ladder writes again: "Let them take courage who are humbled by their passions. For even if they fall into every pit and are caught in every snare, when they attain health they will become healers, luminaries, beacons and guides to all, teaching about the forms of every sickness and through their own experience saving those who are about to fall."[18]

The discerning thought of the eastern fathers recognizes sometimes even in the most extreme forms of human fallenness the thirst, albeit perverted, for life and for the fulness of the human person. We read in the Areopagitic writings: "The profligate is bereft of good by virtue of his irrational desire, but although he neither is good nor actually

---

[16]*Mystic Treatises* 83 (Athens, ed. Spanos), p. 319.
[17]*Ladder*, step 28, PG 88, 1133D.
[18]*Ladder*, step 26, PG 88, 1016B.

desires it, he nevertheless partakes in good precisely through that indistinct echo of union and friendship . . . And he who is given over to the worst of lives partakes in good, inasmuch as he is given over wholly to life and to the life which seems best to him; he partakes in good by the very fact of his longing, of his longing for life and aiming at the best life."[19] The image of God in man and the dynamics of life which form the human person cannot be erased, however much we foul the original beauty of loving distinctiveness and freedom. The truth of the Church illuminates the hell of human failure in order to show man that even the insatiable impulses from which his existence *suffers*—the *passions* of pleasure in their autonomous state—are marks of the alienated personal desire for participation in true life, marks which testify to the nobility of his descent.

This observation may be supplemented by a further quotation from St John of the Ladder, who sees in the autonomous passion of the flesh the same impulse as is expressed in the loving force which, through repentance, can lead man to insatiable *eros* for God. He says, "I have seen impure souls crazed for physical love; but when these same souls have made this grounds for repentance, as a result of their experience of sexual love they have transferred the same *eros* to the Lord. They have immediately gone beyond all fear and been spurred to insatiable love for God. This is why the Lord said to the chaste harlot not that she had feared, but that she had loved much, and was readily able to repel *eros* through *eros*."[20]

8. The encounter between freedom and love

Morbid fear of sin, the egocentric phobia about reducing the worth of our individual self, is the product of a legal and juridical understanding of man's relationship with God. Within the Church, however, it is transformed into love and *eros* for Christ, deriving from personal experience of His

[19]*On Divine Names*, PG 3, 720BC.
[20]*Ladder*, step 5, PG 88, 777A.

grace and love for mankind. The basis for the Church's ethics is identical with the basis of her faith and her life: the identification of life and existence with the fact of personal communion. The Church's ethic is that of personal distinctiveness and freedom, because her truth is the truth of persons—the only reality which constitutes being.

Even in the depths of his fallen state and his existential alienation, man remains a person. He embodies the awesome possibility of measuring himself against God, of opposing to the abyss of divine love the dizzy heights of his own rebellion and denial. "The multitude of my sins and the abysses of Thy judgments, who shall fathom them, O my Savior who savest souls?" Thus runs a line from a troparion for Great Tuesday, known in the Orthodox Church as the troparion of the nun Kassiani, in which the harlot who washed Christ's feet speaks to Him in terms of this fearful comparison. There is the same unsearchable immensity in the two abysses of vastness: in the sin of man and the mercy of God, the measureless bounds of the truth of the personal God and the human person, revealed through the act of repentance. It is hard to surpass Pasternak's comment on the verse quoted above: "What familiarity, what equal terms between God and life, God and the individual personality, God and a woman!"[21]

The recognition of sin can reveal to man the existential dimensions of his person, which are as boundless as even the immeasurable depth of the mystery of the divine life. What we view as sin, however, is frequently the legal and psychological consciousness of guilt which is bound up with the conventional standards of society: it is the feeling that we have transgressed some law, leaving us with the unanswered question of who has ordained it and by what authority. Even more frequently, we transfer the reality of sin to cases of misdemeanors which fall outside the norm of bourgeois decency: crimes, the torture of man by man and flagrantly unjust treatment of people. This shift ensures that most of us can have a sense of being more or less sinless. Add to this the importance attached by present-day man

[21]*Doctor Zhivago,* XIII, 17.

to the rational questioning of established standards and the ease with which he interprets traditional "values" as society's prejudices, and all that remains of sin is the impression of a restrictive check on man, or even of a complex from which he must free himself at all costs.

The Church, however, comes and complicates our simplified interpretation, revealing sin in its existential dimension corresponding to the abyss of the divine life. This is a different way of viewing sin, beyond the scope of our social and objective measurements. This is sin transformed into repentance, man's failure measured according to the greatness of his authentic existence, the truth of his personhood which is an image of the truth of the personal God.

9. The "gospel" of hope

We have stressed the point frequently in the preceding pages: for the Church, sin is not a legal but an existential fact. It is not simply a transgression, but an active refusal on man's part to be what he truly is: the image and "glory," or manifestation, of God. Man refuses to be a person, in relationship and communion with the personal God and the persons of his fellow men. Sin, understood in this way, is not simply a denial of the social categories of "altruism" or "love for others," but means that man makes himself secure in his biological and psychological individuality, which is a mode of existence contrary to nature, distorting his existential truth and contradicting the trinitarian prototype of his nature. Existential distortion inevitably means natural disintegration, corruption and death. Man believes he is combatting corruption and death by clinging desperately to his attempt to safeguard his individual self; to safeguard his prosperity, his standing in society and his moral status. But he only succeeds in adding to the disintegration of his being, in the absurdity and loneliness of his self-centered opposition.

Man's sin, his failure to attain his true existence, is nevertheless a manifestation of one aspect of his *personal* possibilities. If man's fulfilment as a person represents a dynamic and boundless immensity of life, an "uncompleted perfection"—the manifestation of the divine image—, then individuality "contrary to nature" is also a human possibility which is shown to be no less boundless, a negative measure and a distortion of the divine image. Man's yes or no to his existential authenticity reveals the infinite, dynamic magnitude of his personal relationship with God or his individual distance from Him. Thus his daily sins, his failures to attain the "end" of personal fulfilment, are not errors or violations of established conventions. They are dynamic revelations of the distance—in manner, not in space—which separates man from God, contingent manifestations of the way in which man has condemned himself to exclusion from true life.

Formulated in theoretical and objective terms, all this remains without interest if it is not brought to life by the experience of repentance, and embodied in a personal adventure. As the Christian explores the bottomless depths of human failure through immediate experience, he realizes the magnitude of the possibilities of love, and he dares to make the leap of repentance. Thus he meets complete acceptance in the infinity of God's love for mankind: "He who knows the weakness of human nature, the same has had experience of divine power," says St Maximus the Confessor.[22] Salvation is when the two infinite magnitudes come together: here alone does "one deep call to another."

The message that the Church brings specifically for modern man, wounded and degraded as he is by the "terrorist" God of juridical ethics, is precisely this: it assures him that what God really asks of man is neither individual feats nor works of merit, but a cry of trust and love from the depths of our abyss. Or perhaps even one moment of sobriety and agony breaking through the closed, secure subjectivity of our happiness.

This message comes through directly from every aspect of the Church's life: it is an ever-open invitation, a hope and consolation for the man who has come to see within himself, like an abyss, his deprivation of life. It is the message summed up so well by Dostoevsky in *Crime and Punishment*, in the

[22]*Chapters on Love* II, 39, PG 90, 997A.

monologue by Marmeladov as he thinks about the future
judgment:

> "And then Christ will say to us, 'You too come
> forth. Come forth, you drunkards, come forth, you
> weak ones, come forth, you children of shame!' . . .
> And He will say to us, 'You are swine, made in the
> image of the Beast and with his mark; but come
> yet also.' And the wise ones and those of under-
> standing will say, 'Lord, why dost Thou receive these
> men?' And He will say, 'This is why I receive these
> O ye wise; this is why I receive them, O ye of un-
> derstanding, that not one of them believed himself
> to be worthy of this.' And He will hold out His hands
> to us and we shall fall down before Him . . . and we
> shall understand all things! Then we will understand
> all . . . Lord, Thy Kingdom come!"[23]

[23]*Crime and Punishment* I, 2.

CHAPTER THREE

The Gospel's Rejection of Individual Ethics

1. Holy Scripture and the fact of the Church

In the foregoing pages, we have tried to see the real, existential content of morality and sin as the tradition of the Orthodox Church understands them. It looks as if we have made a jump, or as many might think have approached the question the wrong way round in failing to look for the truth about morality and sin first of all in Holy Scripture— in the fount of the Church's doctrine, the written testimony of the first apostolic community.

Nevertheless, it may be essential to make this jump; to assume that the fact of the Church is prior to any written, objective formulation of her truth. This order of precedence does not mean that Scripture is belittled or overlooked. Holy Scripture has a central place in the life of the Church; the worship and asceticism, the life and devotion of the faithful are all imbued with it. But it is only through the experience of the Church, through being organically "grafted" into that experience, that we can recognize the truths of Scripture.

Holy Scripture, then, is not an objectified "source" of Christian truth and revelation, like the "theoretical" texts which outline the impersonal and objective principles of an ideology.[1] Nor are there *two* sources of objective authority,

[1]See Ch. Yannaras, *Truth and Church Unity* (in Greek—Athens, 1977), p. 77.

Scripture and Tradition, as Roman Catholic rationalism would have it. Prior to any written formulation, Christian faith and truth is a *fact*, the fact of God's incarnation and man's deification. It is the unceasing realization and manifestation of this fact, its tangible embodiment in history—in other words, it is the Church.

This order of precedence is a fundamental precondition for approaching the ethics of the Gospel—and, for that matter, the whole teaching of Scripture. The Gospel finds its manifestation in the *fact* of the Church; and if we overlook this fact, we are left with nothing but a disembodied teaching whose significance may be exceptional, but is bound to be relative. (As we know, Scripture formed the basis for all the heretical distortions of the event of salvation, and many who reject Christianity have devoted serious study to the text of Scripture without abnegating their rejection.)

Prior to any written formulation, the historical reality of the Church is the "gospel," the "good news"—the news of incarnate truth and salvation. For this reason, we cannot think of the Bible as the "founding charter" of the Church, containing theoretical "statutes" for the Christian faith and a code of "commandments" for Christian ethics. Christianity is not made up of "metaphysical" convictions and moral directives which always require *a priori* intellectual acceptance. The Gospel of the Church is the manifestation of her life and her experience: and this experience was set down by the eyewitnesses of the resurrection, of the beginning of man's salvation: "... even as they delivered unto us, which from the beginning were eyewitnesses and ministers of the Word" (Lk 1:2).

This is a somewhat extended introductory parenthesis, but it is of vital importance for the subject in hand. Committed as it is to the priority of the Church over Scripture, the Orthodox tradition has never known the temptation to theological schizophrenia. This schizophrenia consists in making a distinction between historical "objectivity" and the certainty born of living experience, between the "historical Jesus" and the "Christ of the Church's *kerygma*," between faith and knowledge, or between ethics and the existential truth of man. The Church is a unified fact of truth and life. Her truth is an experience of life, and her life is truth put into practice and made manifest. The truth and life of the Church is the person of Christ, the mode of existence revealed and inaugurated by the incarnation of the Word. The Church identifies existence with the personal hypostasis, not with biological individuality; and this is why Christ, in the experience of the Church, is "the same yesterday and today and forever" (Heb 13:8). Prior to being doctrine, the Gospel is a manifestation of the fact that God whom none can approach became "Emmanuel," *God with us*; He became the Church, the temporal beginning and the realization within human nature of the trinitarian mode of existence.

Christ is the "head" of the Church, not because He *was* her founder, but because He Himself *constitutes* her body: He forms her trinitarian mode of existence, that ethos of the Church which is to be identified with true life. The ethos or morality proclaimed by the Scriptures is the theanthropic existence of the new Adam, of the "new man" who is Christ. The morality of the Gospel relates to a real, existential transfiguration of man's nature, and not simply to a more complete deontology which leaves human nature existentially unchanged.

2. "A new creation in Christ"

It is characteristic that the word "ethics" is not to be found in the New Testament. We find only the word "godliness" or "piety," which is defined as a "great mystery" and identified with the event of God's "economy," with His work of becoming man for the salvation of mankind: "And without controversy great is the mystery of godliness: God was manifest in the flesh, justified in the Spirit, seen of angels, preached unto the Gentiles, believed on in the world, received up into glory" (1 Tim 3:16). Godliness, or the ethos of the Gospel, is identified with the reality of God's incarnation, and the enthronement of human nature in the life of God—Christ's ascension "in glory."

The union of the divine nature with the human in the person of Christ results in a definitive change in man's existential possibilities. After the fall, it was no longer possible for man's personal distinctiveness and freedom to transcend the natural demands of autonomy and self-sufficiency for the individual biological entity. The relational character of personal distinctiveness is now confined within the limits of our nature, creating the differences and contrasts between existentially individual entities; it is identified with mortal, biological individuality. When the fact of existence is restricted to the autonomy of the individual, this creates a *natural* gulf between man and God which the person's will cannot bridge, condemned as it is to be an individual will.

With the incarnation of God the Word, however, this natural gulf between man and God is removed; the "middle wall of partition" is destroyed (Eph 2:14). In the first Adam, the natural desire for self-subsistence became an autonomous force and condemned his race to expend its existence in the survival of mortal individuality. But now this is reversed: the divine and human natures are joined together and the two natural wills brought into harmony in the person of Christ, the second Adam, and this frees human nature from its self-imposed bondage within the existential limits of mortal individuality. In the person of Christ, human nature *subsists* as a personal hypostasis of communion with the divinity. The personal, theanthropic existence of Christ *hypostasizes* the mortal being of man; it forms a "new creation," a new humanity which *exists* in communion with the Father just as it has been assumed, mortal and bloodstained, by the hypostatic love of the Son.

This "regeneration" of man "in Christ" requires only the cooperation of man's freedom, his assent to Christ's "frenzied love" for him as a person. What God asks of man, existentially alienated and degraded as he is, is an effort, however small, to reject his individual self-sufficiency, to resist its impulses and to will to live as one loving and loved. This is the first step towards participation in the new mode of existence, the new ethos inaugurated by Christ, the new Adam, the father of the new human race. It is the *kenosis* put into practice by Christ as man: the act of emptying out every element of individual autonomy and self-sufficiency, and realizing the life of love and communion.

Conformity to this ethos defines the practical piety of the Church, the practice of asceticism. Asceticism is the endeavor which confirms man's freedom and his decision to reject the rebellion of his individual will and to imitate the obedience of the second Adam. This is obedience not simply in the sense of submission to an external law, but in the sense of faithfulness to the "image" of God which is Christ—of conforming to the trinitarian prototype of life which Christ made incarnate in human nature.

3. The Law as a manifestation of truth and a path of life

From the outlines we have given, it becomes clear that the morality of the Gospel is the absolute antithesis of any kind of individual ethics, since it presupposes the transformation of individuality into an existential reality of communion and relationship. And yet we read in the Bible that there is a "Law" of God, and that man must conform individually to the commandments of this Law. And accustomed as we are to the concept of law which underlies our social and civil coexistence, we are led to think of conformity to the commandments of the Law as an individual achievement, a basis for individual merit and self-sufficiency.

At this point, however, we should recall that the truth of the Law in biblical revelation differs in meaning from the legislation governing a state or social relations; nor does it have the meaning given to the biblical Law in the tradition of the Pharisees. In the Old Testament the truth about the Law and its observance is related to the "agreement" or covenant between God and the people of Israel. According to the book of Exodus, the election of Israel as the "peculiar" and "chosen" people of God was not an arbitrary act: it required the active "assent" of the people, a practical, positive response to God's call.

This practical response is formulated and defined in the next book of the Pentateuch, Leviticus, as "faithfulness to the Law." "When man remains faithful to the Law," says the Haggadah, the rabbinic interpretation and development of the Law, "he is purified and transfigured, and shown to be a child of the Lord of Hosts, the image and glory of Him who made heaven and earth."

The word "Law," used to translate the Hebrew term "Torah," does not correspond exactly to the content of this Hebrew word in the Old Testament: "Torah" is much richer in meaning than "Law" in the sense of a code of obligations imposed by the state or by convention.[2] We shall not embark on the discussion as to whether Plato's "law," the order and harmony which reveals the whole universe as *kosmos* or adornment, corresponds more closely to the biblical Torah or to another biblical term, Hakhmá or Wisdom. If we want to find some sort of analogy, however, we should be nearest the truth comparing the Torah with the rules of the Pythagoreans, and with the rules of artistic creation and musical composition.

If an artist, for instance, wants to express with his brush the beauty of the personal distinctiveness in "things," then he must transcend his subjective preferences as to color, the arbitrariness of his individual sentimental observations, and submit to the laws of color-harmony so as to be able to reveal and express the inner principle or the relationships which go to make up the beauty of the object. And far from destroying the personal quality of a work of art, this obedience enhances it, since it succeeds in expressing the principle of the relationship between the artist and the objects. The biblical Law is closer to this truth than to the notion of laws in a state, or even of the cosmic laws of Plato.

To avoid losing our way in discussions of this kind, we need only call to mind how God gave the Law to Moses, an act identified in the book of Exodus with the revelation to Moses of the divine name. The Law is a manifestation of

---

[2]See Walter Gutbrod, *Das Gesetz im Alten Testament*, in *Theologisches Wörterbuch zum Neuen Testament*, ed. G. Kittel, vol. IV, p. 1029f. Also Walther Eichrodt, *Theologie des Alten Testaments*, part I (Berlin, 1948), p. 31f.

God, a gift of grace—it is not juridical legislation serving a social purpose. It is a *call* to the people of Israel to receive and mediate the name of God, to be manifest as the "radiance" of that truth which is God Himself. In Semitic tradition, the name was not simply what a thing or being was called. It was the expression of its essential hypostasis and, what is more, the manifestation of a personal distinctiveness. The revelation of a name meant communion and relationship with the person whose name was revealed, a possibility of really coming to know him.

This is why, when Moses undertakes the mission entrusted him by God, he asks God to reveal to him His name (Ex 3:13). This name remained hidden from the other nations, and the people of Israel could approach it only within the framework of their relationship, their "covenant" with God. And the covenant was formulated in the Law. In granting the Law, God was placing His name upon the people of Israel. Faithfulness to the Law was the characteristic mark of the "people of God," the way that their life corresponded to His peculiar calling: it manifested the truth of God, His name, incarnate in the body of the chosen people. This is the reality expressed by the injunction in Leviticus: "Ye shall be holy, for I the Lord your God am holy" (Lev 19:2).

Even in the Old Testament, then, observance of the Law was not obedience to some objective legislation which ensured good order in society or virtue in the individual. Observance of the Law was what marked out each Israelite as a member of the people of God. The Israelite had to keep the Law, not to secure individual merit, but because it was this observance alone which secured his participation in the peculiar people who had received the promises of salvation. The aim of being faithful to the Law was not individual justification but manifestation of the truth: it manifested God's covenant with His people, and revealed the truth of the living God. Characteristic are the verses of an evening hymn read in the synagogue: "Lord, almighty king of heaven and earth, I thank Thee for the gift of the Law, through which I am enabled to imprint on my very flesh my love for Thee, and

to adorn my existence with Thy grace and Thy beauty."[3]
With this understanding of the Law as a dynamic revela-
tion of God in human persons, we can understand Christ's
saying that He did not come to "destroy" the Law but to
fulfill it (Mt 5:17). The "new commandment" of the
Gospel is the very person of Christ, the perfect image of
God. Every believer now inscribes this perfect image upon
his own person when he remains true to the Law of the
Gospel, the Law of love which grafts him into the body of
Christ, the Church.[4]

4. Love, the fulfilling of the Law

All the exhortations and commandments in the Gospel
have as their goal love, that dynamic transcendence of egocentric individuality whereby the image of God in Trinity is
realized in the human being. The commandment of love is
the "fulfilling of the Law" (Rom 13:10) not as a more
perfect and effective law, nor as a supplement to the Law,
but as its completion and "end": it is the event in which the
aims of the Law have become a reality and found their
fulfilment.

Consequently, it is a misinterpretation if not a denial
of the Gospel message of salvation to interpret love as an
individual virtue, even the most important such virtue, according to the standards of conventional ethics based on
"good relations," restricting it to "altruism" and "love for
others." The love of the Gospel embodies the self-emptying
of the second Adam; it reinstates life and existence within
the realm of man's created and mortal nature. Love does not
aim simply to improve our social behavior; it has as its

[3]Cf. Oesterley and Box, *Religion and Worship of the Synagogue* (London,
1911), p. 171. See also Hans-Joachim Kraus, *Gottesdienst in Israel* (Munich,
1962[2]); I. Elbogen, *Der judische Gottesdienst in seiner geschichtlichen
Entwicklung* (Frankfurt, 1931[3]).
[4]On this question, see further Jean Daniélou, "Sanctification du Nom et
Avénement du Règne chez les Hébreux," *Cahiers bibliques*, vol. 40, pp.
151-152. *Idem, Théologie du judéochristianisme* (Paris, 1958), p. 40f. Louis
Bouyer, *The Spirituality of the New Testament and the Fathers* (*History
of Christian Spirituality* I, New York, 1963).

aim "that unity which has the Holy Trinity as its teacher," in the words of St Isaac the Syrian.[5]

A direct formulation of this connection between the love of which the Gospel speaks and the trinitarian prototype of our existence is to be found in the "high priestly prayer" of Christ in chapter seventeen of St John's Gospel. Christ prays to the Father for His disciples and for all who shall believe in Him through their preaching, for all the members of His Church, "that they all may be one as Thou, Father, art in Me and I in Thee, that they also may be one in Us" (Jn 17:21); "that they may be one, even as We are one" (Jn 17:22).

This reference to the mode of divine existence, to the trinitarian unity and communion of persons, shows that love is "the first and great commandment" (Mt 22:38). It identifies love with the restoration of God's image in man and man's return to true existence and life: "For love is of God, and every one that loveth is born of God, and knoweth God . . . because as He is, so are we in this world" (1 Jn 4:7 and 4:17). The sundering and "scattering" of God's children is the work of the fall and of death. The work of life and immortality—the work of the Church—is "to gather together in one them that were scattered abroad" (Jn 11:52), to build up the body: "We being many are one body in Christ" (Rom 12:5). The unity of the Church is not merely a sociological fact or a moral achievement; it is a revelation of the truth and a manifestation of life. Only within the existential event which is the unity of the Church do we know man as he truly is, with his personal distinctiveness and the freedom of his love. And we know God and attain personal communion and relationship with Him only to the extent that we accord with the mode of existence whereby the Church is united. The unity of the Church manifests the truth about existence and life "now through a glass darkly" (1 Cor 13:12), since unity is still a dynamic progress from repentance to perfection: "For we know in part . . . but when that which is perfect is come, then that which is in part shall be done away" (1 Cor 13:9-10)—"now I know in part,

[5]*Mystic Treatises* 84, p. 323.

but then face to face" (1 Cor 13:12). But whatever revelation of the truth man does possess, albeit in a mirror and
dimly, is summed up in the unity and love of the Church.

5.   The Gospel's reversal of conventional values

Love, then, is not an easy beginning, but the end which
we are always seeking, the "uncompleted perfection" of
man's moral progress. It begins with repentance, when we
break out of individual self-sufficiency, recognize our human
inadequacy and seek God's grace. The first thing that Jesus
preaches is a message of repentance, because this is the precondition for participation in the Kingdom of God, in the
Church: "Now after that John was put in prison, Jesus
came into Galilee preaching the Gospel of the Kingdom
of God, and saying: The time is fulfilled, and the Kingdom of God is at hand: repent ye" (Mk 1:14-15). Every
page of the Gospels stresses the need for repentance and
faith—the need to escape from imprisonment in our own
egocentricity and to trust in God, giving ourselves over
to Him.

This radical conversion which leads to salvation requires
at the same time a painful loss: Christ affirms that in order
to *save* your soul, you have to *lose* it (Mt 16:25). What
this means is that you have to reject the deep-rooted identification of yourself with your individual nature and with
the biological and psychological self-defence of the ego. It
means renouncing all reliance on human strength, goodness,
authority, action or effectiveness. Whoever wishes to live
must lose his life—the illusion of life which is individual
survival and self-sufficiency—in order to save his life as
personal distinctiveness and freedom: "let him deny himself
and take up his cross." Acceptance of the cross and the
voluntary death of all human self-assurance confers life in
its most powerful and effective form. But, above all, losing
your life means renouncing individual attainments, objective
recognition of virtue and the sense of merit, which are

the mainstays of our resistance to the need for communion with God and trust in Him.

Those who have "trusted in themselves that they were righteous" (Lk 18:9) exclude themselves from the Kingdom. They themselves have shut themselves out of the wedding-feast and remained content with their virtues, with the self-satisfaction afforded by their moral attainments. They have no need for God except to reward their individual performance. This is why the Pharisee, who keeps the Law faithfully, is not justified before God, even though he is "not as other men are, extortioners, unjust, adulterers," but indeed "fasts twice in the week, and gives tithes of all that he possesses"; for he does not justify his existence as a personal fact of communion and relationship with God, beyond corruption and death. The Publican, weighed down as he is by a multitude of sins, is justified because he feels his own inadequacy as an individual and seeks God's mercy, that is to say participation in the life that is grace, a gift of love (Lk 18:10-14).

Rejection of the egocentric satisfaction which comes from the exercise of virtues is a prerequisite for attaining to the repentance preached in the Gospel. This requirement has always seemed a scandalous and provocative reversal of the principles and canons of society's utilitarian ethics. For twenty centuries, the temptation to secularize the Christian message has been summed up above all in the effort to blunt the radical character of repentance in the Gospel, to create a compromise with the formalized code of values required by social utilitarianism.

The Gospel, however, is a straightforward reversal of our rationalistic classification of virtues. Often those recognized by society as "first" are placed "last" by the Gospel, and the last are recognized as first (Mt 19:30). It is the tax-collectors and prostitutes, those who are last in men's esteem, who become guides on the road to repentance, and go into the Kingdom of Heaven before us (Mt 21:31). In the Gospel, there is no yardstick of rationalistic, objective "righteousness" or "justice" by which virtues are evaluated. "And how can you call God just when you come to the passage about the laborers' wages?" asks St Isaac the Syrian. "Where is God's justice? . . . Do not call God just, for His justice is not made known in your affairs . . . He is good, as He says, to the evil and the ungodly."[6]

The people who become citizens of the Kingdom, of the Church of Christ, are not those who are "all right" in their own private religious conscience, not the superficially respectable, the "moral paragons" for the masses. They are the sinners, those who are not afraid to recognize their daily failures and the resistances put up by their rebellious nature, and make no attempt to hide them. These people alone have the capacity to accept the call to repent, to seek refuge in the life-giving grace of God.

Christ states, "I am not come to call the righteous, but sinners to repentance" (Mt 9:13). The consequences of this saying are deeply disturbing for the established ethics of secularized Christianity. The sense of being individually justified, the sense that he is living up to his moral obligations, is in itself enough to cut man off from the call which Christ addresses to him—the call to partake in life and true existence. This is why "all the publicans and sinners drew near unto Him for to hear Him: and the Pharisees and Scribes murmured, saying, This man receiveth sinners and eateth with them" (Lk 15:1-2).

The repentance of sinners is not simply a psychological feeling of guilt: it is man's sense of failure, that sense of inadequacy which shows him ready to receive the grace of God and place personal trust in the divine love. The measure of repentance is not works of merit in expiation; it is the

---

[6]*Mystic Treatises* 60, p. 245; see also 58, p. 234: "Mercy and just judgment in one soul is like a man worshipping God and idols in the same house. Mercy is the opposite of just judgment. Just judgment is the equality of equal measures; for it gives to each as he deserves, without inclining to one part or the other, or having respect of persons when it repays us. Mercy, however, is pity moved by grace, and inclines to all in compassion; it does not requite him who deserves harsh treatment, and it fills to overflowing him who deserves good. And if mercy is on the side of righteousness, then just judgment is on the side of evil. As grass and fire cannot stay together in the same house, so neither can just judgment and mercy remain in one soul. As a grain of sand cannot compare in weight with much gold, so neither can the need for God's just judgment compare with His mercy."

way man abandons hope in his individual powers and throws himself on God's mercy and love for mankind. That is why Jesus says of the prostitute who washes His feet with ointment and tears at the house of Simon the Pharisee, "Her sins, which are many, are forgiven, for she loved much: but to whom little is forgiven, the same loveth little" (Lk 7:36-50). In order to recognize the love of God, man has to feel it shaped to the dimensions of his own abyss. Within these dimensions, the dimensions of death and descent to the depths of hell, the infinity of divine love is revealed.

6. Rebirth and moral restraints

It is perhaps the most characteristic sign of man's fall, of his fruitless persistence in individual moral self-sufficiency, that for twenty centuries now we have managed to reconcile the Gospel with a juridical understanding of the relationship between man and God. The relationship is envisaged as a business deal, with human achievements and divine rewards conferred in return. We use every means and every trick in our efforts to keep the strong wine of the Gospel message in the worn-out wine-skins of our conventional, utilitarian ethics.

Recent critical editions of the Bible inform us that in many manuscripts, Jn 8:3-11 is lacking. This is the scene where the Pharisees bring to Christ "a woman taken in the act of adultery." In every age, the religious conscience has been unable to accept that Christ should assure this woman, who had shown Him no external sign of repentance, that He did not condemn her. He is confronted with the clear commission of a sin, among the gravest in religious and social ethics—a sin which the Law of Moses punished with death. Yet He does not pronounce an indictment, but disarms and shames those who accuse the sinful woman by reminding them of the universality of human failure and sin. Instead of using conventional standards to measure the individual's failure and fall, He points to the need in all men to turn to the grace of God: "He that is without sin among you, let him first cast a stone at her."

The ethics of the Gospel have as their aim the transfiguration of life, not merely a change in external behavior or the punishment of behavior disruptive to social harmony. "You must be born again," says Christ to Nicodemus (Jn 3:7). "Except a man be born again, he cannot see the Kingdom of God—except a man be born of water and the Spirit" (Jn 3:3, 5). The rebirth of man requires that he should die as an individual through baptism and enter into a new life, a mode of existence where life is realized as communion in love and relationship. At baptism the whole of man's life becomes an ecclesial event, a fact of communion and relationship. Thus when a man takes his food in accordance with the Church canons on fasting and feasting, this is not a means to individual survival but becomes a way of partaking in a *common* experience of the use of good things. Time is transfigured into a dynamic cycle of participation in the communion of saints, in the daily festival of their triumph, and in the events of salvation celebrated in the feasts. Space loses dimension and becomes the immediacy of a personal relationship, the unity of living and departed, sinners and saints, an "indivisible union," without beginning or end, measureless and unquantifiable. Marriage is freed from the ontological necessity of biological perpetuation and transformed into an image of the Church, a realization of the trinitarian mode of existence. In his work, in political life and in his everyday dealings with people, man's relationships change: they transform coexistence into the brotherhood of communion, secretly and silently leavening the dead lump of the world.[7]

This transformation of life cannot easily be formalized

[7]"The Christians of the early centuries, when their consciousness of what the Church is was lucid and clear, expressed this transcendence over the relationships created by the biological hypostasis by transferring to the *Church* the terminology which is used of the family. Thus for the new ecclesial hypostasis, 'father' was not the physical progenitor but He 'who is in heaven,' and brothers were members of the Church, not of the family ... A characteristic of the ecclesial hypostasis is the capacity of the person to love without exclusiveness, and to do this not out of conformity with a moral commandment ('Love thy neighbor,' etc.), but out of his 'hypostatic constitution,' out of the fact that his new birth from the womb of the Church has made him part of a network of relationships which transcends every exclusiveness." J. Zizioulas, "From Prosopeion to Prosopon," pp. 315-316.

according to a moralistic pattern. It is a dynamism of life which gives substance to our hope because it exists side by side with the natural impetus towards existential failure. It is a ceaseless test of freedom, since it is only as freedom that love can be realized. This is why the "new life" of the Gospel requires on our part ceaseless repentance and constant renunciation of individual self-sufficiency, together with the pursuit and activation of grace.

The religious consciousness of unregenerate man always insists on seeing repentance as a recognition of individual guilt. The stress on individual guilt, however, is simply a sign of vanity and wounded pride, as St John of the Ladder says.[8] The experience of separation from God, sorrow over the temporary or more permanent loss of His countenance, a taste of the death to which deprivation of the divine life ultimately leads—these are the beginnings of repentance. If we take sin simply as individual guilt and transgression, we deprive it of all existential substance; we turn it into a conventional legal concept, and a psychological complex from which there is no escape. In that case, virtue is merely the individual achievement of keeping the law and remaining true to the moral code—an achievement which satisfies the conscience and thus precludes the conscious need for God's grace, isolating man in the self-sufficiency which brings death.

Whether the path taken is sin or virtue, in either case it is once again the individual who is made into an absolute, this time as a moral unit, and the natural individual relationships in human coexistence which are exalted into ends in themselves. The history of the fall continues even in the structures of moral and religious life. Indeed, the structures of morality and religion are more successful than any other aspect of life in camouflaging and concealing the reality of the fall, the real corruption of man. Taking social utility as their frame of reference, they define sin merely as an objective transgression and virtue merely as a necessary and useful indi-

---

[8] "The proud man will be curious about God's judgments": *Ladder*, step 25, PG 88, 992C.

vidual quality, thus definitely closing the way to repentance. Here we see why the harshest language in the Gospels is reserved for religious people and their rigid forms.

CHAPTER FOUR

A Historical Example: The Challenge of the "Fools for Christ"

1. Mockery of the world

In the life of the Church, there is a historical example which represents the most extreme and extraordinary way of obeying the Gospel preaching about overturning and rejecting individual morality. This is the example of the holy "fools for Christ." In the lives and behavior of these saints, the Church has seen the expression of a particular gift of the Holy Spirit, one of the most acute forms of prophetic preaching.[1]

The fools are usually monks who come down into the "world," into the cities and into "Christian" society, and perform strange and senseless actions—the actions of a madman. Yet these actions always have a deeper meaning: they always aim to uncover the reality and truth hidden behind the practices of this world. The fool goes into taverns and brothels and keeps bad company. He lives on the streets like

[1]Bibliography on fools for Christ is somewhat limited. For my very summary treatment of them here, I have used primarily a study by Ernst Benz, "Heilige Narrheit," in *Kyrios* 3 (1938), pp. 1-55, and the critical edition of the life of St Symeon "who for Christ's sake was called the fool, written by Leontius bishop of Neapolis in the island of Cyprus," published in Uppsala in 1963, by Lennart Rydén (*Das Leben des heiligen Symeon von Leontios von Neapolis*). There is also the written account of the life of St Andrew the Fool for Christ in PG 111, 611ff. I also note two interesting articles by Stephanus Hilpisch: "Die Torheit um Christi Willen," in *Zeitschrift für Aszese und Mystik* 6 (1931), pp. 121-131, and "Die Schmach der Sunde um Christi Willen," in the same periodical 8 (1933), pp. 289-299.

a vagabond, with disreputable people like prostitutes and street-urchins. He appears to fall in with their way of life, whereas in fact he is revealing to them the truth of salvation in a way accessible to them and on their own spiritual level, through extraordinary antics, jokes and absurdities.

He rebukes sinners, and often performs miracles to prevent them falling further. He will usually have the gift of insight, of reading men's hidden depths; and he derides their secret transgressions in public, but in such a way that only the offender can understand the reproach. The fool himself gives the appearance of being very sinful: he provocatively breaks the fasts of the Church before men, while in reality he practises the strictest asceticism in his eating. He poses as a *habitué* of the brothels, but when he is there he admonishes the prostitutes and gives money to save them from vice. At night he returns to the community of the saints, to the seclusion of his prayer and the vision of the face of God; and in the morning, he dons once again the mask of foolishness, "mocking the vain and slanderous world." This is indeed a mockery of the world: it is the most extreme form of asceticism, ultimate self-denial, absolute rejection of the world's standards and complete renunciation of the ego.

The fools come to remind us that the Gospel message is "foolishness," and that salvation and sanctity cannot be reconciled with the satisfaction that comes from society's respect and objective recognition. They present themselves during periods of "secularization" among Christians, when the Christian identity seems to depend on the conventional standards and ideas of a world which measures the true life and virtue of man with the yardsticks of social decorum and deontology.

The fool is a vessel of grace, who has immediate experience of the Kingdom of God and undertakes to manifest prophetically the contrast between the "present age" and the age of the Kingdom, the basic difference in standards and criteria. He refuses any objective recognition of virtue and piety for himself, and takes to the limit his rejection of praise and honor among men. He knows that individual virtue separates man from God because it leads to self-satisfaction;

and also that it separates man from his fellow-men, because they dare not expose to him their need and their weakness.

The fool does not pursue his ascetic way in the secure spirituality of a monastery, but alone, in the world. He grapples at close quarters with the world and the devil, taking up the cross of the Church, the cross of those who are tormented and sinful. This is another form of revelatory "tragedy": of his own accord, he takes on the grotesque mask of foolishness so as to reveal the truth of the person, the artificiality of the nice-looking masks of a conventional decorum which destroys personal distinctiveness and freedom. In the artificial "reality" of a world which changes good into evil and evil into good, and where "the ruler of this world" is on the watch to see that this falsity is maintained, the fool takes it upon himself to leap into the house of the strong man and seize his goods.[2] The only way the saint can make this leap is to go into the midst of the world wearing the mask of foolishness, of social irresponsibility, and uncover the true reality before people's very eyes, tearing apart the veils of conventional morality, established attitudes and deceptive value-judgments. This is not an ironic, Socratic disclosure but a personal awakening, actively forcing people to arouse themselves. Fools for Christ do not choose this foolishness as a form of asceticism, but are chosen for it by God. They do it "involuntarily." That is where their way has taken them. And this is a taste of truth and of dangerous freedom.

2. Taking on another's guilt

In the West, the fools' form of asceticism is unknown. "The West lacked the conditions necessary for such an extreme form of sanctity to appear," writes Ernst Benz, a Western student of the holy fools.[3] Isolated actions parallel to those of the fools in the East are attributed only to St

---

[2]See Mt 12:29.

[3]"Heilige Narrheit," pp. 3, 4. See also Hilpisch, "Die Torheit...," p. 129.

Ulphias (eighth century), St John Colombini (†1367) and St John of God (†1550). In the East many fools for Christ are named, but we do not have historical information about all of them. We know of St Symeon of Emesa (in the time of Justinian, between 527 and 567),[4] St Andrew of Constantinople (880-946),[5] St Thomas the Fool for Christ[6] and St Luke of Ephesus (eleventh century).[7] In the tradition of the Russian and Serbian Churches, there is St John the fool (†1490, recognized as a saint by the Synod of Moscow in 1674), St Basil the Fool (†1552) and St John of Moscow (†1589).

In the *Lausiac History* too, however, and in St John of the Ladder and elsewhere in ascetic writings and church history, we frequently encounter isolated actions and examples corresponding to those of the fools. Thus we read of how St Macarius of Egypt was living as a monk in a hut outside some village, when the parents of a girl accused him of seducing their daughter. They tied a rope round his neck and led him through all the village, crying, "Look at this 'anchorite' who raped our daughter!" They demanded that he should pay compensation and undertake the maintenance of the child which was to be born. Without defending himself, the saint accepted his disgrace and returned to his cell. He began to work twice as hard as before, weaving rush mats and baskets, and saying to himself, "Macarius, now you have a wife, and you must work harder in order to feed her." Every day he would take whatever money he had earned to the girl's house, and received blows and insults in return. This went on until the girl, in the pangs of childbirth, admitted the monk's innocence. Then, however, Macarius fled into the desert to avoid being honored as a saint.[8]

The same story is told of Eustathius of Caesarea when he was still in minor orders, a simple reader, and also of Nicon

[4]See the critical edition by Rydén, and PG 93, 1669-1748.
[5]See PG 111, 628-88.
[6]See PG 86, 2767.
[7]PG 65, 257-260.
[8]*Lausiac History*, ch. 70, ed. Butler, Texts and Studies VI (Cambridge, 1904), p. 165f.

of Sinai.[9] Another monk, Andrew of Messina, later abbot of a monastery, was accused of theft and accepted the accusation without objection until his innocence was proved.[10]

For the monks, this act of taking on another's guilt, voluntarily and without protest, was not simply an opportunity to increase in humility. It was a practical manifestation of their conviction that sin is common to all, an obvious way of participating in the common cross of the Church, in the fall and failure of all mankind. The monk is "apart from all" but also "joined with all," and he sees the sins of others as his own, as sins common to the human nature in which we all partake. Distinguishing the sins of individuals does not have any real meaning, any more than does distinguishing individual virtues. What condemns or saves us is our refusal or our striving to "alter" the rebellion of our common nature into a personal relationship of repentance and communion. Man must imitate the self-emptying of Christ, His renunciation of any individual claim for justification: he must voluntarily take on the failure common to all and bring it to God, embodying in his own person the words of the Apostle Paul, "I fill up that which is lacking in the afflictions of Christ in my flesh for His body's sake, which is the Church" (Col 1:24). Only thus do the saints who live according to the trinitarian mode of existence overcome the fragmentation of our nature caused by sin, altering sin into a humble acceptance of others, a fact of communion and love.

Characteristic is the story of Theophilus and Maria (*c.* 540) related by John of Ephesus. They were only children from aristocratic families in Antioch, both of exceptional beauty, betrothed to each other, "who sought to apply to their own lives the words of the Bible, 'He hath made him to be sin for us, who knew no sin' (2 Cor 5:21)." Theophilus played the buffoon, the jester, while Maria dressed as a prostitute. They roamed the city streets acting as comics, telling jokes and talking nonsense: and people laughed at them, and sometimes even struck them. They sought the contempt of men, the utter degradation of their own ego, in order to gain that

[9]PG 65, 310.
[10]PL 74, 178-179.

ineffable freedom and taste of life which comes as a gift
when the last resistance of egocentric individuality is dead.
On one occasion, a woman asked Maria, "Why do you wallow
in sin, my child"; and she replied without hesitation,
"Madam, pray that God will raise me up from the filth of
sin."[11]

3. Complete abandonment of the ego

The most abundant and striking historical evidence is
preserved in the complete biographies of St Symeon of Emesa
and St Andrew of Constantinople. In the persons of these
two saints we have a complete picture of the holy fools' spiritual gift and the prophetic message they embody.

St Symeon was an anchorite in the wilderness beyond the
Jordan when he received the call from God to live as a fool.
He said to his companion in the ascetic life, "In the power
of Christ, I am going to mock the world."[12] Then he went
down into the city of Emesa "and performed miracles, but
for God's sake he pretended to be a fool": he hid his virtue,
denigrating himself and shunning any respect or honor that
might come from men. For the gifts of holiness were certainly
manifest in him: he had the gifts of healing, foresight and
insight, as well as "pure prayer" and tears.

Thus on one occasion, as his biographer tells us, "on a
Sunday, he took some walnuts and went into the church at the
beginning of the Liturgy, cracking walnuts and putting out
the lamps. When they threw themselves upon him to drive
him out, he went up into the pulpit and from there he pelted
the women with walnuts. With a great deal of effort, they
managed to drive him out; but as he went out he overturned
the tables of the pastry-sellers, and they gave him wounds
which nearly killed him."[13] Actions such as this testify to the
effort he made to refuse at any cost recognition and fame as a
saint. He preferred to be considered a half-crazy monk with-

[11]*Patrologia Orientalis*, vol. 19, pp. 164-179.
[12]PG 93, 1704B; Rydén, p. 142, ll. 25-26.
[13]PG 93, 1708D; Rydén, p. 145, 25-29, and p. 146, 1-3.

out even the rudiments of social decorum—that decorum which safeguards and preserves the ego.

On another occasion, Symeon was working as an apprentice in a wine shop; but his virtue had started to become known, and people were coming to the shop to see him and find in his person a confirmation of the objective type of a virtuous man. Then, in order to avoid men's honor and esteem, Abba Symeon pretended that he felt carnal desire towards the shopkeeper's wife and that he wanted to assault her to satisfy his lust. "While the man's wife was asleep on her own," says the biographer, "and he himself was pouring wine, Abba Symeon went up to her and made as if to take off his cloak. When she cried out, her husband came in and she said to him, 'Throw out this thrice-accursed fellow—he wanted to rape me.' And they struck him with their fists, and drove him out of the shop into the cold."[14] And the shopkeeper put it about all through the city that "he wanted to commit adultery with my wife, if he had had his way."

For the same reason, St Symeon used to keep company with the city's prostitutes and dance with them in the streets, monk of the Church though he was, and would endure their lewd gestures: "He had reached such a state of purity and freedom from passions that he would often caper and dance with a chorus-girl on either side of him, and associate with them and play with them in public; and sometimes the shameless women would put their hands into his bosom and provoke and slap him. But the old man, like pure gold, was in no way defiled by them."[15]

In men's eyes, St Symeon sometimes appeared to transgress even the canonical order of the Church, the basic obligations of fasting: "The righteous man often ate meat, while he did not taste bread all week. As for his fasting, no one observed it; but he used to eat meat in front of all, to deceive them."[16] "In Lent, he would not taste anything until Great Thursday. But on Great Thursday he would sit from morning eating cake, so that the people who saw him were scandal-

[14]PG 93, 1712C; Rydén, p. 148, 1-5.
[15]PG 93, 1724C; Rydén, p. 154, 27-29, and p. 155, 1-4.
[16]PG 93, 1712D; Rydén, p. 148, 10-13.

ized, saying that he did not fast even on Great Thursday."[17] This provocation which scandalized the faithful recalls Christ's "provocative" breaking of the Sabbath: the way He took responsibility for the paralytic "taking up his bed" (Jn 5:1-16), and excused the disciples who "began to pluck ears of corn and to eat" on the Sabbath day (Mt 7:1-16). Christ does not destroy the Law, but shows that the Law is transcended in the Kingdom. And St Symeon is a citizen of the Kingdom: in his person, he embodies the transcendence of the Law, the "transgression," which is a scandal only to those of us who still live in need of the Law, in need of obedience, because we have not yet attained or know nothing about the "end" of the Law which is the freedom of the saints. In Emesa, it seems that Symeon deliberately provoked scandal. Once, he managed to enter the women's public baths—"as it were to the glory of God," notes his biographer, Bishop Leontius of Neapolis in Cyprus— "and they all rushed upon him and drove him out with blows."[18] There are moral and social restraints, like the Law, for those who are subject to the passions. But there is also the reality of the "passionlessness" of the saints; and this is what Symeon reveals, liberating our spiritual vision from the shadow and the narrowness of the Law.

Side by side with their essential content, these extraordinary tactics also had their social dimension, as Symeon's biographer assures us: the saint succeeded in gaining the liking and trust of sinners, of the destitute and disreputable.[19] He saved women who were living in brothels; providing them with money, he liberated them from vice and brought them to lawful marriage or even to monastic life.[20] He also won over unbelievers and heretics, and helped them to return to right faith. "His whole aim was this: firstly, to save souls, whether through the attacks he unleashed on them either in jest or by guile, or again through the miracles which he performed in folly, or through exhortations addressed to them as though he

[17]PG 93, 1728AB; Rydén, p. 156, 23-28.
[18]PG 93, 1713BC; Rydén, p. 149, 1-18.
[19]PG 93, 1713D; Rydén, p. 149, 16-18.
[20]PG 93, 1708B; Rydén, p. 145, 9-15.

were playing the fool. And secondly, to prevent his virtue from becoming known, and himself from receiving praise and honor from men."[21] He advised an archdeacon in the city, "I beseech you never to hold any soul in contempt, and particularly not a monk or a poor man, as has happened. For love knows that among the poor, and especially among the blind, there are people who shine like the sun, cleansed by their endurance and the ills they have suffered."[22]

Symeon also had a blessed end. "The Lord glorified him and translated him [in the body]. Then everyone came to their senses, as if waking from sleep, and told one another what miracles he had performed for each of them, and how it was for God that he had pretended to be a fool."[23]

An exact parallel is to be found in the story of St Andrew the Fool for Christ. He was born a Scythian and came to Constantinople as the slave of Theognostus, *protospatharios* to Leo the Wise (886-911). Theognostus gave him a Greek education and made him steward of his house. Andrew accepted the monastic vocation, and lived as a fool for about thirty years; he died at the age of sixty-six in about 946. He had a particular spiritual bond with Nicephorus, a priest at the church of Haghia Sophia in Constantinople; it was to him that Andrew confided his strict asceticism, and Nicephorus gave the saint his support. His biographer, too, relates that he saw Andrew the Fool in his secret cell transfigured and radiant with the light of divine glory, like Christ on Tabor.

4. Freedom without bounds

The fools for Christ seem to reject the Apostle Paul's admonition to accept any personal deprivation and sacrifice in order to avoid scandalizing the faithful (1 Cor 8:13). But what kind of scandal is St Paul talking about? It is something that causes confusion in the realm of truth, and may thus deprive others of the possibility of participating in truth—

[21]PG 93, 1728C; Rydén, p. 157, 12-16.
[22]PG 93, 1741CD; Rydén, p. 166, 29, and p. 167, 1-3.
[23]PG 93, 1745B; Rydén, p. 168, 68-69.

the possibility of salvation. If by eating food offered to idols you give your brother's "weak conscience" grounds for supposing that there is some connection between idol worship and the truth and life of the Church, then the responsibility for the confusion you cause is great indeed.

The challenge of the fools, however, does not create confusion in people's faith, nor does it obscure the truth of the Church. It simply surprises those who have identified faith and truth with the secularized concept of moral uprightness and conventional decorum. Fools for Christ have the gift, and the audacity, to manifest openly the human fall and sin which is common to us all: this is the reality of our nature, and it is not cancelled out by individual cases of "improvement," nor by concealment behind social externals.

In this sense, every monk in the Orthodox East is a kind of "fool for Christ." He wears a garment of mourning, openly declaring that he accepts our common fall and sin; and he withdraws into the ascetic life, waging war on this fall and this sin on behalf of us all. This same acceptance is the calling of every member of the Church. If we persist in ignoring the Gospel of salvation and continue to identify the regeneration of man with the social recognition of individual virtues, with worldly success in gaining individual moral respectability, then the fault is ours alone—and it is an error which bars us from truth and life.

The prototype to which the Church has always looked is not individual moral self-sufficiency, but the monks' lament of repentance. This lament is ultimately joyful—a "joyful sorrow"—and turns sin into a measure of the acceptance of Christ's love. Man is able to mourn and lament only when he knows exactly what he has lost, and experiences this loss as a personal deprivation, a personal thirst. This is why repentance, the *personal* sense of the loss of God, is also a first revelation, our first acquaintance with His person, our first discovery of the extent of His love.

In the case of the fools for Christ, certainly their shocking freedom from every law, rule, restriction or code of obligations is not simply didactic in its purpose, reminding us of the danger of identifying virtue and holiness with conventional social decorum and egocentric moral rectitude. No one can ever really teach simply by calling into question mistaken conceptions and ways of life: one has to make the fulness of the saving truth incarnate in oneself. The shocking freedom of the fools is first and foremost a total death, a complete mortification of every individual element in their lives. This death is the freedom which can break and destroy every conventional form; it is resurrection into a life of personal distinctiveness, the life of love which knows neither bounds nor barriers.

The example of the "fools for Christ," then, is neither extreme nor inexplicable, as it may perhaps seem to many people. It is the incarnation of the Gospel's fundamental message: that it is possible for someone to keep the whole of the Law without managing to free himself from his biological and psychological ego, from corruption and death. And that on the other hand, it is enough if someone humbly accepts his own sin and his fall, without differentiating it from the sin and fall of the rest of mankind, trusting in the love of Christ which transfigures this acceptance into personal nearness and communion, into a life of incorruption and immortality.

CHAPTER FIVE

The Morality of the Church—
A Liturgical Ethos

1. Faithfulness to reality

Christians are not unaware of sin: on the contrary, their daily asceticism and effort is directed towards fighting it. They are not, however, afraid of it with the egocentric fear of individual guilt, for there is "He that taketh away the sin of the world" (Jn 1:29), Christ "who raiseth up the dead."

What we have here is a faithfulness to the truth of human existence, to the truth of the fall and equally of the regeneration of man, which excludes idealistic illusions, utopian designs and reassuring embellishments. What is here involved is the radically new *quality* of life which makes Christian morality, the Christian ethos, different from the pursuit of even the noblest moral ends. Before all else, Christian morality looks to the personal *identity* of man. Its first and final step is to identify man with his true self, to reject the masks imposed upon him by the egocentric need for external and formal compliance with the demands of social recognition and respectability.

What primarily interests the Christian is not virtue but truth. If virtue becomes autonomous, it may distance man from God. Truth cannot be autonomous and does not cause separation, because it is not a *part* of life but life in its totality. And if man's whole life is a movement away from God, then simply to realize this fact forms an initial relation-

ship with Him. What distances man from Christ and the
Church is falsity of life, the "existential lie" of the masks of
the superego, and conformity to the external formalities of
conventional behavior.

"The change which Christians undergo does not reside in
forms and external formalities" say the Macarian homilies,
"as most people think, imagining that the difference and the
distinction between the world and Christians lies in this, in
forms and formalities . . . For it is in the renewal of the
intellect, in the peace of our reasonings, and in love and
heavenly *eros* for the Lord that the *new creation* of Christians
is distinguished from all other men of the world. This was
why the Lord's coming took place."[1] The passage concludes
by saying that the forms and formalities, the objectified
criteria of individual virtue—"seemingly fine actions," as it
calls them—so far from being identified with the truth of
salvation, may even lead man astray, keeping him far from
salvation and enslaving him to the glory and praise of men.
"Sometimes even seemingly fine actions are performed for
the glory and praise of men; and before God these are
equivalent to injustice and theft and the other sins."[2] We
frequently find statements like this in the writings of the
fathers.

2. The manifestation of the truth of
   God in human morality

Certainly, the change in Christians which is the objective
of the Church can sometimes be measured by the criteria of
social, objective ethics, with the evaluative categories of good
and of virtue. But it is not identified with them—this is the
essential point. Individual virtue does not always indicate a
saving change in man: it may be, by the Church's criteria,
"equivalent to injustice and theft and the other sins." The
Church does not deny the objective moral obligations and
social duties of Christians living in the world. But in no way

[1]*The Fifty Spiritual Homilies of Macarius* 5, 5, ed. Dörries, pp. 49-50.
[2]*Op. cit.* 5, 6, p. 54.

does she confine her own truth and morality within the limits of social behavior and the conventional obligations which govern it.

The Gospel instructs Christians to give the world a practical demonstration of the new ethos of the Kingdom of God through good works. But this practical demonstration is a revelation of truth; it is the "glory," the manifestation of God,[3] the realization of His image in human persons: "Let your light so shine before men that they may see your good works and glorify your Father which is in heaven" (Mt 5:16). The scriptural emphasis on the need for "good works" means precisely this: that the truth should be manifested in its hypostatic realization—as action, which is a reality of life, and not as abstract theory. And the only reality of life, of eternal life, is the personal existence of God, the fact of trinitarian communion. The "good works" performed by the faithful are manifestations of this life, actions which reveal the truth. Without this essential and real content, "all our righteousness is as a filthy rag" (Is 64:6).[4]

Any good work, any objective act of virtue is justified in the Church's eyes only when its object is to manifest God,

[3]The word δόξα ("glory") was used by the Septuagint translators of the Old Testament to convey in Greek the Hebrew term *kabod*, meaning appearance, manifestation, brightness, majesty (see Kittel, *Theologisches Wörterbuch zum Neuen Testament* vol. II, p. 240f., with bibliography). The meaning of the Greek word, however, is originally: opinion, belief, conjecture, and later: others' opinion of someone, good reputation, honor, fame, laudation. Without reference to the Hebrew *kabod*, the biblical expression "δόξα Θεοῦ" (the "glory" of God) would be well-nigh incomprehensible.

[4]In the New Testament, there is an apparent opposition between faith and works: in particular, the Apostle Paul seems to give priority to faith over works (cf. Rom 3:27-28, 4:2-6; Gal 2:16; Eph 2:9, 2 Tim 1:9 etc.) while the Apostle James apparently reverses this priority (Jas 2:14-25). But this opposition only exists if we objectify the terms and strip them of the existential content that they have in Holy Scripture. Faith is an attitude of trust in God which presupposes an initial "annunciation" of the truth of the personal God (a "hearing of faith," Rom 10:17). Without this trust, which constitutes a relationship and communion with God, "works of righteousness" (of goodness and virtue) do not save man. At the same time, however, faith is "dead" if it does not go beyond an ideological certainty, and individual, psychological conviction, and does not express a work and an act of life, and real manifestations of trust in God and surrender of oneself to Him.

to reveal the image of God in man. "Pursue charity," writes
St Isaac the Syrian, "for when this exists within you, you
become an image of that holy beauty in the likeness of which
you were made."[5] For conventional ethics, charity is a "good
deed" which salves the individual conscience, a praiseworthy
example of the virtue of altruism. For the Church, it is a work
of "fellowship" which takes place primarily "within," and
depicts in man the image of the holy beauty of his trinitarian
prototype. Ultimately, says St Isaac, charity or mercy is man's
relationship and communion with the whole Church—with
all God's world, which is His Church and Kingdom. It sums
up the whole world in the "microcosm" of man's "heart."
"What is a merciful heart? A heart which burns for all creation, for men and birds and animals and demons, and for
every creature. As he calls them to mind and contemplates
them, his eyes fill with tears. From the great and powerful
feeling of compassion that grips the heart and from long
endurance his heart diminishes, and cannot bear to hear or
see any injury or any tiny sorrow in creation. This is why he
constantly offers prayer with tears for dumb beasts, and for
the enemies of truth, and for those who hurt him, that they
may be protected and shown mercy; likewise he prays for the
race of creeping things, through the great compassion which
fills his heart, immeasurably, after the likeness of God."[6]

The "merciful heart," then, is where man shows his likeness to God who is compassionate and merciful. It is in this
secret core of his existence that the "change" in man takes
place, the manifestation of the new substance of humanity,
of God's "new creation," the Church. It was for the sake of
this change that "the coming of the Lord took place," as the
Macarian homilies say in the passage quoted above. The
coming of the Lord, God's entry into the world—that un-
approachable mystery—gives rise to a second mystery: human
nature is transfigured, and the "heart" of man is transformed.
The Macarian homilies state again: "Our Lord came to us
for this purpose: so as to change our nature, and transform
and renew and recreate this soul which had been destroyed

[5] *Mystic Treatises* 1, p. 6.
[6] *Mystic Treatises* 81, p. 306.

by the passions through transgression, mingling it with His own spirit of divinity. He came to make a new mind and a new soul, new eyes, new ears, and a new spiritual tongue—to make those who believe in Him altogether new men."[7]

3. The liturgical gathering of those that were scattered

God became man so that the nature of man should be transformed—mind, senses and reason. Man's individual effort and virtue can only "improve" his outward behavior. It is unable to transform his nature, to do away with the existential self-sufficiency of nature bounded by individuality, to transform his mortal and corruptible flesh into the flesh of incorruption. This transformation can take place only if man is grafted into the *body* of Christ, the existential reality which creates life as personal communion, rather than life as individual survival.

This grafting means a "transformation" of man's life within the theanthropic existence of Christ, the changing of the "wild olive" into a "good olive" (Rom 11:17-24). It means total, bodily participation in the body of Christ; eating His flesh and drinking His blood. "Except ye eat the flesh of the Son of Man and drink His blood, ye have no life in you . . . He that eateth My flesh and drinketh My blood, dwelleth in Me and I in Him". (Jn 6:53, 56). The eating and drinking of Christ's flesh and blood changes individuals into members of a unified body, and individual survival into communion of life and unity of life—that unity which exists among the members of a body, and between them and the head. This unity of life in the context of personal communion is the Church.

The Church is a supper, the supper of the eucharist. The realization, manifestation, definition and essence of the Church is the eucharist, where the members of Christ come together and form His body: it is the unifying potential for a communion of persons within an undivided, new nature.

[7]*Spiritual Homilies* 44, 1, p. 291.

"Understand this in holiness," we read in the Areopagitic writings: "when the venerable symbols which signify Christ and through which we partake of Him are placed upon the divine altar, the commemoration of the saints is linked inseparably with this action, showing how the saints are indivisibly joined in heavenly and holy union with Him."[8]

The eucharist unifies the life of persons in the community of Christ's theanthropic nature, and thus restores the image of God's "ethos," of the fulness of trinitarian, personal communion, to man's *being* or mode of existence—it manifests the existential and at the same time *theological* character of ethical perfection in man. The aim of the eucharist is "that unity which has the Holy Trinity as its teacher," in the words of St Isaac the Syrian quoted above.[9]

Manifestation of the trinitarian ethos, the way that the image of God's "ethos" is manifested in man's being, constitutes the liturgical ethos of the Church, the fact of "gathering together in one the children of God that were scattered abroad" (Jn 11:52)—the reality of the Church. In other words, the ethos or morality of Christians is the fact of the eucharist, an existential fact of unity and communion. As the Areopagitic writings note once again, "Although the divine rite of the synaxis is single, simple and unified in its source, out of love for mankind it is multiplied into a holy diversity of symbols, and embraces all the images that represent the Godhead; but in its singleness, through these symbols it unifies those who come to it in holiness, bringing them together once again into the oneness proper to itself."[10]

This, then, is why the Church's ethic is diametrically opposite to any philosophical, social or religious ethic: because it rejects individual virtue, private attainment and individual valuation. The morality of the Church is a liturgical morality, a liturgical ethos of unity and communion, a *personal* participation in the body of God the Word. We know the Church as the *people* of God, the chosen *race*, the heavenly *city*, the *body* of Christ, the new *creation*, the new *Israel*, the *Kingdom*

---

[8]*On the Church Hierarchy*, III, 3, 9, PG 3, 437C.
[9]See above, Chapter 3 n. 5.
[10]*On the Church Hierarchy*, III, 3, 3, PG 3, 429A.

of God, the new *Jerusalem*. All these designations—"the holy diversity of symbols"—identify the truth of the Church not with an ideology, a system or a religious belief, but with a reality of coexistence—with a *liturgy*, λαοῦ τὸ ἔργον or "the work of the people." What makes someone a Christian is not his private virtue or ideas or convictions, but the fact that he participates organically in the life-giving body of Christ, being grafted into the liturgical unity of the Church. Sin is what cuts man off and alienates him from the body of the Church: virtue is what brings him in and grafts him onto the "good olive" of grace.

4. The realization of the New Covenant in the eucharist

The reality of the Kingdom of God, of the Church, is foreshadowed in the Old Testament, and prefigured in the historical existence of Israel. Israel is the people of God, chosen not for its righteousness or the saintliness of its heart, but because it undertook to affirm and manifest God's relationship with the human race in history. It remains God's people however much it shows itself stiff-necked and disobedient to His will. What sets it apart is the call it has received, the covenant which God has made with it. The historical privileges of the Hebrews, their knowledge of the true God and of His will, are guaranteed not by individual piety or virtues but by the primary fact that the Hebrews belong to the chosen people, and coexist in that unity which constitutes a revelation. The Law was not given to them to produce moral improvements in individuals, but as an immediate and practical way of dividing them off from the Gentiles, enabling them to participate and remain in the body of God's people through their way of life.

The historical emergence of Israel prefigures the coming of the Church which is the "new Israel," the peculiar people with whom God puts into effect His "New Covenant," the new relationship of His union with the human race *according to nature*. The Church is the "people of grace": she represents that mode of coexistence and communion which reveals the gift of true, trinitarian life incarnate in human nature. She is the historical manifestation of God's new relationship with mankind as a whole "in flesh and blood." She is the fact of God's incarnation and the deification of man, the eucharistic supper of the Kingdom.

Like the Old Covenant, God's New Covenant with man does not confine itself to a set of duties for the individual, but transfers man's *mode of existence* from individuality to community and communion. Throughout the revelation contained in the Bible, the criteria for truth and salvation involve the general relationship between God and man; and this relationship operates and is ministered within the dynamic framework of the life of a people or a body faithful to God's calling, "a remnant according to the election of grace" (Rom 11:5).

To be more specific, throughout the biblical revelation it is not possible to approach the truth of God as individuals: He cannot be known through individual intellectual ability, through syllogistic reductions or sentimental uplift. Truth is imparted organically, together with the transmission of life and immediate personal experience. God is not the Supreme Being envisaged as an intellectual concept, the "first cause" or the authoritative "first principle" of logical necessity; He is "the God of our fathers, of Abraham and Isaac and Jacob, the God and Father of our Lord Jesus Christ"—the God of our fathers' personal experience, with whom they had a personal relationship. And knowledge of God begins when we live our faith, our trust in the experience of our fathers; it means becoming an organic part of this relationship.

Correspondingly, the ethic of the biblical revelation relates to our personal, experiential entry into a shared reality of life which consists of faithfulness to God's covenant and the obedience to the Law which guarantees this common faithfulness. Here again, we are dealing not with the intellectual acceptance of moral principles and axioms, ensuring moral perfection for the individual, but with faith and trust: it is a matter of sharing organically in our fathers' experience, in the transmission of life and imparting of the truth. The ultimate aim is participation in the community of life, in the existential transformation of individuality into personal distinctiveness, revealed in the context of love and communion.

On this view, the liturgy of the Church is not simply an expression of religious worship, but the core and sum of her life and truth, of her faith and ethics. The life and truth of the Church, her faith and her ethos are a *liturgy*, an organic function of a unified body which receives man in order to save him, to make him whole and restore him to the fulness of his existential possibilities as a person: "What shall the receiving of them be, but life from the dead?" (Rom 11:15).

"Christians, therefore," say the Macarian homilies, "belong to another age; they are sons of the heavenly Adam, a new generation, children of the Holy Spirit, radiant brothers of Christ, like unto their father, the spiritual and radiant Adam; they are of that city, that race, that power. They belong not to this world but to another world."[11] This "other world" of Christians, more real than the "real" world of corruption and death, is life restored to the unity of the one "race" and the true "city." It is the eucharistic liturgy of life which returns to its hypostatic source as thanksgiving, εὐχαριστία; as a loving response which sums up existence, the world and the beauty of the world in personal distinctiveness and freedom.

5. The cosmological dimension of the liturgical ethos

The ethos of the Church is liturgical not only because it unifies the *people* in the common *work* of the eucharistic response, the response of thanksgiving to God's call and covenant, but also because it sums up the inner principle of the world, its meaning and end, in this eucharistic relationship between creation and its creator. This is another way in which Christian ethics differ from any other philosophical, social or political ethics: they have a cosmological dimension, and do not make a distinction between the ethos

[11]*Spiritual Homilies* 16, 8, p. 163.

of man's life and the life and truth of the world. They presuppose that man is the celebrant of life in its totality, in the universal oneness of existence beyond any division or separation between transcendent and mundane, between material and spiritual. Their goal is the unification of "all in all" in the single uniqueness of the divine life.

The unification of "all in all" is brought about with the incarnation of God the Word, and finds its practical manifestation in the eucharist of the Church. The Church's eucharist is a *cosmic liturgy*: it sums up the life of the world and the inner principle of the world in the "principle" of man, in the human word glorifying God, the word which is made flesh in man's life. This is Christ's word of obedience to the Father's will, the "yes" of the Son's assent. The eucharist is man's assent to the assumption of his nature by Christ, an assent which unifies the principle, the "word" of all created nature in the "yes" of Christ's obedience. Man is the celebrant of the eucharistic unity of the world: the restoration of life as communion, communion of the persons within human nature, as a communion of participation in the life of the world. And it sums up the oneness of the life of created things in a movement, an impulse which is eucharistic and loving, turning back towards God.[12]

The connection between man's ethos and the life and truth of the world has specific consequences in the way Christians confront and experience their use of the world, the production and consumption of material goods, technology, economics and political activity. It is not possible to participate in the life of the Church and to despise material reality or remain indifferent to it, to consider that man's salvation bears no relation to matter and the use of the world. True repentance is not simply an intellectual or emotional event; it is an existential change, a change in our mode of existence, and man's existence is organically connected with the life of the world and use of the world. In his moral endeavor, the Christian strives to reject autonomous indi-

---

[12]*The Person and Eros* (in Greek), §§ 33, 34. *Truth and Church Unity* (in Greek), pp. 49, 50. John Meyendorff, *Christ in Eastern Christian Thought* (New York, 1975²), p. 131 ff.: "The Cosmic Dimension of Salvation."

viduality and to transfigure life into a relationship of love and communion. This means coming to see the neutral "objects" of the material world, subject as they are to the need for individual survival and self-subsistence, as *acts* of God's love, *principles* of personal distinctiveness; it means transfiguring them together with one's life into realities of relationship and communion.

Without this transfiguration of the material world into a fact of relationship and the starting-point for a relationship, the Christian ethic no longer looks towards the existential "changing" of man, the salvation of life from corruption and death. It turns into an idealistic system which, like all idealism, is inevitably conventional and essentially irrelevant to real life and its problems. The works of economists in our own century such as R.H. Tawney and A. Fanfani, to name but two significant examples, have shown how a certain understanding of Christianity which divides morality from being, and piety from the truth of existence and life, necessarily leads to an idealistic interpretation of the faith and makes material reality into an autonomous absolute. It opens the way to the polarized phenomenon of historical materialism, the polarization of capitalism *versus* marxism[13]—this modern form of sin and the torture of man.

At the same time, however, the way that the ethos of the Church relates to material reality and life as a whole, the liturgical use of the world within the eucharistic mode of existence, can never be codified or organized into an economic system or a political ideology. The cosmic dimension of the Church's ethos is revealed only in the context of a personal, existential change in man, in the dynamic transcendence of individual self-sufficiency—only when the way man uses the world is transfigured, becoming an act of relationship and communion. For this reason, too, the way in which Christians live out their use of the world cannot be separated from the central core of the "new" life represented by the eucharist. It cannot be separated from the freedom of love, or become

[13]See R. H. Tawney, *Religion and the Rise of Capitalism* (Penguin Books, 1975[11]); A. Fanfani, *Catholicism, Protestantism and Capitalism* (London, 1935). See also Ch. Yannaras, *Truth and Church Unity*, p. 162f.

autonomous in the form of binding principles for a political or economic program. Certainly the ethos of the Church creates a mode of social coexistence, a way of using the world, and consequently a culture, a general attitude of life which is bound to find expression also in the field of politics and economics. But this expression will always be embodied in persons, and identified with the personal adventure of freedom—never with schematic solutions objectively imposed.

The ethos of the Church is one of freedom from any relativity, any bond or criterion belonging to this age. It is the ethos of the freedom of the person; of his unique, distinctive participation in the liturgical communion of persons, the celebration of the total life of the world—in the body of Christ. It is an ethos which reveals the truth and authenticity of life.

CHAPTER SIX

The Kingly, Priestly and Prophetic Ethos of the Eucharist

1. The dynamics of the eucharist

If repentance, the personal awareness of our failure and our fall, is one pole of Christian ethics, then the other is the eucharist, our dynamic participation in the new mode of existence which transfigures man and the world, making them into the Church and the Kingdom of God. Both these truths, the fall and the eucharistic transfiguration, are immediate realities experienced in our lives. Both define the reality of the event of salvation. The salvation of man is not abstract, legal justification, nor an idealistic ascent to spheres of intellectual inquiry or mystical ecstasies ending in complete moral autonomy. Salvation is a *passage*, a crossing from the fall to the transfiguration, from corruption and death to incorruption and life; it is a passover (which means precisely crossing); it is the paschal feast of the eucharist.

The Church experiences the transfiguration of creation and of man in liturgical space and time. This is why the true meaning of the Church was revealed in Christ's transfiguration on Mount Tabor. In the experience on Tabor we have the prefiguration of liturgical space and time, the restoration of nature to its true character as relationship. Space is defined by the immediacy of the relationship, by the inseparable nearness to Christ and communion with Him, and by participation in the truth and glory of God. Correspondingly, the space in

89

which the eucharistic synaxis takes place is the inseparable gathering of the faithful into the oneness of the life of the world, which becomes the *place* for the personal union of created and uncreated—the body and blood of Christ. And in liturgical time, past and future are contracted into the present moment of participation in God's glory: a present, once again, of personal presence. Moses and Elijah on Tabor, the gathering of the "commemoration of saints" at the eucharist, mark the past. The glorified Jesus, the clothing of humanity in divine glory, marks the eschatological future. The liturgical time of the Church is that present moment which contains and sums up past and future in the immediacy of presence.

It is characteristic, however, that the disciples do not remain on Tabor; they do not build their tabernacles there. They go down into the world with the experience and the certainty of the transfiguration. This movement of descent from Tabor into the world, this return from the experience of transfiguration to the protracted sorrow of the world, is the movement which forms the Church. It means taking up the cross of the fall and of sin in the certainty of the resurrection, and with absolute respect for the adventure of human freedom.

The return from the eucharist to the life of common fall and failure which is man's everyday reality neither destroys nor alters the eschatological fulness of the liturgical experience. It is the dynamic affirmation of it, the way the eucharist is personally put into action; it is the struggle of freedom to be transfigured into love, to transfigure every corner of life into eucharist. The realization and revelation of the body of Christ at every eucharistic synaxis is God's continuing entry into the world; it is the dynamic start to the transfiguration of the world and of history. And this transfiguration cannot be set out in objective programs and moralistic formulae: it is in a continuous state of *becoming,* as a living "increase" (Col 2:19) of personal distinctiveness and freedom, and it is realistically implemented in a new way of *using* the world.

2. Eucharistic use of the world

In the opening pages of the Bible, we read that God blessed the material goods of the earth and offered them to man "to eat." Eating, that immediate way in which man takes up the world and is physically united with it so that the good things of the earth are transformed into the flesh and life of man, is identified with the *blessing* God offers to man: it is an actual relationship between man and God. Man's communion with God before the fall was a real relationship of life through every act of eating or drinking, through total, bodily participation in the blessing offered—not through means that were partial, whether intellectual, ethical or religious. Ethics and religion make their appearance once the organic and immediate relationship of life between man and God has been broken: they are attempts to make good the absence of this relationship through acts of individual expiation or merit. Ethics and religion are results of the *fall* of man, his refusal or inability to realize his relationship with the world as a "eucharist," a *thanksgiving* to God—to make an act of thanksgiving out of his very life, out of the eating and drinking which maintain his existence in the world.[1]

The same reality of the fall is evident in the way in which our eating and drinking, and our use of the world in general, is subject to the absolute need and demand for individual survival. Man refuses to see the world as a blessing from God, an actual fact of relationship and communion with Him. He uses the good things of the earth exclusively for the preservation and satisfaction of his individual self-sufficiency. Thus use of the world becomes the sphere in which individuals vie with one another for autonomous survival. The good things of the earth cease to be grounds for relationship and communion, and become objects of dispute and rivalry between individuals intent on preserving their biological existence. In this way, however, man's relationship with

[1]For a more extensive development of this truth, see Alexander Schmemann, *For the Life of the World: Sacraments and Orthodoxy* (New York, 1973).

the world necessarily leads to progressive corruption and death; it is a relationship which deadens life, since it identifies it with the individual survival which is subject to death. Man takes up the world so as to preserve in life his individual being, but the self-preservation of his individuality proves to be an inevitable process of decay, a death sentence.

This transformation of man's relationship with the world, the change of life into death, makes it clear that the fall and sin of man is not a juridical event, the violation of some law or an act of disobedience by the will to the commands of the mind. Sin is the passage from existence "according to truth" to existence "contrary to nature," a denial of the life which is the natural "end" for man and the world. Confusion between life and survival, the obscuring of the truth about existence and freedom, man's refusal or inability to realize his personal distinctiveness and freedom in his relationship with the world, to bring himself and the world to incorruption within that true life which is love—this is man's sin, the inescapable irrationality of human history.

3. The world "made word"

With the eucharistic liturgy, the Church returns to a personal use of the world. She takes up the world from the beginning, using the basic "species" for man's nourishment and life, bread and wine—she takes them as a blessing, as grace and the gift of God, and by this action brings about a new relationship with God, a real and vital relationship of thanksgiving. The world becomes a means of communion between man and God and among men themselves, the "locus" of a common and unified life.

This "transubstantiation" of the world into a fact of communion, of holy communion, is not achieved incidentally through man's behavior towards creation. It has its primary ontological roots in the incarnation of God. It is God Himself who has taken on the flesh of the world, changing the corruptible and mortal nature of flesh and blood into a hypostasis of eternal life, a *natural* union of created and uncreated. In the same way now the bread and wine, man's nourishment and life, are not simply a blessing offered by God, but God Himself, become flesh and offering Himself to those who partake through baptism in the trinitarian, ecclesial unity of personal freedom and love. In the Church, the union of God with man and the incorruption of what is mortal is not a mystical or moral allegory; it is an incarnate life of hypostatic God-manhood, the actual eating and drinking of the flesh and blood of God incarnate.[2] God offers man food which makes life incorruptible and immortal, and this food is the world which He Himself assumed into and made His flesh.

Christ's assumption of the flesh of the world, the changing of bread and wine into the body and blood of God incarnate, is the dynamic beginning of a change in our whole use of the world, in man's overall relationship with creation. Man now has the possibility of assuming the world into himself within the context of a personal, eucharistic relationship with God: he can transform this process of taking into an act of offering the world back to God, and can use the world as material capable of giving flesh to Him who is without flesh, and containing Him who cannot be contained.

The eucharist is that minute quantity of living leaven which secretly gives life to the dead lump of the world. It brings man's free assent into harmony with Christ's act of taking up creation, and transubstantiates the world into a fact of theanthropic communion. It makes life and existence into "word," giving them reason and meaning; it destroys the irrationality of survival as an absolute, condemned to annihilation at death. The eucharist spreads dynamically throughout the life of the faithful, through every aspect of their use and intake of the world; it changes their use and intake into a continuous present of communion and relationship which saves and enhances personal distinctiveness and freedom beyond space, time and necessity.

The eucharist thus defines a new human ethos. The moral

---

[2]"Christianity is food and drink. And the more one eats of it, the more the mind is stimulated by the sweetness; it is uncontrollable and insatiate, insatiably asking for more and eating": Macarius of Egypt, *Spiritual Homilies* 17, 13, ed. Dörries, p. 174.

endeavor of the Christian is a personal extension of the eucharist into every aspect of life. Work, economic life, the family, art, technology, politics and cultural life all become part of man's eucharistic relationship with God. Within the eucharist, man, the world and history find their true identity and at the same time are *made word*: they appear "according to nature" as the Word and Wisdom of God, as the blessed Kingdom of the Father and of the Son and of the Holy Spirit.

4. Tangible experience of salvation

The affirmation of material reality, the process of taking the world and elevating it to its natural end which is the "glory" or manifestation of God, holds a dominant position in the tradition of the Orthodox Church. What could be the meaning of individual salvation or salvation of the Platonic "soul," apart from the salvation of the world and the beauty of the world, the personal distinctiveness of the body and of creation? For man's salvation to be real, it must also liberate his flesh—the whole of creation—from the groaning and travail (Rom 8:22) of subjection to space, time, corruption and death.

"I will not cease to venerate matter, through which my salvation was brought to pass," writes St John of Damascus.[3] Man's salvation becomes reality when God takes up matter, when "clay is seated upon the throne of God."[4] And the liturgical use of matter in the eucharist manifests precisely this participation in salvation, the union of created and uncreated, the cosmic liturgy of the Word. In the Orthodox liturgy the worshipper participates in his entirety, with mind and senses, soul and body, in the manifestation of universal salvation and the Kingdom of God. Starting with the Byzantine church building and turning next to the iconography, the decoration of the church, the royal vesture of the clergy, the dramatic structure of the liturgy, the poetry of the hymns and the liturgical music, we find in the eucharist a synthesis of

[3]*First Homily in Defence of the Holy Icons*, PG 94, 1245AB.
[4]John of Sinai, *Ladder*, step 26, PG 88, 1064A.

all the capacities of sense and mind; and all these serve to manifest the personal beauty of the inner principle in created things, the world transfigured into the personal distinctiveness of a eucharistic response to God's "frenzied love" for His creatures.

The eucharistic liturgy has its own aesthetics, stemming from the same ontology of the Church's truth and ethos. This has nothing to do with the conventional aesthetics of harmonious proportions, with the categories of beauty and ugliness or symmetry and asymmetry, nor with arbitrary individual devices meant to be impressive or imposing. The aim of Orthodox church art is not to delight the senses or the mind, but to reveal to both the truth and the inner principle or "word" of things: the personal dimension of matter, its capacity to manifest the personal operation of God the Word, to give flesh to Him who is without flesh and to contain Him who cannot be contained.

We shall return in a later chapter to the ethos expressed in Orthodox art—that effort to explore the potentialities of matter to *speak* and *manifest* the truth about real existence and life. Here let us concentrate on the fact that the eucharist, with the aid of all forms of art, sets out how man can participate totally in the continuing recovery of a right relationship with the world, a right use of the world. Every form of liturgical art, be it architecture, painting, decorative art, poetry, drama or music, leads to the renunciation of individual aesthetic enjoyment, individual emotional uplift. It is an art which guides the believer to the purification of his individual senses, and purification here means the transfiguration of individual capacities into *personal* capacities; it leads him to loving self-transcendence and personal communion. And this is the hallmark of Orthodox worship: it remains a baptism into the truth, a real *descent* into the elements of the world and emergence into true life—not a mere sprinkling with lofty ideas and moral exhortations.

"Is it such a painful impossibility to apprehend God with the senses?" asks a contemporary European, a typical representative of the religious impasse of our day.[5] It could be said

[5]The Swedish film director Ingmar Bergmann, in his film *The Seventh*

that Orthodox worship is a direct answer to the peculiarly modern quest for immediate, experiential knowledge of God, beyond any abstract intellectual schemes or anthropocentric sentimental elevations. In the Orthodox eucharist nothing is theory, autonomous doctrine or abstract reference: all is action, tangible experience and total, bodily participation.

Let us call to mind the *proskomide,* the part of the liturgy which is concerned with the preparation of the precious gifts. This is a manifestation of the truth of salvation through concrete liturgical actions which repeat the events of the divine economy in perceptible form. The bread is pierced with the lance, and wine and water are poured out as "blood and water": it is the life of the Church, the hypostasis of the new Eve ("Life"), that gushes forth from the pierced side of "the new Adam as He sleeps upon the cross." The star-cover stands "over the place where the young child was," the Lamb "is led to the slaughter," and the holy veil, as heaven—the presence of the Father—covers the entire event of the economy.

Events are relived without rationalistic respect for chrono-logical sequence. The crucifixion of Christ and His nativity, the resurrection and ascension and the whole of the "great mystery of godliness" are concrete, tangible actions, and all form the *present* in the transfigured time of the Church. It takes a total, experiential participation, and a child's freedom to live the truth directly and without the tyrannical primacy of the mind; it takes the astounding wisdom of the heart to represent perceptibly all these events, and each time to mani-fest their present truth. Following on from the *proskomide,* the whole of the Divine Liturgy brings to life as a mystagogic action the teaching work of Christ, His passion, His resur-rection and the enlightenment of mankind.

5. The kingly ethos

The eucharist, then, is the activity, the life and the ethos

Seal; English translation by L. Malmstrom and D. Kushner (London, 1968), p. 28.

of the Church. It is the supreme realization of Christian truth and Christian ethics—the manifestation, in the person of each worshipper, of the authentic ethos proper to man as *king, priest* and *prophet.* "Christianity is nothing commonplace," say the Macarian homilies, "for this is a great mystery. Recognize, then, your nobility, and that you have been called to *kingly* rank; you are a chosen race, a *priesthood* and a holy nation. For the mystery of Christianity is alien to this world."[6] Communion in the flesh of Christ is "the most precious unction," "the heavenly unction; and when the faithful are anointed with it, they become christs by grace, so as to be *kings* and *prophets* of the heavenly mysteries. They are sons and lords and gods."[7]

The kingly ethos revealed and manifested in liturgical life relates to the restoration of the human person's sovereignty over his nature, to the exaltation of that nature into a potential for personal life. Man ceases to be a slave to the demands and needs of an autonomous nature; he is lord and ruler over the "things," the actions and results of actions, in natural creation and in his personal creation, and above all in his own natural hypostasis. "Become as a king in your own heart," writes St John of the Ladder, "sitting exalted in humility: say to laughter 'Go,' and it goes; and to sweet weeping 'Come,' and it comes: and to the body, our slave and our tyrant, say 'Do this,' and it does it."[8]

In traditional societies, the image of the king symbolized that order which permits the truth of life, as communion and harmony in relationship, to be realized. And the image of man as king in the language of the Church expresses the human person's potentiality to transfigure the disorder of autonomous wills and dissention between individuals into the order and harmony of love and communion, into life and truth. And it is the eucharistic use of the world, the denial of nature's autonomy and the liberation of the person from subjection to individual self-sufficiency, which restores the kingly sovereignty of man over nature and the singleness of his life.

---

[6]*Spiritual Homilies* 27, 4, p. 221.
[7]*Spiritual Homilies* 17, 1, p. 166.
[8]*Ladder*, step 7, PG 88, 808D-809A.

In addition, however, man's kingly rank shows the nobility of his descent. In the whole of material creation, he alone
was created to participate in true existence and life, and endowed with personal distinctiveness and freedom. He alone
has the capacity to give life and immortality to creation by
transfiguring matter into a basis for relationship and communion with God. The origin and the "end" of man's existence is God's love, God's mode of existence: this is why the
eucharist, the realization of that end, marks mankind out as
"related" to God, as "a race most like" God, "a kingly race."

6. The priestly ethos

The process of bringing the world to life and "making it
word" is bound up with the priestly quality of man, the
priestly ethos which relates to the human person the potential for bridging the existential gulf between created and
uncreated. If the kingly ethos reflects in man the glory of the
image of God in Trinity, the ontological priority of person
over nature, then the priestly ethos relates to manifestation of
the other mystery of divine existence: to the distinction between the nature and the energies which preserve the reality
of that nature within the existential fact of personal distinctiveness.

The world is formed and brought to life through the
energies of God; the universal liturgy of the Word is accomplished in the whole of creation. This reality is reflected in
the distinction between matter and spirit in man,[9] and in the
way the material world is summed up and endowed with
meaning in the human person. The world is the result of the
divine energies, and the distinctiveness in the beauty of existent things reveals how the creative "words" of divine Wisdom
have a personal character. But only the reason and energy of
man can meet and recognize in created things the polyphony
of the words of the divine energy. At the same time,
man's body is the supreme personal differentiation of the
energies of his nature, and in that very body the principle of

[9]*The Person and Eros* (in Greek), §§ 17 and 21.

man's personal distinctiveness encounters the personal principle or "word" of divine creative energy. In man's body, the sacred liturgy uniting created and uncreated life has its origin and fulfilment.

The image of the priest in traditional societies symbolized man's attempt to bridge the gulf between the trancendent and the mundane, between immortality and mortality, his endeavor to sacrifice the most precious things of this transient life in order to gain eternal survival. And the image of the priest in the language of the Church expresses the human person's capacity for giving life and immortality to the whole of creation in his own body, by uniting it and "grafting" it into the divine life. And it is this eucharistic assumption and employment of the world that brings about the transformation of mortal life into eternal life, the "sacrifice" of what is individual and mortal for the sake of personal life and immortality.

Man is the priest of the natural creation: he partakes in its material state, and summarizes the whole of creation in his person, "like a natural bond, mediating between all the extremes through the parts which are proper to him, and in himself bringing together into one things which by nature are separated by a great distance," in the words of St Maximus.[10] Man's relationship with the world is direct and organic: it is the way he assumes the world into himself, his food, his drink, his clothing and everything his technical skill can accomplish. As we have said before, when this taking serves the rebellious self-sufficiency of the individual, our daily use of the world is a progressive disruption of nature ending in the distintegration of death. Nature is lured into rebellion together with man, since the human person provides the only possibility for nature to have existence. When, on the other hand, man's use of the world takes the form of a eucharistic relationship with God, then material nature is revealed as the "locus" where the energies of God and man meet and interpenetrate, an image of the Word made incarnate and become man. The eucharist is the liturgy of life celebrated through the hypostatic union of created and uncreated; it is

[10]*Ambigua*, PG 91, 1305BC.

the transformation of the "species" of the world into the
flesh of God the Word.

7. The liturgical celebration of life and the distinction between the sexes

The priestly ethos and dignity of man, which finds its
fulfilment in the eucharistic use of the world, unifies man's
life with that of the world, of God and of creation. It leaves
no room for division or partition, and therefore presupposes
that the division of human beings into sexes is transcended.[11]
This means that the priestly ethos and rank is not the exclusive prerogative of the male sex. The eucharistic use of the
world, worked out in the human body itself, unifies the sexes
in a common liturgical celebration of life.

Certainly, the removal of a distinction between the sexes
is related to the eschatological fulness of existence, the Kingdom of God.[12] The life of the Kingdom abolishes the division
of human beings into men and women, because the differentiation of the sexes is a *natural* differentiation—a necessity of
nature which ensures its autonomous perpetuation. It has no
place in the Kingdom because it bears no relation to that
personal distinctiveness and freedom from nature which is
the life of the Kingdom. The differentiation of the sexes does
not represent an ontological distinction, like that between
nature and persons or between nature and energies: it does
not relate to the *mode of existence*, the *image* of God imprinted on man. The distinction between the sexes is a differentiation in natural energies "which no longer looks to the
divine archetype,"[13] but merely foreshadows the fall. This is
why it is done away with in the life of the last days.

The Church, however, lives out the truth of the last days
through the dynamism of human freedom—the dynamics of
the person, who makes life a liturgical celebration as he

[11]See Maximus the Confessor, *Ambigua*, PG 91, 1304D f.; V. Lossky,
The Mystical Theology of the Eastern Church (London, 1957), p. 108;
Lars Thunberg, *Microcosm and Mediator* (Lund, 1965), p. 147f.
[12]See Mt 22:30; Mk 12:25; Lk 20:34-35.
[13]Gregory of Nyssa, *On the Formation of Man* 16, PG 44, 184D-185A.

reveals its ultimate "end." And the dynamics of the person, the fact of freedom, does not deny nature, but presupposes it. It is realized *with reference to* nature, with complete faithfulness to the existential possibilities of nature. Personal distinctiveness and freedom means a change in nature's mode of existence, not the abolition of nature and its existential possibilities.

Consequently, overcoming the distinction between the sexes does not mean for the Church an arbitrary leap into the realm of abstract idealism, nor a moralistic emasculation of human nature, nor yet a rationalistic, and inevitably conventional, equation of the sexes in the sphere of social life. But what it does mean is a dynamic transformation of the natural difference into personal relationship and unity, coupled with complete respect for the differentiation in roles or natural functions represented by the two sexes.

The celebration and operation of the eucharist presupposes a man as priest, because the transformation of life and its deliverance from corruption does not cancel out or violate the way life operates naturally, the differentiation in natural functions represented by the distinction between the sexes. The personal, hypostatic continuity of natural life requires that the man must fertilize the body of the woman. Two distinct natural functions, that of the man who fertilizes and that of the woman who brings life to fruition, are harmonized in the supremely *personal* event which is sexual love. The liturgical celebration of life does not depend more on the man and less on the woman, or *vice versa*. It is groundless, to say the least, to value one role above the other, since both represent a natural necessity which can be transcended only in the freedom of personal love.

The transfiguration of life and its change into incorruption within the Church requires the assumption of natural life, of man's flesh and the flesh of the world. Consequently, it requires a faithfulness to the differentiation in the natural functions which go to make up life. In the *personal* event of the eucharistic celebration, two distinct natural functions are brought together in harmony: that of the man, who performs the ministry of endowing the world with meaning, making it "word," and that of the woman who offers the natural flesh in which life is "made word" and transfigured. God the Word Himself was made flesh in the person of Christ, at once divine and human, but this "supernatural" incarnation did not violate the natural operation of life: a woman gave her flesh to the Word, and thus she herself embodied the participation of humanity, and of creation as a whole, in the *personal* ministry of the "new life" and the salvation of the world. The Mother of God's contribution to the incarnation of the Word was not confined to the role of a "means" or instrument, to the performance of an impersonal function natural to her sex and essential for the birth of the Son of God "in the flesh." From the first moment, the Virgin Mary's contribution as a woman was an act of personal freedom, freedom from any natural necessity. It is precisely this freedom from natural necessity—from desire, instinct and pleasure—and the transformation of the natural function of motherhood into a personal act of free assent, love and self-offering, that makes the Mother of God "Virgin even after childbirth." In Orthodox iconography, the Mother of God holding her child is depicted as the throne of the Godhead, and the faithful see in her person the supreme celebrant of salvation for man and the world.

If, therefore, the Orthodox Church gives the special grace of priesthood, the possibility of celebrating the eucharist and the other mysteries, or sacraments, to men alone, this is not because she belittles the female sex or wishes to maintain social inequality. It is because she has complete respect for the truth of man and his nature, and remains faithful to it, because the salvation which she herself represents is no abstract moralism unrelated to the existential reality of nature. The transfiguration of life within the Church and its deliverance from corruption requires that human nature itself should be brought to its existential authenticity and its true "end," which is personal freedom and distinctiveness. This is why the Church celebrates the "new life" of grace while remaining absolutely true to nature and to the differentiation of functions within nature, the distinction between the priestly roles of man and of woman. This faithfulness preserves the unbounded personal possibilities of true femininity and true manliness from any conventional leveling. The differentiation in roles, however, does not alter the fact that the priestly ethos and dignity relates to both sexes, since both share in the ministry of transforming the differentiated natural energy into a personal self-transcendence and communion in sexual love.[14]

8. The prophetic ethos

Lastly, the eucharist realizes and reveals the truth of the *prophetic ethos,* the way the Church experiences and interprets time and history. The essence of prophecy is not foretelling events which are going to happen, but understanding the course of history, throwing light on its meaning and "end." Prophetically interpreted, history is the dynamic realization of a relationship between man and God, whether positive or antithetical; it is man's acceptance or rejection of divine love, an act of freedom and relationship which judges the world.

Divorced from the prophetic ethos, the experience of history is simply a tragic irrationality, an unjustifiable horror of violence, hatred and exploitation, of slavery, wars, hunger, injustice and misery, since human life in all its aspects is a fall, an unnatural aberration. Only in the eucharist does the new and true use of the world give sense to history, transfiguring the irrationality into the truth of freedom and personal relationship between man and God.

In the eucharist time is not measured objectively as an

[14]In traditions of worship such as the Protestant, where the cosmological dimension and truth of the eucharist is lacking, the demand for the ordination of women makes obvious sense. In such a case, worship is a gathering of brethren, where "there is neither male nor female, there is neither Jew nor Greek, there is neither bond nor free" (Gal 3:28). If divorced from the cosmological preconditions and ramifications of the Church's truth, this concept of brotherhood and equality in no way rules out the priestly ministry of women. The question, however, is how far this concept preserves the ontological content of the Gospel's truth, how far it proclaims the good news of salvation as an existential event, in which the body of man and the flesh of the world both take part. Unfortunately, however, the cosmological dimension of the event of salvation and its ontological content is an area of little concern for the "ecumenical dialogues" of our times.

ordered succession from "before" to "after,"[15] nor as a rhythm
of progressive and inexorable decay; instead, time measures
man's personal relationship with the world and with God,
the dynamics of man's free response to the call of God's
love. At the same time, however, the eucharist is a first experience of the continuous time of personal immediacy, of the
present of love: it does away with the *sequence* and *flow* of
time and also the *corruption* in it, because it removes the
transience of the "moment," transforming the individual desire
for existential survival into a loving fulness of *duration,*
a continuous present of communion, the immediacy of personal Presence.

The prophetic ethos, the experience of time within the
dimension of God's love and the freedom of the person,
forms the third way in which man relates to the life of the
Trinity: the manifestation of the *mode* of divine existence,
which is love. We recognize love in the way God addresses
His personal call to man, the way He intervenes in history
and the way history works itself out as the "economy" of
God. The personal God addresses to the human person a call
to communion and relationship, a call always revealed as a
trinitarian energy; and this call enables us to attain the mode
of divine existence, love as the hypostasis of life.

Precisely, however, because divine love gives substance to
life in the form of personal distinctiveness and freedom, its
intervention in history is not confined simply to a kind of
providence, preserving the forms and patterns of biological
survival. It is an intervention summed up "definitely" and
"finally" in the cross of Christ, in the love which accepts
death, the existential failure of nature, so as to transform
it into resurrection, into hypostatic fulness of life. The prophetic ethos discerns the meaning and "end" of history in
this crucified love which cannot be reconciled with the self-
sufficiency of the objectified, conventional forms of survival;
the love which instead destroys utopian illusions in its very
own flesh, putting to death every individual existential demand

[15]Aristotle, *Physics* IV, 11, 219b 1-3. See also *The Person and Eros,*
§§ 46-55.

in order to realize and reveal the true life of personal distinctiveness and freedom.

It is frequently said that the Church's prophetic duty is to denounce the moribund forms of conventional survival, the structures which preserve social inequality, economic inequity, political oppression or organized exploitation. Nor is this idea mistaken. But there is one essential point: when prophecy denounces corruption in life and the pseudo-forms which safeguard individual interests, the bearer of the prophecy does not divorce himself from the fall of our common nature. He does not speak from the vantage-point of some other form for objectified life, some "improved" form which should replace the corrupt one. On the contrary, prophecy is that word which springs from deliberate acceptance of death, from the mortification—in the very body of the person who proclaims the prophecy—of the antagonistic demands of individual survival. Prophecy is an incarnate expression of the true life which is man's resurrection into the personal adventure of freedom. Prior to being a prophetic word, the prophet's witness is a prophetic ethos, and this ethos is the complete opposite of moralizing, or aggressive criticism, or revolutionary fervor for "purging" and "change." The Church's prophetic intervention in history is not limited to schematic moralizing and demands for revolutionary changes: it is dynamically made flesh by taking up the passion of human freedom as its cross, denouncing not human weakness but confusion in the realm of truth, those artificial cosmetic improvements of death which are put forward and imposed on us as possibilities of life.

The historical "flesh" of the Church, the way she is administratively represented and the institutions which form her organization, is itself often identified with that very "improved" death—with the conservative self-sufficiency and apparent security of conventional forms, with established social and political systems "convenient" for our fallen condition, and with aspects of state authority which are independent of human needs. And yet this alienation in individuals and institutions and the presence of the fall and death in the midst of the objective or historical Church, is precisely what

shows that the Church is free from the deadness of objectified life, formal "piety" and legalistic moralizing. It confirms
her faithfulness to the reality of that mortal and corruptible
nature which Christ took on, the reality of death which can
be transformed into life and resurrection. The unworthiness
of individuals and institutions in the Church is confirmation
of her freedom from any worldly demand for influence which
violates human freedom. It is the incarnate affirmation of
Christ's words that true life and salvation—the Kingdom of
God—"cometh not with observation, neither shall they say,
Lo here! or Lo there!", but it "is within you" (Lk 17:20-21):
it comes about within the framework of personal distinctiveness and freedom.

The Church's prophetic intervention in history and in
current social affairs is not brought about either through the
perfection and efficiency of her administrative institutions
and structures, or through the goodness and "efficacious"
activity of her representatives, or by making objective decisions and taking up positions. It is always realized through the
progress of the saints, by the measure of life-giving death, and
with the ineffable freedom which is granted when the final
resistance of egocentric individuality is put to death. And
there is always present this leaven of the Kingdom, the
communion of saints which leavens the whole lump and
brings to life what is mortal.

9. The "festival of the firstborn"

Man's restoration to the kingly, priestly and prophetic
ethos, the transformation of his life which is revealed in
the eucharistic liturgy, is a dynamic event presupposing
human freedom and daily moral striving on the part of each
Christian to turn the whole of life into a eucharist. The
particular forms that this striving takes, however, and the
means and framework for its accomplishment are rendered
accessible to all within the life of the Church, with its corporate assembly and its shared life; not through self-willed
individual preferences and choices. The fact of the Church

also defines the means whereby we participate in it, through specific actions involving a "loving" use of the world and experience of time.

One concrete way of approaching the transfigured life of the Church is through personal participation in the liturgical experience of time, in the daily, weekly and yearly festive cycles of the calendar. In this context the eucharistic ethos is heortological—it is a festive ethos. For the Church, every day is a feast, the memory of a saint: the Church's joy and triumph over one of her offspring, over a personal manifestation of man's kingly, priestly and prophetic dignity, his triumph over sin and corruption. Each day's festive remembrance of the saints is incorporated in the weekly and annual cycles of feasts of the Lord and the Mother of God, that continuous experience of the "now" of God's historical presence in the world which is the starting-point for the "new creation" of the Church.

Thus the believer's daily ascetic effort is a personal participation in the feasting and joy of the Church, in the "festival of the firstborn" (Heb 12:23). And *personal* participation means renouncing the arrogance of individuality—it means imitating the obedience of Christ and the saints, the obedience of the natural will to the will of personal distinctiveness and freedom. Any distinction between the ethics of the Church and that obedience which is a participation in the Church's love, her feasting and joy, inevitably ends in legal commandments and a conventional system of values, useful perhaps for the purposes of better social coexistence, but irrelevant and alien to the truth and the reality of the Church.

CHAPTER SEVEN

The Asceticism of the Church and Individual Virtue

1. Asceticism, an ecclesial way

The material body partakes in the perfection of man, in his sanctification. Perfection and sanctification signify man's restoration to the fulness of his existential possibilities, to what he is called to be—the *image* and *glory* of God. This "end" for human life involves man's being as a whole, both what we call body and what we call soul; it relates to the totality of the human person.

This is a fundamental truth of Orthodox anthropology, which both interprets the meaning of Christian asceticism and draws a fundamental distinction between this and the legal understanding of individual virtue. Asceticism is not an individual work of merit, an act of constancy in observing some objective code of behavior, or obedience to commandments laid down by some impersonal law or conventional authority. Nor does bodily asceticism confine itself to "suppression" of the body, turning this into an end in itself so that the disdained matter becomes obedient to the superior "spirit."

Christian asceticism is above all an ecclesial and not an individual matter. It is the changing of our nature's individual mode of existence into a personal communion and relationship, a dynamic entry into the community of the life of the body of the Church. The aim of asceticism is to transfigure our impersonal natural desires and needs into manifestations of the free personal will which brings into being the true life of love. Thus the instinctive need for food, the greed for the individual's independent self-preservation, is transfigured in the context of the Church's fasting: submission to the common practice of the Church becomes paramount, turning it into an act of relationship and communion. The Christian does not fast in order to subjugate matter to the spirit, nor because he accepts a division of foods into "clean" and "unclean." He fasts because in this way he ceases to make the intake of food an autonomous act; he turns it into obedience to the common will and common practice of the Church, and subjugates his individual preferences to the Church rules of fasting which determine his choice of food. And obedience freely given always presupposes love: it is always an act of communion.

Nevertheless, the Church's fasting rules do not express a fortuitous or arbitrary division of foods, but summarize a long experience of human nature on the part of the saints who laid down these canons. This experience knows well the rebelliousness of our nature, and understands how to distinguish what use of foods invigorates the autonomous impulse for self-preservation and what weakens it. In this sense, we can accept the connection between fasting and the subjugation of matter to the demands of the spirit, as an image or a figure of interpretation. All that need be made clear is that asceticism in the Church is not in conflict with matter itself, but with the rebellion of material individuality, the rebellious drive for self-subsistence. Asceticism checks the rebellion of our material nature and does not allow nature to become an end in itself —a second purpose within creation, different from that unique end which is the personal hypostasis of life, our participation in the life of trinitarian communion.

One could mention other forms of asceticism in the Church, analogous to the example of fasting: sexual continence, participation of the body in prayer (the prostrations hallowed by the monastic tradition), humbling acts of service, acts of submission and rejection of the individual will, acts of altruism and charity, submission to the liturgical *Typikon* and participation in the mysteries (sacraments). All these are practical forms of resistance to the egocentric individuality identified with the flesh, aspects of man's dynamic struggle to overcome the impersonal elements in his biological nature: his struggle to be fulfilled, through relationship with God and with his fellow men, in his personal distinctiveness which can only be realized through love. And these are not forms of individual resistance or an individual struggle, but of submission by the individual to the universal experience and life of the Church. Individual effort is transformed into a common effort; the struggle becomes an act of communion, taking its place in the life of the whole body of the Church.

Since this is its content, asceticism is not deprivation and a niggardly attitude towards life, nor enmity towards the body and scorn for matter, as Manicheans and puritans have presented it over the ages. Within the tradition of the Church, asceticism is *philokalia,* love for the beauty of that "uncompleted perfection" which is personal fulfilment, the restoration of God's darkened image in man to its original beauty.

2. Rejection of dualism

As it is understood and experienced in the Orthodox East, asceticism presupposes the rejection of Platonic or any other dualism, with its *a priori* scorn for matter and the body, and the value it places on the soul, the spirit of man. The distinction between soul and body is not an ontological distinction, like that between nature and person or between nature and energies; it does not relate to man's *being,* to his *mode of existence.* This is why death, the dissolution of the body, does not put an end to man's existence; it does not destroy his natural hypostasis. Man's existence (soul) is a specific created nature even after death—however much separation from the body ("in which we received our being") constitutes for our nature the greatest possible trial and existential alienation, the painful consequence of man's fall.

[1]"There is one thing in creation [the soul] which has its being in something else, and not in itself; and it is wonderful how it can exist outside that in which it received its being": John of Sinai, *Ladder,* step 26, PG 88, 1036B.

The soul and the body represent distinct natural energies, energies of the one human nature. It is this one nature, and not only the body, which became existentially autonomous and "beast-like"[2] at the fall of man.[3] And the asceticism of the Church relates to this "beast-like" nature: not to the body alone, nor to the spirit alone, but to the common reality of the nature manifested and expressed by both. For this reason the ethos at which the Church's asceticism aims is ontological in content, looking to the "hypostasization" of nature into personal distinctiveness and freedom.

3. Rejection of individuality

Asceticism is the struggle of the person against rebellious nature, against the nature which seeks to achieve on its own what it could bring about only in personal unity and communion with God. The rebellion of our nature attempts to supplant the possibilities for true life which are divine grace, a gift of personal communion and relationship. Every absolute, autonomous natural desire goes back to that first revolt of autonomy: "In the day ye eat of the tree of the knowledge of good and evil, ye shall be as gods" (Gen 3:5). Through asceticism the Christian reverses the movement towards rebellion and self-deification; he resists the tendency in his nature to become existentially absolute, and dynamically puts his personal will into action so as to restore his nature to communion with the grace of life.

This restoration and this resistance, however, presuppose a struggle within man against his very self, against what his nature has become since the fall—in other words, an effort

[2]See Maximus the Confessor, *Ambigua*, PG 90, 397C.

[3]If we reject the ontological distinction between nature and energies, we do not merely leave the reality of matter and the body without an ontological explanation, but we are necessarily led to a schematic Aristotelian *hylomorphism*, to a concept of the soul as the *entelechy* of the body, as happened in the Roman Catholic Church (cf. the Council of Vienne, 1311-1312). And an inevitable consequence of Aristotelian hylomorphism is scorn for matter and an external, schematic understanding of ethical life—ultimately, the juridical moralism of the Roman Catholic Church, and the pietism and puritanism of the Protestants.

which is logically contradictory. For it is undoubtedly a logical contradiction if man resists the needs and demands of his nature, the very nature which is his individuality, his own self. The tragic separation between nature and person, between necessity and freedom, is revealed in every stage of ascetic life; it is the empirical self-knowledge of man since the fall, a self-knowledge which goes back to the very truth of existence, beyond any logical form elaborated by the intellect. The individual nature is what man *is*, yet at the same time it is not man *in himself*. Individual flesh is his nature, yet at the same time something foreign to his *natural* destiny: "this flesh that is mine and yet not mine, this dear enemy," as St John of the Ladder writes.[4] My flesh is mine and yet not mine; it is my human nature, yet also a relentless impulse toward what is contrary to nature, the elevation of nature into an end in itself—an elevation which severs my nature from my personal hypostasis of life and makes it disintegrate into death.

4. Unattainable by nature, yet attainable by grace

The content of Christian asceticism is not control of the mind so as to ensure "moderation" in our needs and desires, nor progressive habituation of the natural will to the observance of some law. It is the struggle for personal freedom from the necessity to which our nature is subject—man's struggle with his very nature, with the death which is "mingled" with human nature. And individual self-control, as the canons of conventional morality would have it, cannot be more than a very limited aspect of this struggle, since the tendency towards what is contrary to nature holds sway primarily in the hidden depths of the human being, in the subconscious and unconscious. The rebellion of nature has to be *put to death* to let nature live out its destiny "according to nature." And this rebellion is rooted in the biological hypostasis of individuality itself: in the natural will, in unconscious desire, in instinct, in the sexual drive and in the blind need for self-preservation.

Thus we have a second logical antinomy, a second scandal

[4] *Ladder*, step 15, PG 88, 885D.

for the criteria of effectiveness which govern legalistic morality: man struggles to mortify the rebellion of his nature, and
yet there is no question of achieving this mortification by
human effort alone. "To defeat one's own nature is an impossibility," as St John of the Ladder assures us from his
experience in asceticism.[5] Keeping to the antithetical parallelism between Christian asceticism and individual virtue, we
might see in this saying of St John's the bankruptcy of all
legal morality and all idealistic humanism. Any systematic
pursuit of "improvement" in man through his own individual
will and effort, of taming his nature through his own powers,
is condemned by nature itself. Man on his own cannot cease
to be what he "naturally" is. His attempt to overcome nature
through his individual powers makes him a prisoner of the
same rebellious autonomy of individuality which brings about
the corruption of nature. This is also why every anthropocentric, autonomous morality ends up as a fruitless insistence
on an utterly inadequate human self-sufficiency, an expression
of man's fall. By contrast, Christian asceticism rejects the
deterministic dialectic of effort and result; it presupposes that
we hope for nothing from human powers. It expresses and
effects the participation of man's freedom in suppressing the
rebellion of his nature, but that work itself is grace, a gift
from God. Thus human ascetic endeavor does not even aspire
to crushing the rebellion of man's nature. It simply seeks to
affirm the personal response of man's love to the work of his
salvation by Christ, and to accord with divine love and the
divine economy, albeit to the infinitesimal extent permitted
by the weakness of his nature.

5. Neglect of asceticism, an alienation of the truth

Here we begin a necessarily critical parenthesis, calling to
mind the distortions produced in Christian piety, especially in
what we call the western societies, by the neglect of asceticism
and more particularly of the physical character of asceticism.
Fasting, which is the most immediate and general act of

[5]*Ladder*, step 15, PG 88, 881A.

asceticism in the Church, is now all but abolished in the West, even on the official level. The center of gravity in Christian piety is shifted further if not exclusively onto what is called "individual moral consistency," onto rationally justifiable areas of behavior, and an obedience to the commands of social utility which is logically self-evident and objectively necessary.

Increasingly, Christian life seems to be nothing more than a particular way of behaving, a code of good conduct. Christianity is increasingly alienated, becoming a social attribute adapted to meet the least worthy of human demands—conformity, sterile conservatism, pusillanimity and timidity; it is adapted to the trivial moralizing which seeks to adorn cowardice and individual security with the funerary decoration of social decorum. The people who really thirst for life, who stand daily on the brink of every kind of death, who struggle desperately to distinguish some light in the sealed mystery of human existence —these are the people to whom the Gospel of salvation is primarily and most especially addressed, and inevitably they all remain far removed from the rationalistically organized social conventionalism of established Christianity.

Today, in this atmosphere, the very word and idea of asceticism is probably incomprehensible to a very large number of Christian people. Anyone talking about fasting and chastity and voluntary restriction of our individual desires is sure to meet with condescension or mockery. This does not, of course, prevent people from having their "metaphysical convictions" and believing in a "supreme being" or in the "sweet Jesus" who had a wonderful ethical teaching. The question is, however, what is the use of "metaphysical convictions" when they do not go any way towards providing a *real* answer—as opposed to one that is idealistic and abstract—to the problem of death, the scandal of the dissolution of the body in the earth.

This real answer is to be found only in the knowledge granted by asceticism, in the effort to resist death in our own bodies, and by the dynamic triumph over the deadening of man. And not just in any kind of asceticism, but in that which consists in conformity to the example of Christ, who willingly accepted death so as to destroy death—"trampling down death by death." Every voluntary mortification of the egocentricity which is "contrary to nature" is a dynamic destruction of death and a triumph for the life of the person. The culmination comes when man shows complete trust by handing over his body, the last bastion of death, into the hands of God, into the embrace of the "earth of the Lord" and into the fulness of the communion of saints.

6. "Bodily knowledge"

The message which is really able to touch man, and perhaps especially modern man in his revolt against the hollowness of conventional moral standards, is none other than the challenge and the call to direct, bodily participation in the truth of the life which destroys death, the truth of personal freedom from the constraint of nature.

In the Church, bodily asceticism has always been the supreme road to *theological knowledge*. It is not possible for man to come to know the truth of life, the truth of God and the truth of his own existence purely through intellectual categories, purely through the conventional concepts which can be expressed in language, relative as they are. When man follows the way of relative analogies and conventional expressions, all he can gain is a relative and conventional knowledge. The universal truth of God's revelation, the truth about the fulness and fulfilment of life, is a universal knowledge gained through personal experience—in the biblical sense of knowledge, which identifies it with sexual relations and intercourse. And as the true sexual relationship and intercourse is a complete participation in body and in soul, and an offering of oneself, so also the *eros* of God, the true relationship and "intercourse" or communion with Him, the *knowledge* of His person, presupposes bodily participation by man, the bodily asceticism of self-offering.

St Isaac the Syrian writes: "If you want your heart to become a place for the mysteries of the new world, first become rich in corporeal works: in fasting, vigils, service, asceticism, patience, the destruction of troublesome thoughts and the rest."[6] And here we have the reason for his exhortation: "For violent activity generates an infinite warmth which kindles in the heart . . . This action and vigilance refine the mind in their heat, and give it vision."[7] The vision of God's countenance, the perceptible experience of the light of His countenance, is the purpose and "end" of asceticism, the dynamic and therefore always uncompleted perfection of knowledge and love: "You cannot love God unless you see Him: and the vision of God comes from knowing Him."[8]

The personal or "erotic" reality of asceticism gives Christian piety the character of a direct, perceptible experience of the incorruption of life, distinguishing it radically and essentially from the conventional nature of the "achievement" of individual virtue. In a way that is perceptible and experiential, the Christian in his daily life repudiates the autonomy of natural survival; he rejects it as an end in itself in order to receive from God's love the gift of life, life as personal and loving communion with Him. Thus bodily asceticism defines in a tangible and concrete manner the eucharistic character of the Church's ethos, the way in which the eucharist, the holy communion, is extended into everyday life.

[6]*Mystic Treatises*, Letter 4, p. 383.
[7]*Mystic Treatises*, Logos 9, p. 41.
[8]Isaac the Syrian, *Mystic Treatises*, Logos 16, p. 58.

CHAPTER EIGHT

Pietism as an Ecclesiological Heresy

1. The historical coordinates

We give the name "pietism" to a phenomenon in church life which certainly has a particular historical and "confessional" starting point, but also has much wider ramifications in the spiritual life of all the Christian Churches.

Pietism made its appearance as a distinct historical movement within Protestantism, at the end of the seventeenth and beginning of the eighteenth centuries, around 1690-1730.[1] Its aim was to stress "practical piety," as distinct from the polemical dogmatic theology to which the Reformation had initially given a certain priority.[2] Against the intellectualist

[1]There is a rich bibliography on pietism, chiefly in the form of monographs dealing with the numerous local pietistic movements and the personalities of their leaders. Although not very systematic, the fullest study of the phenomenon as a whole is still A. Ritschl's three-volumed work *Geschichte des Pietismus* (Bonn, 1880-1886). A recent work, exceptionally informative and well-documented, is Martin Schmidt's *Pietismus* (1972). The Roman Catholic approach, with a concise, objective and reasonably full description of the phenomenon and history of pietism, may be found in Louis Bouyer, *Orthodox Spirituality and Protestant and Anglican Spirituality* (History of Christian Spirituality III, London, 1969), p. 169ff. As for the rest of the bibliography, we note here some basic aids: W. Mahrholz, *Der deutsche Pietismus* (Berlin, 1921); H. Bornkamm, *Mystik, Spiritualismus und die Anfänge des Pietismus im Luthertum* (Giessen, 1926); M. Beyer-Frohlich, *Pietismus und Rationalismus* (Leipzig, 1933); K. Reinhardt, *Mystik und Pietismus* (Berlin, 1925); O. Söhngen, ed., *Die bleibende Bedeutung des Pietismus* (Berlin, 1960); E. Sachsse, *Ursprung und Wesen des Pietismus* (1884); F. E. Stoeffler, *The Rise of Evangelical Pietism* (Studies in the History of Religions IX, 1965), pp. 180-246.

[2]The picture one gets from the relevant bibliography would justify the

and abstract understanding of God and of dogmatic truth, pietism set a practical, active piety (*praxis pietatis*): good works, daily self-examination for progress in virtues according to objective criteria, daily study of the Bible and practical application of its moral teaching, intense emotionalism in prayer, a clear break with the "world" and worldly practices (dancing, the theatre, non-religious reading); and tendencies towards separatism, with the movement holding private meetings and distinguishing itself from the "official" Church.[3]

For pietism, knowledge of God presupposes the "rebirth" of man, and this rebirth is understood as living up to the moral law of the Gospel and as an emotional experience of authoritative truths.[4] Pietism presents itself as a mystical piety, and ultimately as a form of opposition to knowledge; as "adogmatism," in the sense that it ignores or belittles theological truth, or even as pure agnosticism cloaked in morality.[5]

view that the historical roots of pietism are spread throughout the religious and theological tradition of western Christianity, both Roman Catholic and Protestant. There is, nevertheless, a particularly direct historical link between this phenomenon and certain Dutch offshoots of Protestantism, English Puritanism and above all Roman Catholic mysticism. Jansenism in seventeenth century France, the Port-Royal movement, Quietism, Thomas à Kempis' *Imitation of Christ*, Teresa of Avila, John of the Cross, Francis of Sales and Fénélon are considered by most scholars to be immediate forerunners of Protestant pietism. It is typical that Lutheran "orthodoxy" always condemned pietism as pro-Catholic. See M. Schmidt, *Pietismus*, p. 26; L. Bouyer, *Orthodox Spirituality* . . . , pp. 169-170 and 193.

[3]See Karl Heussi and Eric Peter, *Précis d'Histoire de l'Eglise* (Neuchatel, 1967), § 106; M. Schmidt, *Pietismus*, p. 140. The first of the founders of the pietist movement, Philip-Jacob Spener (1635-1705), a Lutheran pastor from Alsace, created the blueprint for this moralistic campaign by organizing the zealous faithful into Bible study circles (*Bibelkreise*) independent of the Church's gatherings for worship. Study of Scripture was meant to lead to practical moral conclusions affecting the individual lives of the members of the movement. Any of the faithful could be in charge of such a "circle." Spener and the other pioneers of the pietist movement (A. H. Francke, 1663-1727, G. Arnold, 1666-1714, N. L. Graf von Zinzendorf, 1700-1760, J. A. Bengel, 1697-1752, F. C. Oetinger, 1702-1782) laid particular emphasis on the universal priesthood of the laity, and were sharply critical of the clergy of their time and the "institutional Church, compromised with the world." See L. Bouyer, *Orthodox Spirituality* . . . , pp. 170-171; M. Schmidt, *Pietismus*, pp. 12-42; *Nouvelle Histoire de l'Eglise* vol. 4 (Paris, 1966), pp. 35-36.

[4]See L. Bouyer, *Orthodox Spirituality* . . . , p. 174: ". . . the dissolution of all defined dogmatic faith and its substitution by unverifiable sentiment . . ."

[5]"[Pietism] considers the practice of piety as the essential element of religion . . . but is accompanied more often by a growing indifference with

Under different forms and in various "movements," it has not ceased to influence Protestantism, and indeed also the spiritual life of other churches, to this day. In combination with humanism, the Enlightenment and the "practical" spirit of the modern era—the spirit of "productivity" and "efficiency" —pietism has cultivated throughout Europe a largely "social" understanding of the Church, involving practical activities of public benefit, and it has presented the message of salvation primarily as a necessity for individual and collective morality.

2. The theological coordinates

Pietism undermines the ontological truth of Church unity and personal communion, if it does not deny it completely; it approaches man's salvation in Christ as an individual event, an individual possibility of life. It is individual piety and the subjective process of "appropriating salvation" made absolute and autonomous, and it transfers the possibility of man's salvation to the realm of individual moral endeavor.[6]

For pietism, salvation is not primarily the *fact* of the Church, the theanthropic "new creation" of the body of Christ, the mode of existence of its trinitarian prototype and the unity of the communion of persons. It is not man's dynamic, personal participation in the body of the Church's communion which saves him despite his individual unworthiness, restoring him *safe* and *whole* to the existential possibility of personal universality, and transforming even his sin, through repentance, into the possibility of receiving God's grace and love. Rather it is primarily man's individual attainments, the way he as an individual lives up to religious duties

regard to dogma": *Nouvelle Histoire de l'Eglise,* p. 35. "Whenever the Church started dogmatizing, so he held, it fell into decadence, and the only way out lay in the fact that each generation produced simple-minded men whose instinctive reaction (bullied by authority) constituted a prophetic re-affirmation of the one pure Christianity, primitive and free from all ratiocination": L. Bouyer, *Orthodox Spirituality . . .,* p. 175.

[6]"At the center stands the individual person: the early Christian image of 'building up' is transformed in an individualistic direction (building up of the inner person)": M. Schmidt, "Pietismus," in *Religion in Geschichte und Gegenwart,* vol. 5, col. 370. *Idem, Pietismus,* pp. 90 and 123.

and moral commandments and imitates the "virtues" of Christ, that ensure him a justification which can be objectively verified. For pietism, the Church is a phenomenon dependent upon individual justification; it is the assembly of morally "reborn" individuals, a gathering of the "pure," a complement and an aid to individual religious feeling.[7]

By this route pietism reached a result opposite to its original intent. Seeking to reject the one extreme of intellectual religion, it ended up at the other extreme, separating practical piety from the truth and revelation of the Church. Thus piety loses its ontological content and ceases to be an existential event—the realization and manifestation of man's existential truth, of the "image" of God in man. It turns into an individual achievement which certainly improves character and behavior and perhaps social *mores* as well, but which cannot possibly transfigure our mode of existence and change corruption into incorruption, and death into life and resurrection.

Piety loses its ontological content; and, in addition, the truth and faith of the Church is divorced from life and action, and left as a set of "principles" and "axioms" which one accepts like any other ideology. The distinction between contemplation and action, between truth and life or between dogma and morality, turns into a schizophrenic severence. The life of the Church is confined to moral obedience, religious duties and the serving of social ends. One might venture to express the situation with the paradox that, in the case of pietism, ethics corrupts the Church: it turns the criteria of the Church into worldly and conventional criteria, distorting the "great mystery of godliness" into a rationalistic social necessity. Pietistic ethics distort the liturgical and eucharistic reality of the Church, the unity in life and communion of the

[7]"The new type of community ... is the formation of groups of reborn individuals, not the community of those called by word and sacrament. The initiative lies with the subject ... Individualism and subjectivism undermine the sacramental perpective": M. Schmidt, "Pietismus," col. 371. "In the confusion between faith and sense experience and the tendency to replace the objective data of faith and the sacraments by an emotional subjective event, he discerns at least latent indifference regarding all established doctrine, and, in a more general way, loss of sight of the Church and its ministry as institutions": L. Bouyer, *Orthodox Spirituality* ..., p. 174.

penitent and the perfect, sinners and saints, the first and the last; they turn the Church into an inevitably conventional, institutional corporation of people who are individually religious.

A host of people today, perhaps the majority in western societies, evaluate the Church's work by the yardstick of its social usefulness as compared with the social work of education, penitentiary systems or even the police. The natural result is that the Church is preserved as an institution essential for morals and organized like a worldly establishment in an increasingly bureaucratic fashion. The most obvious form of secularization in the Church is the pietistic falsification of her mind and experience, the adulteration of her own criteria with moralistic considerations. Once the Church denies her ontological identity—what she really, essentially *is* as an existential event whereby individual survival is changed into a personal life of love and communion—then from that very moment she is reduced to a conventional form under which individuals are grouped together into an institution; she becomes an expression of man's fall, albeit a religious one. She begins to serve the "religious needs" of the people, the individualistic emotional and psychological needs of fallen man.

The utilitarian institutional mentality, a typical product of pietism, has led many churches and Christian confessions to a fever of anxiety lest they should be proved out-dated and useless in the modern technocratic, rationalistically-organized society, and should appear to lag behind in keeping up to date with the world. Frequently they try to offer contemporary man a message as convenient and well-fitted as possible to his utilitarian demands for prosperity. "Humanistic" ethics—the principle of keeping up appearances—takes precedence over truth, over the salvation of existence from the anonymity of death. The miracle of repentance, the transfiguration of sin into loving desire for personal communion with God, the way mortality is swallowed up by life—these are truths incomprehensible to the pietistic spirit of our age. The Gospel message is "made void," emptied of its ontological content;

the Church's faith in the resurrection of man is made to appear vacuous.

3. The moral alienation of salvation

When the piety of the Church is transferred to the plane of individual ethics and separated from her truth, this inevitably results in a blurring of the difference between the truth of salvation and the illusion of salvation, between the Church and heresy. The idea of heresy or schism loses all real content, and is confined to abstract, theoretical differences understood only by "experts" who discuss them at meetings and conferences, exchanging the thrust and parry of confessional articles and formulations which fail to correspond in any way to the life of human beings.

Increasingly pietism equates the spirituality and piety of the various churches and confessions, taking them on the level of individual, or socially useful and efficacious, ethics, while disregarding even fundamental dogmatic differences. The piety of a Roman Catholic, a Protestant and frequently even an "enlightened" Orthodox, do not present substantial differences; practical piety no longer reveals whether the truth one lives is real or distorted. Dogma does not appear as a "definition," laying down the limits within which the Church's experience is to be expressed and safeguarded. Christian piety appears unrelated to the way we experience the truth of God in Trinity, the incarnation of the Word, and the energies of the Holy Spirit which give substance to the life of the members of the Church.

The model of Christian piety in the different churches and confessions is increasingly equated with that of a more "perfect" utilitarian ethic, with an individual morality which takes precedence over the fact of the Church. The only distinctions in piety are variations in religious customs and religious "duties." Even the liturgical act is incidental to individual piety, a complement, aid or fruit; it is thought of as an opportunity for "edification" or a religious duty. The eucharist, the original embodiment of the fact of salvation, is distorted by the pietistic spirit; it is construed as a narrowly "religious" obligation, a duty to pray together and perhaps to listen to a sermon which usually confines itself to prescribing how the individual should behave. The eucharist is not the event which constitutes and manifests the Church, the changing of our mode of existence and the realization of the ethos of the "new man."

Ultimately, even participation in the sacraments takes on a conventional, ethical character. Confession turns into a psychological means of setting individual guilt-feelings at rest, and participation in holy communion becomes a moral reward for good behavior—when it is not a scarcely conscious individual or family custom bordering on magic. Baptism becomes a self-evident social obligation, and marriage a legitimization of sexual relations without regard to any ascetic transfiguration of the conjugal union into an ecclesial event of *personal* intercourse or communion.

4. The moral assimilation of heresies

A typical and entirely consistent extension of all this blurring and alienation of the ontological character of the Church's truth is the modern movement towards the so-called "union" of the churches, and the much-vaunted priority of the "love" which unites the churches over the "dogma" which divides them. One could say that this movement was historically justified, since it often looks as if union has been accomplished on the level of a common, non-dogmatic piety —on the level of pietism. What used to divide the Church from heresy was not abstract differences in academic formulations; it was the radical break and the distance between the universality of life and illusions of life, between realizing the true life of our trinitarian prototype and subjugating this truth to fallen man's fragmentary mode of existence. Dogma "defined," or showed the limits, while the Church's asceticism secured participation in that truth of life which defeats corruption and death and realizes the image of God in the human being.

When piety ceases to be an *ecclesial* event and turns into an individual moral attainment, then a heretic or even a non-Christian can be just as virtuous as a "Christian." Piety loses its connection with truth and its ontological content; it ceases to be related to man's full, bodily participation in the life of God—to the resurrection of the body, the change of matter into "word," and the transfiguration of time and space into the immediacy of communion. Piety is transformed into an entirely uniform manner of being religious which inevitably makes differences of "confession" or tradition relative, or even assimilates the different traditions, since they all end in the same result—the moral "improvement" of human life.

Thus the differences which separate heresy from truth remain empty verbal formulations irrelevant to the reality of life and death, irrelevant even to piety. They are preserved simply as variations in religious customs and traditional beliefs, with a purely historical interest. It is therefore natural for the distinct Christian confessions to seek formal union—respecting, of course, the pluralism in religious customs and theoretical formulations—since they are already substantially assimilated in the sphere of "practical life." This is the obvious basis for the unity movement in our times—when, of course, it is not guided by much more stark socio-political considerations.

Socio-political considerations, however, have influenced church life in every age; they are the sins of our human nature which has been taken into the Church. And they are not a real danger so long as we are aware that they are sins; they do not succeed in distorting the truth and the fact of the Church. The danger of real distortion lies in heresy: when we take for truth and salvation some "improved" version of the fragmented mode of existence of fallen man. And the great heresy of our age is pietism. Pietism is a heresy in the realm of ecclesiology: it undermines or actually denies the very truth of the Church, transferring the event of salvation from the ecclesial to the individual ethos, to piety divorced from the trinitarian mode of existence, from Christ's way of obedience. Pietism denies the ontological fact of salvation—the Church, life as personal coinherence and communion in love, and the transfiguration of mortal individuality into a hypostasis of eternal life.

Pietism undermines the ontological truth of the Church or totally rejects it, but without questioning the formulations of that truth. It simply disregards them, taking them as intellectual forms unrelated to man's salvation, and abandons them to the jurisdiction of an autonomous academic theology. Pietism preserves a formal faithfulness to the letter of dogmatic formulation, but this is a dead letter, irrelevant to life and existential experience.

In that particular, this real denial of the truth of salvation differs from previous heresies. It does not reject the "definitions," the limits of the Church's truth; it simply disconnects this truth from the life and salvation of man. And this disconnection covers a vast range of distinctions and nuances, so that it is exceptionally difficult to "excommunicate" pietism, to place it beyond the bounds within which the Church's truth and unity are experienced. But this is precisely why it is perhaps the most dangerous assault on this truth and unity.

5. The individualistic "culture" of pietism

Pietism is definitely not an autonomous phenomenon, independent of the historical and cultural conditions which have shaped western civilization over the last three centuries. The spirit of individualism, rationalism and utilitarianism, the priority given to rationalization, the myth of "objectivity" and the "values" it imposes, the connection of truth with usefulness and of knowledge with turning things to "practical" account—all these are factors which have influenced and shaped the phenomenon of pietism, and have equally been influenced and shaped by it. Corresponding currents and tendencies, like the Enlightenment, humanism, romanticism or positivism, are part of the web of interdependence formed by these same factors which ultimately make up the mentality and the standards of our modern culture, setting an imperceptible yet decisive seal on people's character and temperament.

This assertion poses an exceptionally difficult problem for Christian theology. If the way of life in western civilization, the only civilization which can really claim to be called worldwide, presupposes and imposes the cult of the individual, what place remains for the experience and realization of *ecclesial* truth and life? If the technocratic consumer society throughout the world presupposes and develops the primacy of intellectual ability in the subject, the autonomy of his will, the rationalistic regulation of individual rights and duties, "objective" backing for individual choices and for the economic safeguards assured for the individual by trade unions, and a rationalistic linkage of the individual with the group—then the individualistic religion of pietism is the inevitable consequence. Indeed, it is the only possibility for religious expression in western culture—the necessary and sufficient condition for religious life. There seems little or no scope for experience and historical realization of the Church's truth, the trinitarian mode of existence: no room to live our salvation through a practical subjection of the individual to the experience of communion which belongs to the Church as a body, and to realize the ethos or morality of the Gospel through self-transcendence on the part of the individual and through the freedom and distinctiveness of persons within the communion of saints.[8]

It is no accident that the first pioneers of pietist ideals consciously envisaged an ecumenical movement which was to restore "genuine Christianity" throughout the world.[9] Pietism

[8]Precisely because the Church is not a religious ideology but the continuous assumption of the flesh of the world and the transformation of it into the theanthropic flesh of Christ, it is impossible for the ontological truth of the Church's unity and communion to "coexist" passively with a culture centered on the individual, a culture of objectification. The Church lives and functions only so long as she is continuously and dynamically assuming individualistic, objectified existences in order to transfigure them into unity of life, into personal relationship and communion. But this means that on the historical and social level, the life and unity of the Church operates as a radical and direct rejection or subversion of the cultural "system" of individualism and objectification. Otherwise, the Church would be subject to the way of life imposed by the "system," so that she herself would be alienated both as a reality of truth and salvation, and as an institutional expression of this reality.

[9]"Pietism originally was an ecumenical, world-wide phenomenon . . . Above

spread with exceptional speed over a remarkably wide area. From Germany it passed at once to England, where the ground had been prepared by Puritanism, and to the Netherlands and Scandinavia; it spread eastwards as far as Russia, and took hold in America with the first generations of settlers, as also in the missionary churches of Africa and Asia. But the factual details of how pietism spread so rapidly and the ecumenical ambitions of its founders are only a part of its far more general and organic identification with the tendency towards expansionism and universality innate in western civilization.

It is certain that pietism holds a central place in the web of mutual influence between the factors which have shaped the peculiar character of western culture. However much this might seem both a generalization and a paradox, it could be maintained that pietism has played one of the most significant roles in the historical development of "western-type" societies. This assertion becomes more comprehensible if we accept the view of scholars who attribute to pietism the birth and development of the system of the autonomous economy, or *capitalism*[10]—a system which today is decisive in determining the economic, political and social lives of people all over the world.

The initial historical link between pietism and capitalism is well known. The linchpin of the capitalist ideology may be identified with the pietistic demand for direct, quantifiable and judicially recompensed results from individual piety and morality—in this case, from hard work, honesty, thrift, rationalistic exploitation of "talents," etc. Work acquires an autonomy: it is divorced from actual needs and becomes a religious obligation, finding its visible justification and "just deserts" in the accumulation of wealth. The management of

all it understood itself to be of ecumenical scope, the representation of true Christendom over all the earth": M. Schmidt, *Pietismus*, p. 11.

[10]See R. H. Tawney, *Religion and the Rise of Capitalism* (Penguin Books, 1975[11]); Max Weber, *Die Protestantische Ethik und der Geist des Kapitalismus*, in *Die protestantische Ethik*, I (Hamburg, 1973[3]); E. Troeltsch, *Die Soziallehren der christlichen Kirchen und Gruppen* (Tübingen, 1965); H. Hauser, *Les débuts du Capitalisme* (Paris, 1927); A. Fanfani, *Catholicism, Protestantism and Capitalism* (London, 1935); H. M. Robertson, *Aspects of the Rise of Economic Individualism* (Cambridge, 1933).

wealth similarly becomes autonomous: it is divorced from social need and becomes part of the individual's relationship with God, a relationship of quantitative deserts and rewards.[11]

Confirmation of the conclusions thus formulated could be based not only on the inevitably relative agreement among students of the phenomenon of capitalism, but also on reference to direct historical examples. Perhaps the most representative example is that of the birth and development of the United States of America. This superpower of our times, which is also the most powerful and important factor in the operation of the world capitalist system, has its roots in the principles and the spirit of pietism. The successive waves of Anglo-Saxon Puritans and pietists who first emigrated to America with the millenarian vision[12] of a Puritan "promised land"[13] identified trust in God with the power of money,[14] and religious feeling with the economic efficiency of work (work ethics), and ultimately hallowed as ethics whatever ensured individual security and social prosperity.[15] By the

[11]"Convinced that character is all and circumstances nothing [the morally self-sufficient] see in the poverty of those who fall by the way, not a misfortune to be pitied and relieved, but a moral failing to be condemned, and in riches not an object of suspicion—though like other gifts they may be abused—but the blessing which rewards the triumph of energy and will": Tawney, *Religion and the Rise of Capitalism*, pp. 229-230.

[12]Millenarist tendencies and expectation of the Messiah are characteristic of pietism, "... a sort of renewed 'chiliasm,' that is to say the immediate expectation of a kingdom of God on earth which it would be within our power to produce": L. Bouyer, *Orthodox Spirituality* ..., p. 174. See also M. Schmidt, *Pietismus*, pp. 130-132 and 160; and Charles L. Sanford, *The Quest of Paradise: Europe and the American Moral Imagination* (Urbana, Ill., 1961).

[13]See Robert Bellah, *The Broken Covenant—American Civil Religion in Time of Trial* (New York, 1975), especially pp. 7-8 and the chapter "America as a Chosen People" (p. 36ff.); Conrad Cherry, *God's New Israel: Religious Interpretations of American Destiny* (Prentice-Hall, 1971); H. Richard Niebuhr, *The Kingdom of God in America* (New York, 1937).

[14]"In God we trust" is the inscription on every coin and dollar note. See also Moses Rischin, ed., *The American Gospel of Success* (Quadrangle Books, 1965); Howard Mumford Jones, *The Pursuit of Happiness* (Ithaca, N.Y., 1966).

[15]See Robert Handy, *A Christian America* (New York and Oxford, 1971), especially the chapter: "Components of the New Christian Civilization: Religion, Morality, Education," especially pp. 33-40; William McLoughlin, *Isaac Backus and the American Pietistic Tradition* (Boston, 1967); Irvin G. Wyllie, *The Self-made Man in America* (Free Press, 1966).

very fact of their existence, the two hundred and fifty or so different Christian confessions in that country make the truth of the Church body take second place; in defining the quality of a Christian, priority is given to the peculiarly American idea of individual ethics (civil religion).

Going by the example of America and the pietistic basis of the "gospel of wealth" which took shape there,[16] one might venture to make a further assertion. The whole of mankind lives today in the trap of a lethal threat created by the polarization of two provenly immoral moralistic systems, and the constant expectation of a confrontation between them in war, perhaps nuclear war. On the one side is the pietistic individualism of the capitalist camp, and on the other the moralistic collectivism of the marxist dreams of "universal happiness." At least the latter refuses to cloak its aims under the forged title of Christian, while the name of Christianity continues to be blackened in the sloganizing of even the foulest dictatorships which support the workings of the capitalist system, upholding the pietistic ideal of individual "merit."

If the witness of an ecumenical council of the Church were to have any meaning in our day, its chief purpose would be to denounce this torture of man, this imprisonment in an adulterated and falsified idea of Christian piety: the corrosion and destruction of the truth of salvation and the reality of the Church by generalized pietism.

[16]See Andrew Carnegie's famous essay "The Gospel of Wealth," reprinted from *The American Review* 148 (1889), pp. 653-664, in Gail Kennedy, ed., *Democracy and the Gospel of Wealth* (Boston, 1949).

Additional Note: Some specific products of pietism are the Halle movement (founded by August-Hermann Francke), the Moravian Brethren (Herrnhuter Brüdergemeine—founded by N. L. von Zinzendorf), the Methodists (founded by John Wesley, 1703-1791), the Quakers (founded by George Fox, 1624-1691), and in the nineteenth and twentieth centuries a host of "Free Churches," missionary societies, schools of preaching, "inner mission" movements, Protestant monastic brotherhoods, etc. See M. Schmidt, *Pietismus*, pp. 243-60.

In Roman Catholicism we rarely hear of autonomous groups or movements of pietists, perhaps because pietistic tendencies and initiatives were officially adopted by the Roman Catholic Church in the form of orders, societies, sacred confraternities, etc. In Roman Catholic mysticism, certainly, pietism has always found the conditions for its natural generation. The in-

dividual approach to virtue, anthropocentric sentimentality and the transference of religious feeling to the "interior" of the individual are all hall-
marks of Roman Catholic mystics, whether as individuals or in organized
and officially recognized groups. The link with the body of the Church
is of secondary importance and sometimes of purely legal and formal significance. "Bei ihnen kam alles auf die inneren Menschen, nichts auf die
aussere Form der Kirchlichkeit an": M. Schmidt, *Pietismus*, p. 26.
   Of the Orthodox churches, the Russian Church was the first to be in-
vaded by the spirit of pietism. Early in the eighteenth century, Bishop
Feofan Prokopovich (1681-1736), professor and later rector of the Theological Academy in Kiev, represented in Russia the pietistic Halle movement (see Schmidt, "Pietismus," article in *Die Religion in Geschichte und
Gegenwart*, vol. 5, col. 372; R. Stupperich, "Protestantismus in Russland," in the
same volume, col. 1248). Prokopovich's influence was very widespread and left
a distinct mark on the Church and spiritual life of Russia, from the moment when
Peter the Great (1672-1725) took him on as a close collaborator, after promoting
him to the archbishopric of Novgorod, and let him fundamentally shape his
religious reform. (See Igor Smolitsch, *Geschichte der russischen Kirche,
1700-1917* [Leiden, 1964], p. 94ff; and Reinhard Wittram, *Peter I—Czar
und Kaisar*, vol. 2 [Göttingen, 1964], p. 189ff.) The religious reform of
Peter the Great had as its aim the systematic westernization of the Russian
Church both in structure and in spiritual life. And under the influence of
Feofan Prokopovich, many areas of Russian church and spiritual life were
shaped precisely in accordance with the spirit and the criteria of Protestant
pietism. At the same time, his theological "system" and his writings imposed on the academic study of theology in Russia what Florovsky calls
"the domination of Latino-protestant scholasticism" (*Puti russkogo bogoslo-
viia* [Paris, 1937], p. 104; the reference is from I. Smolitsch, *Geschichte
der russischen Kirche*, p. 577. See also H. Koch, *Die russische Orthodoxie
im Petrinischen Zeitalter* [Breslau, 1929]; Cyprien Kern, "L'enseignement
théologique supérieur dans la Russie du XIXe siecle," *Istina*, 1960; Igor
Smolitsch, *Russische Monchtum, 988-1917* [Würzburg, 1953], p. 383ff.)
The influence of Feofan Prokopovich's theology reached even as far as
Greece, at least through Theoklitos Farmakidis, "the first to teach dogmatic
theology at the Ionian Academy on Kerkyra in 1824, following the text
of the Russian Feofan Prokopovich": Manuel Gedeon, *The Cultural Progress
of the Nation in the Eighteenth and Nineteenth Centuries* [in Greek—
Athens, 1976], p. 206.
   Actual pietistic movements in Russia were probably very few; the best
known is the Moravian Brethren, from 1740 in Sarepta on the Volga (R.
Stupperich, "Protestantismus in Russland," col. 1250). What is more striking is the way in which the Church's mentality as a whole was undermined.
In combination with the stress on sentiment introduced into Russia by the
religious romanticism of the nineteenth century, and the corresponding
prevalence of baroque in church art which distorted basic theological presuppositions in Russian Orthodox worship, a general climate of pietism often
shapes the atmosphere and complexion of Russian church life.
   Pietistic influence is apparent even in the figures most representative of
Russian spiritual life. The most important spiritual figure in eighteenth
century Russia, St Tikhon Zadonsky (1724-1783), is also a typical representative of pietistic and Roman Catholic influences. "He was strongly
influenced by contemporary western piety, both Counter-Reformation Catholic

piety and Protestant piety with an emphasis on pietism ... We find in [his works] a direct echo of St Augustine and the *Imitation of Christ,* as of Lutheran works such as Arndt's *True Christianity* ... and Anglican ones such as the *Meditatiunculae subitaneae* by the Puritan Bishop Hall": L. Bouyer, *Orthodox Spirituality* ..., pp. 37-38.

In the form of an organized movement, pietism appeared in the Romanian Orthodox Church just on the eve of World War II, under the name of "the Army of the Lord" and with the priest Joseph Trifa at its head. There, however, the Church reacted swiftly; she excommunicated the founders and excised from her body this danger which threatened to alienate her tradition and her life.

In Greece, pietism made its appearance as a symptom of a more general "europeanization" of the country. Quite early, around the eighteenth century, Humanism and the principles of the Renaissance and the Enlightenment exerted an obvious influence on Greek scholars and church writers who turned to the West for their higher education. Rationalism and moralism, as direct results of European thinking and theology, reached the Orthodox Greek East through the writing and teaching of the "enlightened Teachers of the Nation," learned preachers and writers from the period of Turkish domination. At least in the works of Vikentios Damodos (1679-1752), Elias Miniatis (1669-1714), Evgenios Voulgaris (1716-1806), Nikeforos Theotokis (1730-1800), Theoklitos Farmakidis (1754-1860) and Neofytos Vamvas (1770-1855), there is manifest influence from western theological positions of their day: moral eudaemonism, the "religion of sentiment" (Schleiermacher), the connection of Church and "culture" (*Kulturchristentum*), the identification of spiritual regeneration with moral regeneration, the juridical understanding of morality (see Ch. Yannaras, *Orthodoxy and the West—Theology in Greece Today* [in Greek—Athens, 1972], especially pp. 57-95, with bibliography).

With the establishment of the independent Greek state and the imposition of German and Protestant models on the organization of the Church of Greece (which became "autocephalous" in 1833) and of theological education, western influences prevailed in Greek academic theology and in "official" church life—though not without exceptions and reactions. The phenomenon could perhaps have been contained there, since popular spirituality and piety remained untainted by western alienation. But from the very first decades of our own century, pietism made its appearance in Greece in the form of a specific movement whose intention was to bring in the broad masses of the people. Initially it seemed that the aim of the "movement" was the renewal of church life, with the systematic organization of sermons, catechism classes, religious publications and confession. But it very soon separated itself and its activity from the life of the Church, the life of the parishes and the jurisdiction of the local bishops. It was organized as an independent effort, with a system of administration and organization independent of the church hierarchy, and with its own spiritual and theological direction.

It is quite extraordinary how closely the modern Greek pietist movement copied its German and Anglo-Saxon prototypes. Preaching and teaching were based on exactly the same premises: the theological truth of dogmas was ignored or passed over in silence and replaced with the teaching of ethics, a rationalist apologetic, utilitarian rationalism and moral eudaemonism, and stress on individual virtue and the cultural necessity of religion. Fol-

lowing Spener's method to the letter, the "movement" organized a vast
number of Bible study circles meeting in houses all over Greece. This led
to the formation of a kind of private worship outside church—in imitation
of the Protestant "service of the word" (*Wortgottesdienst*)—with the lay
element alone. It consisted of reading from the Bible, always with a moral
conclusion, *ex tempore* prayers and sentimental songs, usually from Protestant
collections of hymns. The Greek pietist movement, exactly like the Protestant
ones, came to be dominated by a strongly military discipline: its members
were forbidden to go to public spectacles or recreation centers, to smoke, or
to read books or other material of their own choosing. They have developed
more or less a common style of dress, and cultivate a militant missionary
spirit to gain followers.

To the general public, the pietistic movement in Greece is known as the
Zoe movement, after the first "Brotherhood of Theologians" which began
its organized efforts in 1911. Later, however, there emerged offshoots of
this same organization (the Fellowship of Academics "Aktines," the Student Christian Union, the Christian Union of Working Youth, the Women's
Fellowship "Evseveia," the Fellowship of Nursing Sisters "Evniki," the
Christian schools "Elliniki Pedeia," etc.). There were also parallel movements which copied the Zoe model in principles and structure (the Brotherhood of Theologians "O Sotir," the organizations of Metropolitan Avgoustinos
Kandiotis of Florina, etc.).

Making their moralistic criteria into absolutes, these movements in Greece
turned into complete religious units, divorced from the life of the Church
and society. They developed into closed, autonomous religious groups,
entry to which could be secured only by objectively recognized "suitability"
and moral rectitude. Divorced from the life of the parishes and from local
bishops, these pietistic groups consolidated their independence by taking
the form of secular "associations" with recognition from the state. They
were thus able to control the numbers and the morals of their members,
and organize a kind of "para-ecclesial" life in open opposition to the
official Church. They acquired buildings of their own for catechism meetings and, where possible, their own churches. They have their own clergy,
who are formally attached to the local bishop but are in reality directed
down to the last detail by the administration of the organizations. They
thus have their own confessors and separate confession, in the buildings
belonging to the organizations rather than in the churches—and even their
own separate liturgies, where entry is controlled and only members of the
organizations are allowed in.

It may perhaps be useful to add some mention of the position taken up
by the pietistic organizations in Greece on the question of ecumenism, a
position which contradicts their principles. The organizations came out in
fanatical opposition to the idea of church unity, although the idea of
union had to a great extent been embodied by these same pietistic movements. It was they who had been exclusively responsible for transferring to
Greek Orthodox territory both the practice of western piety and also, on
many points, such western dogmatic teaching as was essential for their
moralism. Such points of doctrine include the legalistic theory of the satisfaction of divine justice through Christ's death on the Cross, denial of the
distinction between God's essence and energies, rejection of hesychasm and
the neptic tradition, an apologetic devised with utilitarian ends, the general
priesthood of the laity as an autonomous absolute, a legal understanding

of the transmission of original sin, etc. We are bound to conclude that their stance against church unity is simply the result of a tragic confusion in spiritual criteria, and shows the movements' lack of theological self-awareness, or else is nothing but a conventional attempt to outdo everyone else in conservatism. Either way, it cannot be a matter of deliberately upholding Orthodox spirituality and the Orthodox tradition, since the organizations could be said to ignore these quite provocatively and to distort them systematically.

It would require a separate study to analyze the various forms these distortions take: the abolition of the holy icons, which are replaced with Renaissance art (both in their catechetical work and in the buildings belonging to the organizations), the almost exclusive use of Roman Catholic and Protestant manuals and religious literature for the spiritual nourishment of the faithful, the polemics against monasticism and the Holy Mountain, the institution of "lay brotherhoods" (like the western "orders"), neglect and erosion of the authority of the episcopate, etc. See further Christoph Maczewski, *Die Zoi-Bewegung Griechenlands* (Göttingen, 1970); V. Yioultsis, "A Sociological View of the Religious Brotherhoods" (in Greek), in *Sociological questions in Orthodoxy,* ed. Prof. G. Mantzaridis (Thessaloniki, 1975), pp. 169-203; A. Alexandridis, "A Phenomenon of Modern Greek Religious Life: The Christian Organizations" (in Greek), in *Synoro* 39 (1966), pp. 193-204; Ch. Yannaras, *Orthodoxy and the West—Theology in Greece Today* (in Greek), p. 95ff.; idem, *The Privilege of Despair* (in Greek—Athens, 1973), pp. 80-92; idem, *Chapters on Political Theology* (in Greek—Athens, 1976), p. 114ff.; idem, *Honest to Orthodoxy* (in Greek—Athens, 1968), pp. 68-73.

Nevertheless, the most positive sign in the history of Orthodoxy in Greece over the last century must surely be the progressive weakening and ultimate disintegration of the pietistic movements. It is extremely encouraging how the Orthodox consciousness has reacted to this foreign intervention in its living body. Over approximately the last two decades, the pietistic movements have undergone a relentless series of internal problems; they have suffered splits and lost their followers, and have really ceased to be a substantial presence in the spiritual life of the country. At the same time, there has been an awakening of theological consciousness in the Church in Greece, and the initial fascination which pietism exerted over a majority of lay theologians and clergy has been significantly curtailed.

This awakening is summed up and expressed in a truly unique manner, and in organic continuity with the Orthodox patristic tradition, in a text which is among the most important products of modern Greek theology and spirituality. This is the declaration of the "Holy Community" of the Holy Mountain on the academic approach to theology independent of the Church's experience, and the pietism of the religious organizations which corresponds to it. This memorable Athonite text was published in the periodical *Athonitikoi Dialogoi* (1975, pp. 20-27) *a propos* of Prof. P. N. Trembelas' work *Mysticism—Apophatism—Cataphatic Theology,* vols. 1-2 (Athens, 1974):

The help of the logic and language of Western theologians and the spiritual opinions that spring from the experience of a closed, pietistic mentality, are both things that leave no place for the mystery of the mystagogic coinherence of Orthodox theology and living experience . . .

The tragic state of our times does not allow us to concern ourselves with pietism and the obsolete theology of the workshops of scholasticism, that characteristic curse of the West which is effectively nourished by the Western tradition and which suffers from its divisions and passes on its sickness . . . Especially today, when young people all over the world, in their barren journey through the desert wilderness of modern so-called civilization remain dissatisfied with a dry scientific approach, with the paltry productions of an insipid pietism . . .

The theology of the universities and the various Christian movements needs to be rebaptized into the mystery of our living church tradition; this will give them new strength and new methods of work and evangelism . . .

A scholastic and spiritually jejune theology is useless for the salvation of man. And a dogmatically spineless pietism which thinks that deification is an improvement in character should by its very nature be rejected. Such a theology is at its last breath; and such a way of life is powerless to withstand the general crisis of our era. The two together, theology and pietism, form one of the causes and the consequences of the spiritual decadence of our times.

If the theology of the Church were like this, it would create not fathers and confessors who spoke the words of God, but cold academic researchers and disputants of the present age. And if the spirituality of our tradition were like this, it would not create the neptic fathers as "gods by grace" and "lamps of discernment," but morbid sentimentalists who were prey to psychic hallucinations.

Why should we wander pointlessly in sterile concern with a cerebral and superfluous theology and an unreal, insipid pietistic way of life? Both of these are unknown to our holy tradition, alien to the wishes and needs of man and unworthy of them.

Our pietistic ideas about sanctity as "improvement in character" are shocked and rendered powerless when set side-by-side with the holy experience of our saints, who received Christ in their hearts "as light, in a real and substantial way; seen invisibly and comprehended incomprehensibly, with formless form and appearance beyond appearance."

We feel as Orthodox that we do not simply belong to the East geographically, nor do we fight the West in a geographical sense. We belong to the Church of the uncreated divine Light that knows no evening, which saves both East and West.

From henceforth, then, "let no profane hand touch" the mystery of Orthodox theology, but "let the lips of the faithful" sing without ceasing in praise of the Church, the Mother of God which brings forth gods according to grace; for only in her and through her saints are we led unfailingly to life and knowledge.

CHAPTER NINE

The Ethical Character of the Mysteries

1. Fulness of life in the mysteries

After our painful digression on pietism, we return to the Church's teaching about how man attains moral perfection. In the chapter preceding this digression, we had been saying that Christian asceticism is distinguished from the pursuit of individual virtue because it is not a private achievement but an *ecclesial* event, a work of communion and *personal* participation in the unity of the Church's life. Here we shall add that asceticism can find the completion of its purpose only in the mysteries of the Church.

In the language of the Church, we use the term "mysteries," or "sacraments" for seven specific ways in which the individual life can take its place organically, or dynamically return to its place, in the oneness of church life; they are the ways in which man participates personally in the mode of existence of the church body. And these possibilities for participation are at the same time also events which manifest and realize the truth of the Church. If we use the word "mystery" for these events, it is not to attribute to them an occult character, but to underline the truth that entry into the life of the Church, the ceaseless, dynamic act of approaching and participating in it, cannot be confined to perceptible symbols. The conventional language of our everyday discourse and our scientific relativism is not adequate to define it. Man

137

has to participate totally and experientially if he is to come to know the possibilities of that life which is brought to fruition in the Church.

In the mysteries man's personal freedom encounters the love of God. His personal asceticism, or his personal failure and sin, are made good by the grace of God—the gift of true life. Man brings to the Church his free will: that is to say, his daily effort, unsuccessful though it may be, to free himself from slavery to autonomous individuality and to exist "according to nature," "according to truth"—in communion and relationship with God and with his fellow men. And in the mysteries of the Church he finds that his own fruitless efforts are made good by grace, and his personal will achieves total fulfilment.

Through this dynamic progress, this "mysterious" interpenetration of human freedom and God's grace, the image of the "new man" and the citizen of the Kingdom is progressively manifested in the person of the Christian: the ethos of human existence liberated from death is revealed. What man brings to the Church is not an intellectual desire for immortality, but every aspect of his natural life, of his fall and failure, which reflects his deeper thirst for life. And every such offering finds in the Church an appropriate welcome, a corresponding *mystery* of encounter between human life and God's grace, the gift of God's life. Each one of the mysteries of the Church provides man with a way of making his offering in a dynamical way and being incorporated into her life-giving body, her theanthropic nature and her authentic ethos. It is a transfiguration of the life "contrary to nature" into life "according to nature," and of the corruptible time of individual existence into the time of personal relationship, which has been made incorruptible.

Here, then, is the reason why the mysteries of the Church are the sum and perfection of her ethics, the aim of personal asceticism and the sphere in which it takes its place. It is in this sphere that the identification of the *ethos* or *morality* with *being* is put into effect and made manifest: the achievement of moral perfection is revealed as a "wondrous change" in man's existence. Here the Law which is our tutor and the rules of asceticism find their real "end," which is life in its sacramental immediacy and totality. If natural life—distinctiveness in appearance, the immediacy of sense experience or human reason—is a mystery inaccessible to the "objectivity" of logic and the conventionalism of everyday speech, then how much more of a mystery is moral life, which is the restoration of natural life to its existential fulness and incorruptibility. If we draw the bounds of Christian ethics outside the realm of the mysteries of the Church, we shall inevitably end up with the shadows of conventional social requirements, with the fleshless, spineless ethic of legalistic "improvements" with no taste of real life and no correspondence in a real transfiguration of man.

2. The baptismal birth

The eucharist is undoubtedly the prime and fundamental mystery of the Church, the action which constitutes the Church and manifests it. In the personal life of each Christian, however, the first mystery by which he is presented to the Church and incorporated in it is baptism. At baptism, the Church grafts a new human person into her body, into her new theanthropic nature: she makes it part of the oneness of the life and personal communion of the saints. Each natural birth manifests the capacity of human nature to perpetuate itself as a succession of individual beings subject to corruption and death; and in a corresponding way, baptism manifests the capacity of Christ's theanthropic nature, which is the Church, to bestow incorruption and perpetuate, not nature, but personal distinctiveness, forming natural personal existence into a hypostasis in the true life of loving communion.

It was through water that the first life came forth; the first, unimaginable differentiation of living nature from lifeless matter. And through the water of baptism there emerges the new life, the radical differentiation of life and communion from an individual survival bounded by death. The bishop or presbyter of the Church assembly invokes the personal opera-

tion of the Holy Spirit—who puts into practice the common
will of the Trinity, as with the incarnation of the Word and
the formation of the Church—to free creation from slavery to
corruption and death. Creation here is summed up in the
water, the primal element of natural creation, which is
revealed as life-giving matter, the primal element of the new
creation. At baptism, as in every mystery, we see a realization
of the new nature of the Church—the presence of the eucharistic body, the parish or diocese, and the communion of saints
in which the new Christian takes his place. At the same time,
baptism fulfils and manifests the new creation of the world:
it displays the reason and meaning of creation, its natural
"end" which is the "glory" or manifestation of God, the
manifestation of the work of the Holy Spirit which is the
recreation and renewal of life.

In baptism, as in every mystery, the Church is dynamically
living out her existential prototype—the "great mystery of
godliness," the event of God's union with man. The incarnation of God the Word and the possibility of theanthropic life
began with the free, personal assent of man in the person of
the most holy Virgin; it began with a dynamic movement of
obedience and self-offering. Baptism, too, is a birth and a
personal embodiment of the theanthropic mode of existence
which begins with the same free, personal assent, with obedience and self-offering from man in the person of the newly-
baptized or his sponsor.[1] Before the whole assembly of the
Church, man rejects his enslavement to the rebellion of sin;
he "renounces satan" and "joins himself to Christ."

The renunciation of satan and acceptance of Christ is
not merely a verbal confession; it is a direct, perceptible
action. The person who is coming into the Church is plunged
into the water of baptism: he is bodily conformed to the
death and resurrection of Christ, to Christ's mode of existence.
He is buried as the "old man," and rises through triple
immersion into the life of his trinitarian prototype. He buries

[1]In this sense, the Mother of God is godmother to all of us who are
members of the one body of Christ, receiving us into the new life of
grace; she has personified and embodied the "end," conscious or unrecog-
nized, of our personal freedom and our acquiescence in salvation, and the
profound, existential thirst for life which we all share.

"in the quickening waters the death of disobedience and the sting of error," and comes out of the font "radiant with the light of the knowledge of God." Baptism is the supreme mystery of "knowledge," of the *enlightenment* of man.

The triple descent into the water of baptism and triple emergence from it is not a type or an instructive allegory, but the tangible experience of a real event. At baptism, human existence ceases to be a result of biological necessity. In contrast with the natural birth, which forms a biological unit subject to the facts of nature, baptism raises existence to freedom from natural necessity, to the personal distinctiveness which subsists only as an ecclesiological hypostasis[2] of communion and loving relationship. Man ceases to be an individual species, a closed circuit of purely biological succession, a mere social unit. He joins the communion of saints, which is a manifestation of God in Trinity. He himself receives the name of a saint, and from this first moment of baptism he is potentially realizing in his own person the revelation and "glory" of God. "Build him up upon the foundation of Thine apostles and prophets," the celebrant prays, "that he may not be overthrown; but implant him firmly as a plant of truth in Thy holy, catholic and apostolic Church." This direct, hypostatic entry into the body of the Church is "knowledge" and enlightenment.

[2]"The hypostasis of ecclesial existence is constituted by the new birth of man, by baptism. Baptism as new birth is precisely an act constitutive of hypostasis. As the conception and birth of a man constitute his biological hypostasis, so baptism leads to a new mode of existence, to a regeneration (1 Pet 1:3, 23), and consequently to a new 'hypostasis' ... Not only with regard to God, but now also with regard to man the basis of ontology is the person: just as God 'is' what He is in His nature, 'perfect God,' only as person, so too man in Christ is 'perfect man' only as hypostasis, as person, that is, as freedom and love. The perfect man is consequently only he who is authentically a person, that is, he who subsists, who possesses a 'mode of existence' which is constituted as being, *in precisely the manner in which God also subsists as being* ... Thanks to Christ, man can henceforth himself 'subsist,' can affirm his existence as personal not on the basis of the immutable laws of his nature, but on the basis of a relationship with God which is identified with what Christ in freedom and love possesses as Son of God the Father. This adoption of man by God, the identification of his hypostasis with the hypostasis of the Son of God, is the essence of baptism," J. Zizioulas, "From Prosopeion to Prosopon," pp. 311, 313, 314.

Thus baptism marks the beginning and also the culmination of the new human ethos inaugurated by the Church, the
transformation of man's nature[3] and his mode of existence—
his ontological transfiguration. "Put off from him the old
man, and renew him unto life everlasting; and fill him with
the power of Thy Holy Spirit, in the unity of Thy Christ:
that he may be no more a child of the body, but a child of
Thy Kingdom." At baptism the Church expresses her fundamental truth which we have reiterated frequently before:
that the renewal of human morality is not a result of individual conformity to certain codes of behavior, nor a matter
of character improvement; it is the reality of a transformation
of nature, the reality of the death of the "old man" or
autonomous individuality and the resurrection of the person
into the communion of saints.

3. The unction of royal adoption

Chrismation is a separate mystery which accompanies
baptism: it seals and confirms the personal mode of existence
inaugurated when nature is made new at baptism, when the
natural distinctiveness of the individual is raised to a hypostatic identity of freedom and love. At chrismation the
candidate is not simply partaking in the possibilities of the
common reborn nature of Christ's body; but he is being sealed
with the seal of personal adoption, of a personal and unique
relationship with the Holy Trinity, through the personal
presence of the Holy Spirit in the secret depths of his being.
This is why the Orthodox Church insists on giving chrismation immediately after baptism; she thereby remains faithful
to the truth of the regeneration of both our nature and our
individual distinctiveness.

The anointing is performed with *myron,* in the way that
the kings of Israel were anointed in the Old Testament,[4]

[3]"Our Lord came for this: so as to change and transform nature."
Macarius of Egypt, *Spiritual Homilies* 44, 1, ed. Dörries, p. 291.

[4]See R. de Vaux, *Les Institutions de l'Ancien Testament,* vol. I (Paris,
1960), pp. 160-163. D. Lys, "L'onction dans la Bible," *Études Theologiques*

and so in a way that perceptibly manifests the restoration of man to his kingly rank and ethos, his princely position in creation. The anointing of kings resulted in a change, not in nature, but in the anointed person's relationship with the whole body of the people. In the distinctiveness of the royal person, the people perceived the central axis of life as communion and unity, and at the same time the prefiguration of the expected Messiah who sets life free and restores it to the fulness of God's promises. Correspondingly, the Church sees in the personal distinctiveness of each anointed Christian a new possibility for realizing the true life of loving communion, and at the same time an icon of Christ who sets life free and restores it to the fulness of the divine mode of existence.

The seal of chrismation is placed on all the members of the human body in order to demonstrate the universality of the human person, the total participation of the body in the "royal" distinctiveness of the person liberated from the necessity of his nature. From the moment of chrismation, the human body is the imprint of the gift of the Holy Spirit, manifesting the stamp of that distinctiveness which is not confined to individual dissimilarity, but is grace, a gift of natural self-transcendence, the call of love and the response of love.

4. Personal realization of the transformation in our nature

All the mysteries of the Church relate to the same ethical dimension, the restoration of life to the fulness of freedom and love. Each mystery which follows baptism and chrismation in the life of the Christian grafts him anew into the dynamic fulfilment of the human ethos which begins at baptism. This fulfilment of the ethos is a dynamic process that is never completed,[5] because it involves the fulness of that life which has no end or limit since it is identified with love

et Religieuses 55 (1954), pp. 3-54. J. de Fraine, "Onction," _Dictionnaire Encyclopédique de la Bible_ (Éditions Brépols, 1960), col. 1282-1285.

[5]"And there is no limit to the process of perfection, because the per-

and freedom. And the mysteries of the Church are not magical events, automatic transformations of man's individual nature unrelated to the dynamic realization of personal freedom.

No transformation in nature is possible outside the sphere of its *personal* realization, since nature only exists in persons, and once it becomes existentially independent of the life of personal distinctiveness and freedom it is inevitably led into corruption and death. The mysteries of the Church take up the person's initial movement or decision to rid himself of the existential autonomy of his nature and incorporate it into the life of personal coinherence and loving communion, which is the ontological precondition for distinctiveness and freedom. Progressively and dynamically this brings nature to life within the bounds of a personal freedom supported by the grace of God; it transforms nature into a hypostasis of life, into *personal* existence.

The incarnation of Christ gives human nature the possibility of realizing the divine mode of existence, the relationship between the Son and the Father. But this realization is the work of personal freedom, an imitation of Christ's obedience. And at the same time it is grace, a gift of life, the rebirth of existence through the energy of the Holy Spirit which takes up the initial movement of personal freedom into the community of the life of God and the saints. The resistance of our rebellious nature is not abolished automatically; and it is this which confirms freedom and grace as an existential act of obedience and love, a reality which progressively and imperceptibly forms nature into *hypostases,* giving life to created being until finally "mortality is swallowed up by life" (2 Cor 5:4).

What man strives to do is to put into action *personally* the ontological moral transformation which has its beginnings in his baptism, to cooperate freely in the task of his moral transfiguration—in the work of "building up" the person and depicting the image of God in his existence. With

fection of the perfect is indeed endless. Therefore repentance is not restricted either in seasons or in actions, even till death." Isaac the Syrian, *Mystic Treatises* 55, p. 220.

this end in view, he looks at the resistance of his rebellious nature, the inadequacy and limitations of his freedom, and the tragic divide between person and nature. But at the same time he also considers the power of life which is God's love, that transfusion of life which is the grace and energy of the Holy Spirit. The tragic opposition of these two impulses, of personal freedom and the autonomy of nature, remains even after baptism and chrismation; but this does not negate the reality of man's regeneration in baptism, the dynamic fulfilment of baptismal death and resurrection. It merely confirms the truth that our regeneration and resurrection is grace, a gift of life which does not cancel out freedom and its consequences in nature, nor distort the ontological unity of person and nature. No change in nature is a given fact, independent of its existential realization within the bounds of personal freedom and distinctiveness. Man's rebellious freedom has made nature "wild"; but freedom in obedience to the will of God, supported by the charismatic energy of the Holy Spirit, "tames" nature, bringing it progressively and dynamically into harmony with the existential regeneration accomplished at baptism—with the process whereby the person becomes an organic part of the trinitarian mode of existence belonging to the communion of saints.

It is *natural,* then, that even after baptism man should fail in his attempt to transcend his autonomous individuality. He does not always succeed in controlling the absolute desires and needs of his individual nature; he fails in his asceticism, in the exercise of his freedom. But the Church receives him back, and herself takes up his failure; she recognizes in his fall the signs of his personal struggle, and accepts it as a measure of the tragedy of his freedom, as confirmation of the truth of his person. The way in which, after any and every fall, man is accepted back into life, into the love and communion of the Church, equally constitutes a *mystery,* an event in which human freedom is taken up once again by the grace of God; and this is the mystery of repentance and confession.

5. Repentance, the transformation of death into resurrection

Repentance, like baptism, manifests the truth of the Church and her theanthropic life. It is a participation in the death and resurrection of Christ, a regeneration of the person into freedom from natural necessity, that freedom which plumbs the depths of death with the measure of God's love. The categories used to express this event are literal: they are not metaphorical, nor reducible to psychological equivalents. The death in question is man's sin, his failure to *exist* as personal distinctiveness and freedom; it is the tragic reality of his rebellious and fragmented nature. But when this failure is recognized and brought to the Church, this is an act of humility, of communion and love—it is a return to life. I bring to the Church my failure and my sin, and by this action I demonstrate practical opposition to my natural tendency towards self-satisfaction and self-sufficiency. I call the Church to be a partaker in my inadequacy: I ask and receive the love of the Church, the love of God which is not a "feeling" of pity or a legal absolution, but life. It is grace, the gift of transforming my alienated person into an image of the Son of God, the Son of the Father's love.

On the cross Christ transfigured death, the ultimate consequence of our nature's autonomy, into obedience to the will of the Father's love, into communion of life with the Father, the fount of life. And the mystery of repentance imitates this offering of death to the Father's love "in the person of Jesus Christ" (Eph 2:18, 1 Pet 3:18). Confessing our sins, we affirm our adoption by God, the fact that "even when we were dead in our transgressions and sins, He hath quickened us together with Christ" (Eph 2:5). We are the "beloved of the Father" as the Son is "beloved of the Father," with the same love which gives life and constitutes existence[6] —"living as from the dead." And with the image of adoption upon our persons, "we have boldness at the entry of the holy ones": we are taken up directly by the love of the saints and

[6]See Jn 14:21-23, 17:23 and 26; Eph 1:6.

the Mother of God, and become organically joined to the life-giving body of the Church.[7]

It is evident, then, that repentance and confession form an event radically different from a psychological process of relieving or "sorting out" our guilt feelings, which it is often thought to be today. The experience of repentance which leads to confession is essentially different from a sense of guilt or a guilt complex. It is one thing for man to recognize his failure, his inadequacy to realize the life of personal distinctiveness and love, and quite another to be conscious that he has transgressed some law which is of value in itself, and to feel a sense of guilt for offences which lower him in his own individual estimation. Man has first to go beyond the level of his individual psychological requirements, beyond the needs of his psychological ego for individual justification and moral self-sufficiency: only then can he be raised to the life of the mysteries, to the truth and reality of the life which the Church embodies.

The purpose of repentance, as of every mystery, is to realize the truth of man, which also means manifesting the truth of God; it is not to restore the individual to "virtue" and psychological self-sufficiency. The whole of the Church's ethics look to truth, not to virtue. Virtue may serve truth, but truth is never subjugated to the purposes of virtue. "Virtue exists for truth; truth does not exist for virtue," writes St Maximus the Confessor. "Thus he who practises virtue for the sake of truth is not wounded by the darts of vainglory. But he who concerns himself with truth for the sake of virtue

[7]"The grace which raised us up after we had sinned is greater than that given when we were not in existence, which brought us into creation . . . O measureless goodness, into which He brings the nature of us sinners in order to reshape it. Who can speak of His glory? He raises up him who has betrayed and blasphemed Him and He renews irrational dust, endowing it with understanding and reason; and He makes the dissipated and unfeeling mind and the dissipated senses into a rational nature capable of thought. The sinner is unable to understand the grace of his resurrection. Where is that gehenna which can afflict us? Where is the hell which terrifies us in many ways and overcomes the delight of His love? And what is gehenna compared with the grace of His resurrection, when He raises us out of hell and makes this corruptible body put on incorruption, and raises in glory him who had fallen into hell?" Isaac the Syrian, *Mystic Treatises* 60, p. 246.

has the conceit of vainglory as his associate."[8] This statement sums up the whole of Christian ethics, and differentiates it radically from every other version of morality, whether religious, philosophical or legal. And the same statement also summarizes the end and purpose of the mystery of repentance.

Man's repentance bears no relation to the proud distress of the wounded ego. The individual sense of sinfulness is not repentance. Repentance is a recognition of our sins understood in the light of God's mercy, in terms of our relationship with Him. This relationship is already a measure of the truth of the "new man"; it means reliving our baptismal regeneration, renouncing death and uniting ourselves to life in a practical way. "Against Thee alone do we sin, and Thee alone do we worship," says a prayer read at Vespers on the Sunday of Pentecost. This possibility, then, is given us by Christ's incarnation, and made incarnate by repentance: we are enabled to transfigure our sin into a relationship and communion with God, in the same way as worshipping His person is a relationship and communion with Him. And every sin we commit has immediate *existential* reference to Him alone; it is a violation and a rejection of the life which He constitutes. We do not sin before ourselves or before others; sin is not a failure in our obligations, a violation of impersonal codes of behavior. We sin before God alone, and in every case our sin is a relationship with Him—a relationship of communion and life through repentance, or else a relationship of rejecting the life He gives.

The cross of Christ, that apparent triumph for human sin, is the salvation of man, the transformation of death into a measure of the acceptance of God's love—into life and resurrection. And in the same way every sin, even the most depressing fall, is transfigured by repentance into a manifestation of man's adoption by God. Through the mystery of repentance the sinner's relationship with God is the same as that of the crucified Christ with the Father. By repentance man realizes the same relationship with God as Christ has with the Father freely and through love, as Son of God. Thus through the successive stages and the dynamics

[8]*Ambigua*, PG 90, 369A.

of repentance, man builds up the same mode of existence which forms the unity of the trinitarian communion.

However unfathomable the hell of human sins, once brought to the Church it is transfigured into adoption; into a manifestation of the love of God, of the truth of the personal God who descended even to the nethemost hell of human apostasy in order to draw up the human person and restore him to the life of freedom and love. The more tragic and intractable the sin brought to the mystery of repentance, the greater the triumph of the Church, the affirmation of the Church and her truth. Man will fail again after confessing his sins. To a greater or lesser extent, the force of his nature's rebellion will subjugate his freedom; it will drag the divine image in his person into the corruption and ugliness of the desires and needs of his individual nature. But the believer will bring himself once more to the Church so as to repeat the act of triumph and joy, the dynamic "pressing forward" (Phil 3:14) of his adoption by God.

Are we therefore to "continue in sin, that grace may abound?" (Rom 6:1). This is the usual objection from moralists in every age, as the Apostle Paul sums it up in order to reject it utterly, "God forbid!" If, say the moralists, man can approach the mystery of repentance without being bound by an obligation to show some objective "reformation" and not to repeat the same offences, then everyone can sin without a second thought and ask God's forgiveness afterwards. But however much such reasoning appears to have its pastoral and educational uses, it does not cease to be typically legalistic and totally unrelated to the reality of that life which the mystery represents. The requirement of objective "reform" and the fear that people are likely to take advantage of the forgiveness of sins are based alike on the juridical understanding of both sin and salvation. Sin is seen as the violation of codes of behavior, and the way we are received back and adopted is seen as individual justification and the calculated cancellation of our debts. When a man becomes aware of his sin, the deadness of his life and the way he is tormented by this living death, and brings all this to the Church, how is it possible for him simultaneously to enjoy this deadness and this torment, and mock the possibility of life while preserving it as a contingency for abstract justification at some unspecified point in the future? Supposing, however, that even this can happen: the healing of such perversion in the sensory organs of life cannot result from binding conditions and obligations to show some objective "reform," which inevitably keep man confined to the impasse of individual effort and individual morality. It can only come through gradual understanding and dynamic experience of the truth of the mystery, through bringing one's sins to the Church again and again until one gains real humility, and this humility encounters the love of the Church—until *life* does its work, and the deadened nature is raised up.

Repentance is not a more or less difficult decision taken by the will alone, albeit accompanied by psychological contrition and promises of "reform." It is a total, personal attainment of the fall of man and the truth from which he has fallen—ultimately, an experience of the life which is communion with God. This is also why "this perception of one's sins is a gift which comes from God," as St Isaac the Syrian writes: "for repentance is a second regeneration from God."[9] And it is not fortuitous that the dynamic vanguard of the life of the Church, monastic life—a life of ascetic exercises and labors, of pains and unceasing struggle—has as its goal nothing other than repentance, that repentance which comes from God. Its goal is to plumb the depths of man's fall with the measure of God's love, and to discover the light of His countenance.

6. The juridical alienation of repentance

When the truth of the *person* is underrated or ignored in the realm of theology, this inevitably leads to the creation of a legal, external ethic. Man's ethos or morality ceases to relate to the truth of the person, to the dynamic event of true life and its existential realization. His moral problem is no longer an existential one, a problem of salvation from

[9]*Mystic Treatises* 71, pp. 280, 281.

natural necessity; it is a pseudo-problem of objective obligations which remain existentially unjustifiable. Then repentance too is distorted by elements alien to it, unrelated to the reality of the mystery.

The distortion has its roots in the notion that the mystery is a means to expiation and justification for the individual, a way of setting the psychological conscience at rest. In the framework of this conception, sin is nothing more than individual guilt, and can be classified according to objective gradations; it become a legally predetermined "case" requiring expiation or redemption through imposition of the penalty provided in the corresponding "rule." If the truth of the mystery does not go beyond admission of guilt and enforcement of the rule provided, this is enough to transform confession into a kind of rationalistic legal transaction, an act which is psychologically humiliating yet necessary in order to redeem the moral self-sufficiency of the egocentric conscience. In the framework of this transaction, "remission of sins"—a phrase which refers directly to the existential transfiguration of man accomplished through repentance—is identified with legal "justification" and release from the pangs of guilt. And the educative penances, which are always intended to guide us to physical participation in the realization of our freedom, are interpreted as a price for the redemption of our sins.

In the Roman Catholic West of the Middle Ages, there was a whole theology created to support this individualistic "religious" need for objective "justification," for a transaction with the Godhead,[10] the aim being to provide the

---

[10]A look at the "canons on justification" formulated by the Council of Trent [1545-1563] (see *Conciliorum Oecumenicorum Decreta*, ed. Instituto per le scienze religiose, Bologna 1972⁴, p. 679), might be enough to give the reader a concise picture of this legal transaction or exchange which constitutes the Roman Catholic Church's official teaching on the salvation of man and his relationship with God. And the Council of Trent was not making some innovation: it was simply summarizing the existing western tradition, from Augustine (the fount of every distortion and alteration in the Church's truth in the West) down to its own day. See also Thomas Aquinas, *Summa Theologiae* I.II q. 21 ad 3. H.-G. Pöhlmann, *Rechtfertigung* (Gütersloh, 1971), pp. 139-182. Johannes Brinktrine, *Die Lehre von der Gnade* (Paderborn, 1957): this is the third part of a dogmatic work which is particularly interesting and valuable because it sets

fullest possible support for moral self-sufficiency, and by extension for social order. Thus was formulated the theory of "the satisfaction of divine justice through Christ's death on the cross";[11] and this theory passed both into Protestantism,[12] and into Eastern Orthodox writers in the climate of "europeanizing" tendencies and pietistic influences on the

out the unadulterated, traditional and officially recognized dogmatic teaching of Roman Catholicism, without the modern embellishments and evasions. Characteristic is a passage on p. 230: "Good or bad works at present give rise to a certain inequality in the moral order, but equality will be reestablished through reward with respect to good works and through punishment with respect to bad works."

[11]This theory was first formulated by Anselm of Canterbury (1033-1109), drawing mainly on Tertullian: man's sin is a disturbance in the divine "order of justice," and at the same time an affront to God's honor and majesty. The greatness of the guilt for this disturbance and this affront is measured according to the dignity of Him who is affronted; so God's infinite majesty and justice require an infinite recompense by way of expiation. Man, limited as he is, could not possibly provide such an infinite recompense, even if the whole of mankind were to be sacrificed to satisfy divine justice. Therefore God Himself undertook to pay, in the person of His Son, the infinite ransom for the satisfaction of His justice. Christ was punished with death on the Cross in order to make atonement for sinful mankind. See Michael Schmaus, *Katholische Dogmatik*, vol. II, part 2 (Munich, 1955[5]), p. 64. The theory was further developed by Thomas Aquinas (see Schmaus, *op. cit.* p. 358), and established as the official doctrine of the Roman Catholic Church by the Council of Trent (see *Decretum de iustificatione*—Sessio VI—with the characteristic formulation: "Dominus noster Iesus Christus, qui... sua sanctissima passione in ligno crucis nobis iustificationem meruit et pro nobis Deo Patri satisfecit," *Conciliorum Oecum. Decreta* [ed. Bologna], p. 673). See also L. Heinrichs, *Die Genugtunslehre des hl. Anselmus* (Paderborn, 1909); A. Deneffe, "Das Wort *satisfactio*," *Zeitschrift für katholische Theologie* (1919), p. 158ff.; Osmo Tiililä, *Das Strafleiden Christi* (Annales Academiae scientiarum Fennicae B, 48, 1, Helsinki, 1941).

The connection between the theory of "the satisfaction of divine justice through Christ's death on the cross" and the mystery of confession becomes quite clear in Schmaus, *Kirchliche Dogmatik*, vol. IV, part 1 (Munich, 1957), pp. 531-532: "Also on Christ was a judgment executed... He assumed the punishment of death imposed by the Father... Those sinning after baptism must become like unto the suffering Christ through some sort of punishment or suffering which they take upon themselves."

[12]See *Confessio Augustanae* art. IV: *De iustificatione*, ed. J. C. Müller, *Die symbolischen Bücher der evangelisch-lutherischen Kirche* (Gütersloh, 1900), p. 86ff. Calvin, *Institution de la Religion Chrétienne*, II (Paris, Belles Lettres, 1937), p. 251ff. In the teaching of Luther and Calvin, it is not simply divine justice but *God's anger* which is assuaged by Christ's sacrifice on the cross. "In fact Luther leaves no doubt that the appeasing of God's anger was necessary": Otto Hermann Pesch, *Theologie der*

East in recent centuries.[13] The image of God is identified with the archetypal "sadistic father" who thirsts insatiably after satisfaction for his "wounded justice," and, by logical extension, delights in the torment of sinners in hell.[14] This legalistic version of the event of salvation ultimately ends with the redemption of sins becoming totally objective, so that the price can even be paid in money—as happened in the medieval Roman Catholic Church, with the notorious indulgences which caused Protestant Christianity to reject the sacrament of repentance altogether.[15]

Rechtfertigung bei Martin Luther und Thomas von Aquin (Mainz, 1967), p. 127. See also P. Bläser, *Rechtfertigungsglaube bei Luther* (Münster, 1953), p. 34; H.-G. Pöhlmann, *Rechtfertigung*, p. 220. The difference between the reformers and Roman Catholic doctrine on this question is confined to their interpretation of how man makes his own the results of Christ's expiatory sacrifice: it is not good works which ensure this, but faith alone. "Ideo primum volumus hoc ostendere, quod sola fides ex iniusto iustum efficiat, hoc est, accipiat remissionem peccatorum." *Confessio Augustanae* art. IV n. 72, ed. Müller, p. 100. "Dicimus hominem sola fide iustificari": *Institutio* 1.3. c II. n. 19. But this justification of man purely through faith in the expiatory power of Christ's death on the cross does not mean that his sins are blotted out, but merely that they are not charged to him. Man remains in *essence* sinful: "Non ita accipiendum est, quod iustificatis et renatis nulla prorsus iniustitia (post generationem) substantiae ipsorum et conversationi adhaereat, sed quod Christus perfectissima obedientia sua omnia ipsorum peccata tergat, quae quidem in ipsa natura (in hac vita) adhuc infixa haerent . . . Peccatum adhuc in carne, etiam in renatis, habitet": *Formula Concordiae*, ed. Müller, p. 614. See also O.-H. Pesch, *Theologie der Rechtfertigung . . . .*, p. 79ff.

[13]See P. N. Trembelas, *Dogmatics*, vol. II (in Greek—Athens, 1959), p. 168; E. Matthopoulos, *The Destiny of Man* (in Greek—Athens, 1966[12]), p. 350; S. Papakostas, *Repentance* (in Greek—Athens, 1953[10]), pp. 78-79.

[14]See Olivier Clement, *Theology after the "death of God"* (in Greek—Athens, 1973), pp. 53-54 and 56-58: "For Augustine—and a part at least of the western tradition followed him—the agonies of the damned contributed to the bliss of the elect. It should be noted that these ideas of Augustine's were among the avowed causes of the atheism of a man such as Camus. Thus the religion of victory over hell became at some point a religion of hell . . . The doctrine of personal judgment, with hell as a possibility and no chance of a reprieve at the moment of death, took shape in the West in the fourteenth century. The Reformation put an end to prayers for the dead . . . Is not the atheist frequently held up as a liberator by parricide, someone who destroys the idol of that childish idea of God which Freud denounced by the name of the 'sadistic father'?"

[15]On the origin and development of the practice of redeeming sins with money, see Willibald Plöchl, *Geschichte des Kirchenrechts*, vol. II (Munich, 1962), pp. 283-285, with extensive bibliography on p. 288. Plöchl relates the theological basis of the institution of indulgences to Thomas Aquinas,

Confession certainly does aim at a *change* in man's life.
For confession signifies repentance, μετάνοια, which means
a transformation of the mind—the culmination and ultimate
end of asceticism, man's concrete effort to make his rebellious
individual will obedient to the will of the communion of
saints. But a change and an existential alteration such as
this is not an individual achievement which cancels out or
redeems individual misconduct.[16] On the contrary, it is realized only with the passage from the individual mode of existence to the real existence which is loving communion and
relationship.

The change in man's life which accompanies repentance
is an event which presupposes an encounter between personal
freedom and the grace of God. It presupposes the dynamism
of asceticism, the ceaseless testing of human freedom; but
it is the encounter with grace which makes the change in man
a living reality, beyond any rationalistic definition. And this
comes about in the way that life always does: "It is as if a
man should cast seed into the ground; and should sleep, and
rise night and day, and the seed should spring and grow up,
and he knoweth not how. For the earth bringeth forth fruit
of herself" (Mk 4:26-28).

To persist in using objective attainments to define the

who set out three "reasons for the justification" of that institution: God's
honor, the benefit of the Church and the benefit of the individual.

The sale of pardons was one of the reasons why Calvin rejected the
sacrament of confession right from the start (see Calvin, *Institution de la
Religion Chrétienne*, vol. II (Paris, Belles Lettres, 1937), p. 171ff., while in
Lutheranism the mystery was progressively undervalued and ignored, to
vanish completely around 1800. See K. Ramke, "Die Privatbeicht bei Luther
und im Alt- und Neuluthertum," in F. Heiler, *Die heiligen Sakramente,
Beichte und Absolution* (1935), pp. 232-245. Cf. *ibid.* in P. Schäffer, *Das
Sakrament der Busse und seine Stellung in Vergangenheit und Gegenwart*,
pp. 204-228.

[16]The Council of Trent defined three basic elements in the sacrament
of confession: *repentance, confession* and *reparation* (see Sessio XIV, cap.
VIII: De satisfactionis necessitate et fructu, *Conciliorum Oecum. Decreta*
[ed. Bologna], pp. 708-709). Reparation, according to Schmaus, *Kirchliche
Dogmatik*, vol. IV, part 1 (Munich, 1957), p. 586, "belongs essentially
to the sacrament. It is the resolve to give body to repentance, not only in
word, as happens in the confession of sins, but also in work, and to submit
oneself to God's punishment." Cf. p. 584: "Never did the Church of God
know a surer way of averting the punishment of God, than when men

mystery of the "new life" and transfiguration of man which is repentance—this is the most tragic form of persistence in the fall, in the individual mode of survival. Our will and effort to rid ourselves of sin is imprisoned in the confines of individual self-assurance; in the presumptions of the fall, which is the existential alienation of man. Thus confession becomes an aspect of the life of existentially unliberated man, of the conventional life of this world.[17]

7. The ministry of spiritual fatherhood

Within the framework of confession, the tradition of the Church recognizes the ministry of "spiritual direction," embodied in the figures of venerable priests or simple monks with years of spiritual experience, an experience of personal

take upon themselves these works of penance with real anguish of soul." See also J. Brinktrine, *Die Lehre von den heiligen Sakramenten der Katholischen Kirche*, vol. II (Paderborn, 1962), p. 57ff.

[17]The Council of Trent officially established confession as a *judicial* act and excommunicates those who deny its juridical character (see Sessio XIV: Canones de sanctissimo poenitentiae sacramento 9, *Conciliorum Oecum. Decreta* [ed. Bologna], p. 712). See also M. Schmaus, *Katholische Dogmatik* vol. IV, part 1, p. 265: "Das Bussakrament als Gericht." On p. 530, he writes: "The judgment of the Church brings to manifestation the judgment of God. It is the epiphany of God the Judge... In the bishop sitting in judgment appears the heavenly Father sitting in judgment." Also P. N. Trembelas, *Dogmatics*, vol. III (Athens, 1961), ch. 8, 4: "Absolution as a judicial operation, and the character of penances." On pp. 273-274, he writes: "It is quite clear that exercise of the power to bind and to loose, and the remission of sins or the withholding of remission in confession are operations of a judicial character. The priest looses the penitent from the bonds of sin, or does not so loose him, and imposes on him educative punishments according to the circumstances, exercising the full power of judgment which the Father gave to the Son, and the Son gave to the Church." In contrast with these juridical ideas, the Orthodox believe that in confession, in the mystery of repentance, God's fatherly love is constantly being revealed to the faithful. "Fear Him because of His love, not because of the harsh name which is attached to Him": Isaac the Syrian, *Mystic Treatises*, p. 245. He is fearsome because of His love, which we do not deserve. He awaits us prodigals with open arms outside His house. He does not reproach, He heals. The atmosphere of confession in the Orthodox Church is conveyed by the compassionate words of Abba Isaac: "If you desire to heal the sick, know that the sick have need of care rather than reproach" (p. 234). And there have always been good spiritual fathers, healers who are full of love for mankind.

asceticism and profound knowledge of man. These are the spiritual "elders," the *gerontes* or *startsy*, people who have the gift of "discerning" the depths of the human soul, the secret crevices of human existence, and who know the most hidden and obscure aspects of the resistance human nature puts up to the grace of God. They have the ability to penetrate the depths of the human soul and draw out the secret roots of the passions, the entrenched defences of individual self-sufficiency, and yet also the hidden sighs of man's thirst for life and truth. This ability is not only the result of long experience in the understanding of man; it is also a particular gift bestowed by God, the gift of insight and the gift of intercession.[18]

The relationship with a spiritual guide such as this constitutes spiritual fatherhood, a free and often life-long surrender of our will, thoughts, desires and temptations to the discerning knowledge and direction of the spiritual elder. Ultimately, it is a relationship and a bond which "hypostasizes" the person in the unity of the Church's life—it is a *birth* into life, not mere instruction: "for though ye have ten thousand instructors in Christ, yet have ye not many fathers: for in Christ Jesus I have begotten you through the Gospel" (1 Cor. 4:15).

The spiritual father transmits life as he transmits his experience, the experience of the Church. The Christian comes to know the life of the Church embodied in the person of his spiritual father, and becomes attuned to his asceticism, to his prayer. Thus the process of grafting the believer into the body of the Church remains an act of freedom, while at the same

[18]See, for example, some biographies of holy spiritual guides of recent years (all of them in Greek): *Father Arsenios the Cappadocian* (Souroti, Thessaloniki, ed. *Hesychasterion* of St John the Divine, 1975). This biography, by Father Paisios of the Holy Mountain, is a remarkable piece of writing—a direct, empirical witness to the communion of saints which makes up the Church, destroying the limitations of time, space, corruption and death. Archimandrite Elias Mastroyannopoulos, *Saintly Figures of Modern Greece* (Athens, ed. Tinos, 1977); Nun Martha, *Papa-Nikolas Planas* (Athens, ed. Astir, 1974). *Papa-Dimitris Gangastathis* (Thessaloniki, ed. Orthodoxos Kypseli, 1975). Also the chapter entitled "The Startsy," in Dostoevsky's *Brothers Karamazov*; Ch. Yannaras, "'Gerontes' and the 'intelligentsia,'" in *The Privilege of Despair*, p. 67ff.; Sotiria Nouhi, *The Elder Ieronymos of Aigina* (Athens, Eptalofos, 1978).

time being stripped of any element of personal achievement; it is exclusively and solely an act of communion and relationship. In other words, the life of the Church becomes accessible through a living event; one does not come to know it as an individual, as when adopting some ideology or "system." The Christian is "led by the hand" into knowledge, prayer and asceticism—into the life and truth of the Church; he becomes attuned to the experience of his spiritual father—particularly, in monasticism, to the experience of *prayer of the heart,* which is the breathing of the Church's body—to his experience in the realm of "discernment of thoughts and spirits," on the road to "divine *eros.*" Experience and knowledge are transmitted in love and accepted in humility: it is a double dynamic impulse which reflects the unified mode of existence of the Church as a whole, the "celebration of exchanging knowledge," and the likeness to God attained through trinitarian communion in love.

Parallel to the "apostolic succession" of the clergy which maintains the unity of the Church in her organic historical continuity, there is also the succession of spiritual fatherhood which preserves the unity of the Church's spiritual experience, the orthodoxy of the Church's mind and life. Naturally this institution of spiritual fatherhood and discerning guidance bears no real relation to the moral and psychological "paternalism" towards the conscience of others which has become associated with the mystery of repentance in recent centuries.

8. Marriage and the "loving power" in nature

In our attempt to determine the ethical character of the mysteries—their dynamic quality and their power to transfigure life—we must stop to consider the example of marriage. This too is a mystery of the Church, an event in which the truth of her life is manifested and realized, and a reality in which our fragmented nature is transfigured into an image of trinitarian communion.

As in the case of every other mystery, marriage is not a religious "addition" to the natural life of the individual but a liberation of life from natural constraint: it transfigures natural existence into a hypostasis of personal distinctiveness and freedom. This is why the mystery of marriage should on no account be thought of as a ceremonial blessing bestowed on natural sexual relations, a religious seal of approval for the natural institution of the family.

Natural sexual relations and the natural institution of the family certainly have their value in the life of fallen man. It is indeed possible for sexual attraction and the bond between man and woman to preserve the natural basis and precondition for the "loving power" which God has bestowed on human nature, so that it can realize its existential "end" and become a hypostasis of life.[19] In the objectified world of the fall, the world of safeguards for the subject and entrenched egocentric individuality, *eros* or sexual love remains one last possibility for a life of *relationship* and *knowledge*. On the horizon of our consciousness, there suddenly emerges the uniqueness and distinctiveness of the loved one; we are astonished at the revelation of an experience which surpasses understanding and feeling alike, and so we escape from the realm of utilitarian evaluations.[20]

[19]St Maximus the Confessor sees the natural precondition for man's "loving power" in the "power towards desire": "Apart from the power of desire, there is no yearning, of which the end is love. For to be in love with someone is a property of desire. And apart from the power of ardor which steers the desire towards unity with the object of its delight, in no way can there be peace—if indeed peace is the undisturbed and total possession of that which we desire": *Theological Chapters* II, 74, PG 90, 1248CD—*Scholion on Questions to Thalassius*, PG 90, 460C. Desire for St Maximus relates not to sensual pleasure, but to pleasure of the *mind*—and the mind in his parlance means man's *personal* powers. The relation of desire to sensual pleasure is an existential corruption, but this corruption does not destroy the natural preconditions for real *eros*.

[20]It is characteristic that with pairs of lovers in mythology and the classic prototypes of loving fulness formed by art, it is almost always impossible for the love to last any great length of time, and the heroes prefer to confirm their love by dying rather than accept individual survival and separation from the person they love. Concealed in this preference is the truth that the only way of hypostatic existence and life "in truth" is self-transcendence in love and loving self-offering, as revealed by the cross of Christ. Since we are on the subject of attempts by art to express the most profound truth of man through the experience of love, we should perhaps mention Tolstoy's short story "Alyosha," a true masterpiece. It describes the life of a poor servant, despised by all for his physical ugliness and

In the language of the Bible, the word *knowledge* is identified with sexual relations, and in the Old Testament God's relationship with His chosen people is expressed through the image of the conjugal bond. Indeed, in every religion and every primitive cultural tradition sexual attraction always serves as an archetypal symbol, as an inexpressible, mystical "sign-post" to the mystery of existence beyond death and corruption, the great miracle of life in its cosmic dimensions. Life is realized through the loving union of the masculine "word," the reason or principle, with the "feminine" substance of the perceptible world; through the union of intelligence with perception, of wisdom with nature. The "word"—wisdom, freedom and distinctiveness—fertilizes nature, transfiguring the dissolution and corruption of the perceptible world and turning it into pregnancy with life, a realization of life. And conversely, it is perceptible nature which gives the "word" a concrete, existential reality, shaping it into a creative energy and a potential for fecundity corresponding to the perceptible flesh of the world, which is the only thing that can preserve life as a natural reality.

In the language of the Old Testament, however, the love relationship between God and His people is something more than an archetypal symbol referring to the cosmic workings of life. It preserves the clearest rejection of the personal mode of existence after man's fall and his subjugation to autonomous natural necessity—it is the call of the personal God, summoning personal man to communion and relationship. In the same way, the natural institution of the family, faithfulness in the conjugal relationship and the concerns that come through having children manifest and preserve after the fall the most immediate possibility for transcending the ego and abnegating the absolute demands of individuality;

natural artlessness. They heap upon him the heaviest tasks and the most humiliating forms of labor, and he endures it all, humble and unconcerned. Then, one day, love intervenes in his miserable life. The cook of the house falls in love with him, and then he realizes that for the first time "there is someone who needs poor Alyosha, not for what he does, but for what he is." This sentence contains perhaps the most complete definition of the natural potentialities of *eros.*

they convey some taste of the life of love and self-offering.[21]

Yet natural sexual relations, like the natural institution of the family, do not cease to constitute and express also the ultimate subjection of personal freedom and distinctiveness to impersonal natural necessity, to the relentless impulse in nature to perpetuate itself through a succession of mortal individuals. The "amazement" in sexual love certainly gives us a taste of what it means to transcend the laws of corruption and death. This is not a lasting transcendence, however; it does not perpetuate personal distinctiveness and freedom. It perpetuates nature, the autonomous biological necessity of reproducing mortal individuals which can give the parents nothing more than a psychological illusion of an existential "extension."

The function of perpetuation, what today we call "sexuality," is unavoidably bound up with death, and no "ethics of sexuality" can remove the subjugation of the sexual impulse to the natural necessity of perpetuating death. This is why the Bible states that in the Kingdom of God, the realm of true life, sexuality ceases to exist, as does the distinction between the sexes. "The children of this world marry and are given in marriage. But they which shall be accounted worthy to attain that world, and the resurrection from the dead, neither marry nor are given in marriage. Neither can they die any more; for they are equal unto the angels and are the children of God, being the children of the resurrection" (Lk 20:34-36); "there is neither male nor female" (Gal 3:18).

9. The mystery of true *eros*

In the mystery of marriage, the Church intervenes to give

---

[21]Even in the New Testament, it is said that "the woman shall be saved in childbearing" (1 Tim 2:15). The meaning of this statement certainly cannot be that subjection to the natural necessity of childbearing *saves* woman, but that the natural possibility given to woman for transcending her individual self-sufficiency is to be found in childbearing. The natural distribution of her life to her children may be transfigured into a truth of love and self-offering, into freedom from natural necessity and consequently into *salvation*—"if they continue in faith and charity with sobriety," as St Paul adds in the same verse.

sexual love its full dimensions, to free the loving power in man from its subjection to natural necessity, and to manifest in the unity of man and wife an image of the Church and the gift of true life.

In this mystery, as in every other, man brings his natural life to the Church in order to graft it into the Church's mode of existence, the way in which she makes nature immortal. Within the mystery marriage is not simply a reciprocal relationship and a knowledge which goes no further than the "loving power" in nature. The relationship and knowledge of the partners becomes an ecclesial event, realized not only through nature but also through the Church. It is an experience of participation in the communion of saints: the man encounters and knows the woman, and the woman the man, not simply within the natural relationships of sexual love and the family, but in the context of those relationships which constitute the Church as an image of her trinitarian prototype.[22] This does not mean a "spiritualization" of marriage and depreciation of the natural relationship, but a dynamic transformation of the natural sexual impulse into an event of *personal* communion, in the same way as the Church always brings about communion: as grace, a gift of personal distinctiveness and freedom.

Thus marriage ceases to perpetuate nature alone, and is transfigured into a personal relationship of coinherence in love—a relationship of persons who have received their existential hypostasis through their participation in the eucharistic unity and communion of the Church. The individual uniqueness and dissimilarity which emerges and is realized through the natural sexual relationship progressively gives place to the personal distinctiveness of a member of the communion

[22]See also J. Zizioulas, "From Prosopeion to Prosopon," p. 319 n. 52: "It would be a mistake to consider marriage nothing more than the confirmation and blessing of a biological fact. Connected as it is with the eucharist, it serves as a reminder that although the newly wed couple have a blessing to create a family of their own, the ultimate and real network of relationships which constitutes their hypostasis is not the family but the Church, as expressed in the eucharistic synaxis. This eschatological transcendence of the biological hypostasis is hinted at also by the 'crowning' of the couple, but its existential substance is lost as soon as the marriage service is separated from the eucharist."

of saints, to the identity of the *name* given to the Christian by his participation in baptism and the eucharist. This progressive transfiguration of natural *eros* into "true *eros*"[23] constitutes the ethical or dynamic character of the mystery, the *asceticism* of marriage, to which we shall return. Gradually, through a reciprocal relinquishment of the individual will and an acceptance of the other's will, the unity of man and wife comes to be built not on the natural premise of the individual sexual impulse but on the premise of ecclesial communion, which is self-transcendence and self-offering. Marriage draws its identity not from the natural relationship, but from the relationship in the realm of the Kingdom.

Through this dynamic "becoming," marriage approaches the fulness of love, "the totality of love."[24] The human body becomes a fact of communion existentially transcending both individuality and duality, and encompassed by the unity of the Church's life. The human body is accounted worthy to realize the image of Christ's body, which is a fact of communion in the context of the eucharist—"a peaceful transmission of divine similitude."[25]

Marriage is defined by St Paul as "a great mystery . . . concerning Christ and the Church" (Eph 5:32). The way the existential unity of human nature is realized in the framework of marriage is a mystery inaccessible to any objective psychological or sociological approach: for nature on its own is incapable of being existentially unified, since the individual entities are condemned to separation at death. The unity of man and wife in church marriage, however, has its starting-point in the body of Christ, in the relationship between the body and the head (Eph 5:23). The constitution of the body —the unity of the members' life—is a result of their relationship with Christ, the head of the Church. This means that the unity is fundamentally grace, a gift of personal freedom and love which can only be accomplished "in Christ"; for

[23]See Dionysius the Areopagite, *On Divine Names* IV, 12, PG 3, 709BC. *The Person and Eros*, § 52.

[24]See Maximus the Confessor, *Scholia on the Divine Names* 4, 17, PG 4, 269CD.

[25]Dionysius the Areopagite, *On the Ecclesiastical Hierarchy* III 3, 11, PG 3, 428B.

sin is not removed automatically or by magic, but can only be transfigured through *repentance* into a relationship of freedom and love. Nor is the gift of unity simply a psychological or subjective experience; it is realized *naturally*, as the reality of a life which has its hypostasis in the theanthropic nature of the Church, in the body of Christ.

The relationship between man and wife in marriage does not deny or scorn its biological origin and fulfilment. It merely refuses to confine itself as an existential event of unity within the limitations of the life of discrete biological hypostases condemned to separation at death. It looks to that unity which gives existence and relationship a hypostasis in the eschatological fulness of nature: Marriage hypostasizes sexual love and the body in a way that is ecclesiological, transfiguring the physical relationship into a unity of persons in freedom and love, through their relationship with Christ in the eucharist. However much death remains a most painful experience of parting, it cannot destroy this unity which becomes a reality each time in the cup of the eucharist, to be fulfilled once and for all in the last times, in the Kingdom. The ecclesiological hypostasis of the partners' natural union, realized in the mystery of marriage, conquers death, because it transcends the division between biologically individual entities—it is the communion in Christ's flesh and blood which unifies their life. Through the natural relationship of marriage the two are united "into one flesh," and through the eucharistic relationship of the mystery of marriage this one flesh, the shared life of the two persons, is made incorruptible and immortal.[26]

[26]"The ascetic character of the ecclesial hypostasis does not come from a denial of the world or of the biological nature of existence itself. (It is not the 'principle' of nature which has need of change, but the 'mode of existence.') It implies a denial of the biological *hypostasis*. It accepts the biological *nature* but wishes to hypostasize it in a non-biological way, to endow it with real being, to give it a true ontology, that is, eternal life. It is for this reason that I stated that neither *eros* nor the body must be abandoned, but must be hypostasized according to the 'mode of existence' of the ecclesial hypostasis. The ascetic character of the person, derived as it is from the eucharistic form of the ecclesial hypostasis, expresses the authentic person precisely when it does not deny *eros* and the body but hypostasizes them in an ecclesial manner": John Zizioulas, "From Prosopeion to Prosopon," p. 321.

When we speak of the eschatological fulness of the personal and physical unity of the partners in the mystery of marriage, we are talking about a dynamic event corresponding to Christ's assumption of humanity—about "the substance of things hoped for" and at the same time about the immediacy of the saints' experience: nature is taken up despite its "spots" and "wrinkles" (Eph 5:27) and incorporated into the trinitarian mode of existence, the life of the Godhead. "Husbands, love your wives, even as Christ also loved the Church, and gave Himself for it" (Eph 5:25). This assumption and acceptance comes about through surrender of self and *self-emptying*, through a love which is not of the order of social "altruism" but an existential change, a process whereby individuality is "emptied" of self-determination in its conduct and relinquishes its autonomous resistances. Thus in church marriage the natural self-offering of sexual love becomes a dynamic, progressive assumption of the other partner: a reciprocal *personal* assumption of the other's individual nature, the acceptance of its autonomous resistance and of the deadly consequences of its "brutalized" existential self-sufficiency. In other words, the natural self-offering of sexual love is transfigured in church marriage, becoming a dynamic imitation of Christ's cross and conformity to His voluntary assumption of our nature's death—a conformity whose fruit is resurrection and incorruption.

10. The ascetic character of marriage

Sexual love, the natural "loving power" in man, is undoubtedly something that shapes our lives; it is the central axis for the formation of personality and its conscious, subconscious and unconscious layers. Man's very existential identity, the peculiar characteristics of his personality, depends on the attitude he develops towards the biological demands of his sexual impulse, on his readiness to transcend himself and offer himself, on his degree of sensitivity to sexual love, and on the way he cultivates his capacity to love and be loved. Many centuries before Freud discovered the significance of the libido, or psychoanalysis "liberated" sexual life from its "social restraints" and made it a separate area of man's life insulated from the whole—showing it as an end in itself, tragic and unfulfilled—the Greek church fathers had connected man's existential problem with the orientation of his natural sexual impulse: whether it turns towards sensual pleasure or towards giving life a hypostatic reality as communion and relationship.[27]

Through the thought of the fathers, it become clear that the Church recognizes in sexual love man's existential identity, but does not equate it exclusively with the reproductive process. Or, at the very least, she does not restrict *eros* to its natural starting point, the distinction between the sexes. The "greater" possibility for realizing "true *eros*" lies neither in the psychological and physical aspects of the reproductive process, nor in institutional marriage, but only in the Church's *asceticism*. The mystery of mariage *saves* natural *eros*—which means *making it a hypostasis* in the life of the Church— precisely because it grafts it into the asceticism which is the eucharistic mode of existence. Under its guidance natural love becomes like the love of Christ, which accepted crucifixion; and so it realizes in itself the miracle of Christ's cross.

For this reason, marriage in the Church has very little to do with the social institutionalization of the reproductive process. It certainly does not aim to give this process legality or metaphysical authority, or to "improve" and facilitate the natural relationship with moral obligations whose purpose is to "harmonize" the characters of the partners. An entire mythology has grown up around the bourgeois ideal of the "Christian family"; and this can serve a variety of worthy ends, but it has nothing to do with the mystery of marriage in the Church. Furthermore, the Gospel uses particularly harsh words about the natural institution of the family, despite its undeniable usefulness, demanding from Christians abandonment and even "hatred" of their kinsfolk: "If any man come to me, and hate not his father and mother and

[27]See Gregory of Nyssa, *On the Formation of Man* 18, PG 44, 193. Maximus the Confessor, *Theological Chapters* V 98, PG 90, 1392A (=*Ambigua*, PG 91, 1353A), John of Sinai, *Ladder*, step 5, PG 68, 777A.

wife and children and brethren and sisters, yea, and his own soul[28] also, he cannot be my disciple" (Lk 14:26). These words of the Gospel remain incomprehensible if we are unaware of the aim they have in view. And that aim is freedom from natural necessity, from the exclusiveness of the biological bond created by carnal relationship and natural kinship. Within the bounds of the eucharistic body, which are also those of the mystery of marriage, carnal relationship and natural kinship are not done away with; they simply cease to be confined to the biologically-determined exclusiveness which reinforces individuality. The immediacy of the natural relationship is generalized: it is no longer the immediacy of individual dependence, nor an exclusiveness subject to the laws of the biological bond. The gift of personal freedom, which is love, itself creates within the Church relationships of natural immediacy. In this sense, the Church community of persons is an extended "family." Right from the beginning of the Church's historical life, the relationships between members of the eucharistic body, which constitute the Church's mode of existence, have always been expressed in terms of the relationships created by marriage and natural kinship.[29] The natural foundation and potential for the free and universal personal relationships created by the Church is that of carnal union and biological kinship. But before this potential can be transformed into a fact of personal life and relationship, beyond any restriction from corruption and death, man has to practice asceticism as an active rejection—or, literally, "hatred"—of the way his natural potentialities for relationship are subjugated to biological individuality treated as an existential absolute.

[28]Meaning the whole network of relationships which goes to make up the biological hypostasis. "These sayings do not signify a simple denial. They conceal an affirmation: the Christian through baptism stands over against the world; he exists as a relationship with the world, as a person, in a manner free from the relationship created by his biological identity. This means that henceforth he can love not because the laws of biology oblige him to do so—something which inevitably colors the love of one's own relations—but *unconstrained* by the natural laws. As an ecclesial hypostasis man thus proves that what is valid for God can also be valid for man: the nature does not determine the person; the person enables the nature to exist; freedom is identified with the being of man": John Zizioulas, "From Prosopeion to Prosopon," p. 315.

The mystery of marriage, then, looks to "true *eros*," and this is why it has more in common with the asceticism of the monks than with the social institutionalization of the reproductive process. Through the mystery, the natural relationship is not moralized or spiritualized: it is transfigured into a potential for personal relationship with the whole body of the Church, free from natural laws. When the Church crowns the newly-wed couple as "martyrs," *witnesses* to her truth, she is affirming that the final "end" of marriage is one with the ultimate fulfilment of her own life: the relationships of the Kingdom, the freedom of personal love from subjection to natural necessity. But this identification, while establishing marriage as a mystery, indicates at the same time the need to transcend the natural institution and to pass dynamically from the natural to the eucharistic relationship, to the ascetic realization of true *eros*.

In church life, marriage has always been an image and prefigurement of the perfect personal relationship and communion in love which forms the Kingdom of God, the eschatological realization of salvation. And the truth of the Kingdom represented and prefigured in marriage presupposes that the distinction between the sexes has been transcended (Mt 22:30, Mk 12:25, Lk 20:35), and with it the exclusive *possession of another*, since that is ultimately what natural kinship is. True *eros*—through self-emptying and self-offering —for one person in the communion of marriage creates a hypostatic possibility of relationship with all the members of Christ's body.[30] The symbolism of the Song of Songs, which

[29]See Mt 23:8-9: "All ye are brethren. And call no man your father upon the earth: for one is your Father, which is in heaven."

[30]"*Eros* becomes a movement of free love with a universal character, that is, of love which, while it can concentrate on one person as the expression of the whole nature, sees in this person the hypostasis through which all men and all things are loved and in relation to which they are hypostasized ... The person's capacity to love in just one person all things and all men is a property of God, who as *Father* hypostasizes and loves just one Son, the Only-begotten, and yet can love the whole of creation and give it hypostasis 'in the Son' ('by Him all things consist,' Col 1:18)": John Zizioulas, "From Prosopeion to Prosopon," p. 321. Here we should perhaps mention the example of many married saints who soon came to live as brother and sister. And this absence of carnal relationship was not a deprivation, but a manifestation of the ceaseless coinherence in true *eros*

so exercised patristic exegesis, goes beyond mere allegory. In the person of the beloved woman, the whole Church acquires substance for the man. The woman's body and her natural beauty sum up the beauty and truth of the world, of all creation. The experience of this hypostatic immediacy can be secured only by the true *eros* of the self-denial of the cross and ascetic self-offering.

On this view, we can understand that the ascetic *virginity* of monks is not the opposite of marriage or something substantially different from it, but the perfect realization of its truth, the greatest possible affirmation of its existential worth. Virginity is *eros* free from the natural constraint of lust and pleasure, that same *eros* which grafts marriage into the life of the Kingdom. True virginity and true marriage are reached by a common road: the self-denial of the cross, and ascetic self-offering. This is why it is chiefly in the persons of ascetics and monastics that the Church recognizes her saints, those guides and mentors on the common road to life "according to truth," incarnate realizations of her ultimate "end." And if amongst the saints of the Church there are some few married people, it is not fulness of natural love or their "perfect marriage" which has ranked them among the first-fruits of the Kingdom—just as it is not merely the celibacy of the ascetics which guarantees their sanctity—but their asceticism and imitation of the cross of Christ.

For the same reason the whole life of the Church, her worship and her ethics, follow the asceticism of the monks, without laying down special rules of *ascesis* and worship for the life of married people. It is not that this universal and uniform asceticism has been established in Church life for incidental historical reasons: it is a matter of the Church's faithfulness to her truth and her existential identity, that same

which had no need of external physical actions. In the same way, their true union in Christ through marriage feared no separation or death. This real marriage, which appears to be a non-marriage, is the same as the real knowledge of spiritual experience which is manifested as unknowing, "unknowing above all knowledge." Some typical examples of married saints are St Ammoun (4 October), Galaction and Episteme (5 November), St Zacharias (17 November), Andronicus and Athanasia (9 October), St Melany (31 December), Chrysanthus and Daria (19 March), and the Emperor Marcian and Pulcheria (10 September).

truth which also marks out marriage as "a great mystery concerning Christ and the Church."

This ascetic and eschatological identification of virginity with marriage, however, remains obscure, incomprehensible and perhaps scandalous so long as man's existential demands do not go beyond the relief and comfort provided by the institutionalized forms which lend support to individual life. The mystery of marriage, like the truth of the monastic or celibate life, presupposes the extreme existential demand for life and personal identity beyond corruption and death—a level of existential thirst impossible to reconcile with ephemeral satisfactions or illusions of life within the confines of a biological individuality subject to death.

11. The crisis in the institution of marriage

Amidst the fundamental rearrangements of the last thirty years, particularly in western societies, the institution of the family—an institution whose roots are lost in the depths of pre-history—has for the first time been called into question both theoretically and in practice, in a radical and absolute fashion. The frequency and ease with which marriage is dissolved, and the rapidly increasing number of divorces, chiefly in "developed" societies, may perhaps be an indication of how widely the institution is questioned in practice. Even without the statistical evidence, however, it is clear that the way of life imposed on us in the culture of autonomous technology and consumption undermines the institution of marriage, or even precludes it completely. It is a way of life definitely centered on the individual, and seems to preclude the possibilities of individual self-transcendence and personal relationship. Relationship is a form of subjection: you subjugate or are subjugated. This is why the rejection of marital faithfulness is advertized as a liberation whose necessity is self-evident, as a release from subjection to conventionalism and routine and as an opening onto life, which is a ceaseless adventure of breaking through conventional forms.

It had perhaps to do with the rural way of life that for

centuries the institution of marriage functioned as an organic
necessity, bringing man into harmony with the whole rhythm
of the life of the world; it was an obvious, practical expression
of man's faithfulness to his worldly hypostasis. The meeting
of a man and a woman and the creation of a family was an
act of total, existential obedience to the universal rhythm of
life, to sowing, growth and fruiting; it was not simply an
individual choice arbitrarily made by the intellect or emotions.
Marriage and the family were man's obvious duty, the main
content of his life.

In western culture, however, it seems as if the cord linking
man with the cosmic dimensions of life is finally being cut.
Life is thought of in the context of individual existence, and
the truth of the world in the context of the intellect. The only
possible way of relating to the world is by subjecting it to
individual needs and desires, a subjection achieved by the
power of the intellect materialized in the machine. In the
same way even love, the supreme possibility for relationship
with the cosmic totality of life, is subjugated to individual need
and desire. Modern western man's individualistic mode of
survival leaves nothing to life apart from individual preference, judgment, decision, choice and pleasure.

Imprisonment in complete subjectivity and the simultan-
eous attempt at absolute objectivity, with the individual as
the center in either case, have turned western man into an
idea devoid of content, a unit of autoerotic satisfaction. We
live in a culture of autoeroticism, a hysteria of erotic thirst
beginning and ending with the ego, the individual; with the
nullification of any relationship and ignorance of the truth
of man as a person. Inevitably marriage too is distorted into
a rationalistic contract serving utilitarian ends, or preserved
as a mutual attraction founded on natural eroticism, for
ephemeral individual satisfaction.

The crisis in the institution of marriage within western
societies cannot be unrelated to the way the truth of the mystery of marriage has become alienated in the spiritual life of
the Christian churches. Within the framework of what we
call "secularization," the conventional interests of social
utilitarianism frequently strip marriage of its content as a

mystery; they turn it into a formal ratification or a liturgical blessing of the natural, social union of two persons of opposite sexes. The mystery ceases to be a gift of freedom from natural necessity, a real possibility of personal relationship and participation in the ecclesial totality of life, or an ascetic affirmation of the truth and distinctiveness of the person.

If the alienation of marriage were caused exclusively by the weakness or immaturity of those who approached the mystery—if it were their own naive approach which was devaluing and weakening the possibilities of life in the mystery —then the symptom would point to nothing more than the accepted fact of the common fall and failure of man. But it is not a question of human inadequacy alone; also involved is the policy of institutionalized church organizations which uses the power of state authority to make this mystery of the Church a formal and obligatory precondition for the social and civil recognition of a marriage. In other words, it is a matter of "official" ignorance or denial of the truth of the mystery of marriage. This still expresses the same given fact of man's common failure and fall, but has perhaps more immediate consequences in the alienation of the event of salvation, the transformation of the Church into a conventional social institution and an expedient for the state. One might call to mind the biblical sense of "blasphemy," meaning mockery of God's love and majesty, when people who are atheist or indifferent to religion, but formally keep the description "Christian" on their civil identity cards, are obliged to play a laughable role within the holy body of the Church: that of a formalized participation in a mystery in which the Holy Spirit is given.[31]

The dissociation of marriage from the truth of the mystery is characteristically expressed in its estrangement from the eucharist. It is no longer the eucharistic assembly, the whole body of the Church, which receives those who come to the mysteries and grafts them into life. Instead, it is the priest who gives grace individually, in successive ceremonies on the same day and in the same church. This distortion in the truth

[31][Translator's note: at the time of writing, there was no civil marriage in Greece.].

of the mysteries is so fundamental, and goes so deep, that one wonders in what sense these ceremonies relate to man's salvation from his corruption and death as an individual, severed as they are from the body of the Church; and what they have to do with the Church's mode of existence, with participation in the communion of saints.

If we accept the truth of the mystery of marriage, we must also accept its consequences, however painful they may be for the prevailing moralistic and social understanding of the institution. And a fundamental consequence of this truth is that the church mystery of marriage cannot be laid down as an essential precondition for conjugal life in every case, even in what are known as "Christian" societies (although there are no real Christian societies left). The mystery of marriage is a manifestation of the Church's truth; it is not a means of "satisfying the religious needs of the people," nor does it serve the conventional purposes of social utilitarianism. To serve these ends, modern states have the institution of civil marriage, which binds the sexual relationship socially and morally into the framework of an honest conjugal life. Civil marriage can be laid down as an essential social or moral condition for any cohabitation, but the mystery of marriage cannot. The mystery is offered by the Church only to those who want to experience the transfiguration of the natural sexual relationship into a cross, and asceticism of freedom and loving self-denial, a participation in the ultimate freedom of true life.

In opposition to the culture of individualism, the era of post-Freudian "liberation" of instinct and the rejection of formalized institutions and conventional structures, the Church has to affirm the mystery of marriage as the supreme possibility of freedom and relationship: of the true freedom won through ascetic self-transcendence, and the true relationship which we experience through the voluntary death of the ego.

CHAPTER TEN

The Church Canons
and the Limits Set to Life

1. The Church and the law

The ethos of the Church is the life of personal distinctiveness and freedom; it is the love which gives to existence a hypostasis of eternal life, beyond any natural restriction or individual predetermination. When man is grafted into the eucharistic mode of existence of the Church body, then no ready-made definition can correspond to the dynamism of the ways in which life is transfigured "from glory to glory" (2 Cor 3:18). No casuistic subjection of man to objective provisions in laws or canons of life can exhaust the distinctiveness of the *name* given him by the Church within the communion and relationship of love.

This does not apply only to personal participation in eucharistic unity and communion; man's failure to transcend the rebellious impulse to existential autonomy in his natural individuality—sin in its various forms—is also something that defies objective definition, and in this way preserves the uniqueness and dissimilarity of the tragic opposition between person and nature, the personal adventure of freedom.

Yet the Church herself in ecumenical and local councils, through the wisdom of her fathers and saints, has ordained a host of canons and provisions which regulate her life. And what they regulate is not only external relationships having to

do with her administrative structure and the good order of her
human organization, but also the conditions for each member's participation in her body or personal severance from it.

The existence of canons and legal regulations in the
Church's life must be interpreted correctly, because otherwise
it undermines the very truth of the Church, the truth of
personal distinctiveness and freedom which constitutes true
life in the context of loving communion and relationship.

From New Testament times onwards, the problem of the
Church's freedom from every law, even the Law appointed
by God for the historical education of Israel, has been a
particularly acute one. It is enough to call to mind St Paul's
struggle with the "Judaizers" who wanted the Law to be
preserved in the life of the Church; to recall the theology of
his epistles, and their insistence on salvation "by faith" and
not "by law." We must not, however, fail to notice that Paul
does not react by rejecting the Law and its educative character;[1]
he only opposes the *precedence* of law over faith and the
legal interpretation of faith, of the new relationship between
God and man in Christ.

It is plain that for St Paul, the Law goes with the fall of
man; it marks off the fall from what is not the fall, evil from
good. It defines and manifests the reality of sin,[2] man's failure
to live in communion and relationship with God. The existence of the Law manifests our distance from God; it proves
that there exists between God and man a "middle wall of
partition." Even supposing man keeps the whole of the Law,
the "middle wall of partition" is not removed, because the
partition, which is sin, consists not in violation of the Law
but in that separation from God which the Law marks out
and affirms. And because violation of the Law does not exhaust the reality of sin, observance of the Law could never
do away with sin. The existence of the Law itself precludes

---

[1]"Do we then make void the Law through faith?" God forbid: yea, we
establish the Law" (Rom 3:31).

[2]"For by the Law is the knowledge of sin" (Rom 3:20). "For where
no law is, there is no transgression" (Rom 4:15). "But sin is not imputed
when there is no law" (Rom 5:13). "I had not known sin, but by the
Law . . . For without the Law, sin was dead" (Rom 7:7-8). "The strength of
sin is the Law" (1 Cor 15:56).

justification "by works of Law," since the Law is the "power
of sin": it is the Law that makes possible the concrete realization of sin in the form of transgression, and this is why
it simply "worketh wrath" (Rom 4:15). It is in this sense
that Paul asserts that "a man is not justified by the works of
the Law—by the deeds of the Law there shall no flesh be
justified" (Gal 2:16, Rom 3:20, Gal 3:17).

Christ alone is the end of the Law (Rom 10:4) and freedom from the Law (Rom 8:2), precisely because He did
away with the precondition for its existence when, in His
theanthropic flesh, He destroyed the "middle wall of partition" (Eph 2:14), the existential distance between man and
God. Thus the Law is not annulled but "fulfilled," in the
sense that it finds its fulness in love (Rom 13:10). The Law
continues to manifest and affirm sin, but now the acknowl-
edgement of sin is not proof of condemnation and death,
not a "curse," but a measure of acceptance of God's love:
the Law reveals God's "frenzied *eros*" for man.

Christ abolished the Law by showing that love is above
the Law. If the Law subjugates man to transgression and
consequently to death, the love of God "in the person of Jesus
Christ" frees transgression from its consequence, death, and
transforms transgression of the Law into a potentiality for
repentance and loving relationship with God—a potentiality
for eternal life. Man's salvation, his participation in eternal
life, is not a legal event; it is a participation in God's love
which gives substance to life. The dilemma which St Paul sets
before the Judaizers is between the ontological content of
salvation and the legal interpretation of it: is it the Law
that "gives life to the dead," transfiguring our mortal being
into a hypostasis of eternal life, or is it the love of God?[3]
If it is the Law, then "Christ is dead in vain."[4] If it is love,
then life and salvation are grace, a gift of freedom from
observance of the Law.[5]

[3]"No man is justified by the Law in the sight of God...If there had
been a law given which could have given life, verily righteousness should
have been by the Law" (Gal 3:11 and 21).
[4]"If righteousness comes by the Law, then Christ is dead in vain"
(Gal 2:21).
[5]"By grace ye are saved...and that not of yourselves: it is the gift

Christ showed that love is above the Law when He made Himself subject to the Law and to death, and showed that the Law was powerless to kill the life which is love and acceptance of death. "We have a law, and by that law he ought to die," say the Jews to Pilate as they hand Christ over to him (Jn 19:7). With these words, yet without a full understanding of their significance, they set out the fundamental meaning of Christ's sacrifice: in accordance with man's law, He is subject to death, to separation from life—He "ought to die." This obligation to die *constitutes* the Law and shows it to be a "curse": "for as many as are under the Law, are under a curse" (Gal 3:10). From the moment there is law, there is separation from life, an obligation to die. But Christ subjects Himself to the Law, to the obligation to die, and transforms this obligation into obedience to God's love, into relationship and communion between mortal flesh and the life-giving love of God. Thus Christ's submission to the Law and to death makes law and death part of another mode of existence, of the love which gives substance to life. The cross of Christ, that ultimate consequence of the Law, the fulfilment of the curse and of death, is the end of the Law and transcendence of the Law.

Christ "was raised from the dead," putting death to death and abolishing the Law "in His flesh" (Eph 2:15)—the reality of law, sin and death are "swallowed up by life" (1 Cor 15:54, 2 Cor 5:4). "Wherefore, my brethren," writes St Paul, "ye also are become dead to the law by the body of Christ; that ye should be married to another, even to Him who is raised from the dead, that we should bring forth fruit unto God (Rom 7:4). The way we are conformed at baptism to the death and resurrection of Christ and incorporated into the body of the Church is "newness of life," freedom from the Law.[6] The children of the Church are not children of

of God ... for we are His workmanship, created in Christ Jesus" (Eph 2:5-10). "... But the gift of God is eternal life" (Rom 6:23). "For ye are not under the Law, but under grace" (Rom 6:14). "... being justified by His grace" (Ti 3:7).

[6]"Therefore we are buried with Him by baptism into death: that like as Christ was raised up from the dead by the glory of the Father, even so we also should walk in newness of life" (Rom 6:4).

Hagar, of slavery to the Law, but children of Sarah; they are children of the freedom of God's promises, of the loving relationship and communion with God (Gal 4:22-31). Salvation is an organic entry into the communion of saints, the body of the Church, "built upon the foundation of the apostles and prophets, Jesus Christ Himself being the chief corner stone; in whom all the building fitly framed together groweth unto an holy temple in the Lord" (Eph 2:20-21).

2. The canon of martyrdom and the witness of the canons

In her first, apostolic council (Acts 15:6-29), the Church vindicated St Paul's theology, rejected the observance of the Mosaic Law, and refused to admit legal substitutes for salvation; she repelled the danger of being turned into a "religion" and an "ethic" of the present age which "passeth away." It is nevertheless characteristic that the apostolic council retained what was "necessary" from the regulations of the Law: it commanded the Christians converted "from the Gentiles" to abstain from "meats offered to idols, and from blood, and from things strangled and from fornication" (Acts 15:18-29). In retaining these four regulations from the Law, the Church defined for the first time an objective, social distinction between Christians and pagans; it was the beginning of the canons of her historical life.

In the first three centuries, there was no need for a clearer definition of the bounds of church life, of the objective limits safeguarding the visible unity and homogeneity of the life of the Church's body. For all the faithful there was a constant possibility of martyrdom, and this kept church life in harmony with the fullest possible affirmation of the truth of salvation. Martyrdom is the supreme canon of the Church's life, a practical witness manifesting the mode of existence which differentiates the "new creation" of Christians from the way the "world" lives; and it is the measure for understanding the truth of all later canons enacted by the Church. We must therefore insist on this as a fundamental prerequisite for understanding the canons.

The witness of the Christian martyrs goes beyond the heroism of self-denial for the sake of certain ideals which a person believes to be higher in value even than his individual survival. History has seen many forms of such idealistic heroism and extreme self-denial, and all merit absolute respect; but they bear no direct relation to the witness of Christian martyrs. The martyrs of the Church embody the truth of the Church, the truth of the true life which is communion and relationship with God—which is the ultimate self-transcendence of natural individuality, and love for Christ who alone gives a hypostasis of eternal life to man's personal distinctiveness. It is not a question of ideological fanaticism, or of faith in ideas which aim to improve our common life; what we have seen is the concrete realization of a mode of existence which is the complete antithesis of individual survival, and has its historical prototype in the cross of Christ.

Subsequently, every canon of the Church has aimed at the same "martyr-like" self-transcendence of natural individuality and autonomous survival, the same realization of life as communion and relationship, as obedience to the love of God according to the prototype of self-denial in the life-giving death of the cross. Every canon provides a witness to, and a possibility for, personal relationship with the whole body of the Church and the subjection of individuality to the common participation of all the faithful in the oneness of the Church's life. Nor is there room for a different interpretation of the canons. If this is not their truth, if the difference between the church canons and any other religious, moral or social legislation does not lie in the definition of the *ontological* fact which the Church embodies—that of personal distinctiveness and freedom—then their existence becomes a scandal in that it contradicts the gospel of salvation.

3. The canon of *ascesis* and the ascetism of the canons

As the Church's historical life went on, after the period of persecutions and martyrdoms the canons began to multiply all the more as participation in the life of the Church came to be more or less taken for granted in any member of society. The "necessary things" laid down by the apostolic council gradually increased in number; the preconditions for participation in the general ethos of the Church body or for severance from eucharistic unity became ever more specific.

Certainly up to the seventh century, the canons of the ecumenical councils, which have universal authority in the life of the Church, still avoid marking out limits for the individual morality of the faithful and defining cases of individual sins which entail excommunication, exclusion from the church body. The canons of the first four ecumenical councils deal almost entirely with matters of church order: the jurisdiction of the clergy, the validity of ordinations, behavior towards heretics, and the like. The very few individual misdemeanors which are singled out bear a direct relation to the eucharistic structure and functioning of the Church: for example canon 17 of the First Ecumenical Council, *On clergy practising usury;* canon 2 of the Fourth Council, *That ordination should not be performed for money;* canon 16 of the same council, *On virgins and monks, that they should not enter upon marriage.* In the last case, there is the very characteristic addition: "if they are found to be doing so, let them remain without communion. But we have decreed that the local bishop has authority to exercise clemency towards them . . ."

Only from the end of the seventh century, and specifically from the Quinisext Council, also called the Synod in Trullo (692), do we see the start of a striking increase in the number of canons relating to general cases of individual sins. These deal with exhibitions of bad social behavior by clergy and laity alike, and also with the relation between natural, and particularly sexual, life and participation in the life of the

Church, as likewise with the determining of penances for social offences, etc. Thus while the canons established by the first four ecumenical councils number in total just 66, the Quinisext Council alone formulated 102 canons. In addition, it endorsed and established as canons with universal authority for the Church an exceptionally large number of regulations made by earlier local councils, and of opinions expressed by individual fathers, mainly on questions of moral behavior. Inevitably sins were listed in greater detail, and the corresponding sanctions to be imposed by the Church were specifically fixed. Later scholars have seen in the work of the Quinisext Council the first formation of a *system* of canon law, the first creation of a code of church legislation (*codex canonum*) analogous to the legal codes of the state.[7]

Does this mean, then, that we must recognize in the work of the Quinisext Council a compromise on the part of the Church with considerations of social usefulness? Is the event of salvation being falsified, and changed into individual obedience to legal forms and commandments?

Neither the historical data from this period nor the criteria for the truth and life of the Church permit us to reach any such conclusions. The texts of the council themselves set out unequivocally the one and only aim and purpose of the canons: "for the cure of souls and the healing of passions."[8] The canons are established to be healing and therapeutic in character, not legal and juridical. They do not exist for the purpose of judging man, tormented as he is by sin, and condemning him by subjecting his failure to the impersonal casuistry of a merciless law. The canons define and delimit the healing, therapeutic action of pastoral instruction in the

[7]See V. Laurent, "L'oeuvre canonique du concil in Trullo, source primaire du droit de l'Eglise orientale," *Revue des Études Byzantines* 23 (1956), 19, 20. A. Christodoulos, *Essay on Ecclesiastical Law* (in Greek—Constantinople, 1896), p. 57ff. Bartholomaios Archontonis, *On the Codification of the Holy Canons and Canonical Regulations in the Orthodox Church* (in Greek—Thessaloniki, Patriarchal Institute for Patristic Studies, 1970) p. 47.

[8]Canon 2: "This also seemed to this holy council excellent and most important: that from now on the canons received and confirmed by the holy fathers for the cure of souls and the healing of passions, and so passed on to us, should still remain sure and steadfast."

Church, the way in which the Church guides man to the fulfilment of his possibilities for life.

In the language of the Church, healing means disengaging
man from the *natural* impetus of his individual existence
which makes the needs and desires of such existence into
absolutes, forms an end in itself, and by itself exhausts the
possibilities of life and pleasure all on its own. The first step
towards this disengagement is for man to become aware of
the existential failure and condemnation represented by the
autonomy of his individuality, to recognize within himself
the profound deprivation of life to which egocentric survival
leads. In order to reach such maturity of self-knowledge, man
needs to submit himself to certain objective standards which
determine the severity of his sins, the magnitude of his failure
to approach the truth of life. These objective standards and
aids to self-knowledge are what the Church's canons offer with
their evaluative appraisal of transgressions.

The canons, however, are not simply an aid to self-knowledge. The "cure of souls and healing of passions" is effected
in the body of the Church through grafting individual existence into the overall reality of life and unity in the Church's
body. When the canons lay down special penances for particular cases of sin, they are assessing the significance of the
various forms of human failure within the context of the
Church's common struggle to delimit and avoid death, her
common asceticism. The penances imposed by the canons do
not represent penalties to buy remission, but the measure of
the Church's ascetic consciousness, the length of the journey
which personal freedom has to traverse in order to accord with
the trinitarian mode of existence within the church body.
Simply to recognize our distance from the truth of life and
to submit to the canons, to the standard of the Church's
ascetic consciousness, is an act of participation in the Church,
the first and greatest step towards communion with the very
body of life. Precisely because of their exemplary and advisory
character, in the practice of the Church the penalties laid
down by the canons have always been relative and subject to
economy. The application of the canons is, and always has
been, a matter of economy; this does not necessarily mean

that canonical penalties are reduced, but it does mean that they are adapted as closely as possible to the distinctiveness of each personal failure.

It is impossible to understand the existence and operation of the canons in the body of the Church without taking account of their *ascetic* character. The canons are the conditions for asceticism, the prerequisites for a participation in the life of the Church which is ascetic and dynamic, not conventional and formal. At this point, it should be stressed that the truth represented by the canons of the Church cannot be understood in isolation from the spiritual and cultural climate which gave birth to them. The period which gave birth to the canons represents a level of spiritual achievement which remains not only unattainable, but even incomprehensible without the standard of the asceticism they express. It may require direct experience in the field of art to understand how many canons or rules the Byzantine painter or poet had to obey in order to create in a strict given framework the heights of art which Byzantium has bequeathed to us. The more flourishing the art, the more numerous and implacably strict are its canons. One has the impression that Byzantine artists deliberately created additional restrictions on the expression of individual inspiration and initiative, in order to obtain a maximum of individual self-transcendence and the manifestation of a personal, and therefore universal, experience of truth.

We live today in a culture diametrically opposite to that of Byzantium; a culture where the individual dominates and where safeguards for individuality are given an institutional form. So it is exceptionally difficult to understand that what happened with art in Byzantium also happened with the whole of life: the greater the height of spirituality and culture, the more numerous and implacably strict were the canons of asceticism. We, perhaps, may see in these canons a system of law. But the Byzantines saw in them the preconditions and possibilities for an ascetic realization of personal freedom and distinctiveness, for the real manifestation of the beauty of life. The measure of our understanding of the canons is a measure of our spiritual maturity.

4. The distinction between natural perpetuation and personal regeneration

It is within this same perspective that we should see the attitude represented by the canons towards problems and areas of life such as the natural process of motherhood, and sexual behavior in general. The conscience of modern western man seems to be particularly sensitive on these matters. According to the criteria formed within our western culture by modern "liberalism" and "humanism," sexual life is *par excellence* the private area of individual life admitting of no legal interference, an area where hereditary factors, social influences and profound existential demands shape the psychological identity of the subject. More especially, the natural process of motherhood is a "sacred" area of life, an object of deference and concern on the part of social institutions.

This modern attitude towards motherhood and sex may be idealistic and impracticable, but it is certainly has general acceptance as a theoretical position; and it is hard to dispute or reject it when one considers how many centuries of struggle have preceded it in Europe—struggles to stop sexual life being considered, and indeed actually being, grounds for a traumatic sense of guilt in the individual, and maternity being connected in people's minds with unenlightened, repressed complexes.[9]

Given, then, the modern criteria of humanism and liberalism formed in the long struggle against medieval survivals of Manicheism, against Roman Catholic legalism and Protestant puritanism, the canons of the fathers and saints of Byzantium relating to sex and the process of motherhood conjure up for western man scenes and presumptions from the dark historical subconscious of the European, precisely

[9]See Peter Gay, *The Enlightenment—An Interpretation*, 2: *The Science of Freedom* (London, 1973), pp. 96, 189-190, 194-207. Philip Sherrard, *Christianity and Eros* (London, 1976). André Biéler, *L'homme et la femme dans la morale calviniste* (Geneva, 1963). M. Rade, *Die Stellung des Christentums zum Geschlechtsleben* (Tübingen, 1910). Th. de Félice, *Le protestantisme et la question sexuelle* (Paris, 1930). John Marbove, *The Puritan Tradition in English Life* (London, 1956). Fritz Tanner, *Die Ehe im Pietismus* (dissertation, Zürich, 1952).

184 THE FREEDOM OF MORALITY

because they express an attitude different from today's absolute and rebellious affirmation of this area of life. These canons of the Orthodox Church, however, approach the problem on a level beyond today's cultural criteria, and represent a historical tradition unconnected with the obscurantism and morbid repression which gave rise to the reactions of modern liberalism and humanism.

It is a fact that there are canons which characterize the new mother as "unclean."[10] They forbid holy communion for the duration of the physiological function which prepares for motherhood, the menstrual period.[11] They require abstention from conjugal relations before and after holy communion.[12] They refuse the priesthood to anyone who has been raped as a child, even if the act was demonstrably against his will.[13] They regard extramarital sexual relations as an obstacle to priesthood, even after repentance which may have led to the gift of working miracles, the gift of raising the dead.[14]

Considered "from without," outside the milieu and the conditions of life which gave them birth, all these canons remain incomprehensible; they are a "scandal" to modern western man's way of thinking. But this external view, even though it may be to some extent inevitable today, is incapable of capturing the spirit and ethos of the fathers who laid down those canons. It is not possible at once to undervalue the human body and sexual life or even to despise them, and yet to insist, as do the fathers and particularly the ascetics of the desert, on the value of the "loving power" in man and

[10]Canon 38 of St Nicephorus the Confessor, Patriarch of Constantinople: "That a woman who has recently given birth should not enter the room where her baptized baby is."
[11]Canon 2 of St Dionysius of Alexandria: "That women should not receive communion during menstruation." Canon of St John the Faster: "On menstruating women." Canons 6 and 7 of St Timothy of Alexandria: "That a menstruating woman should not be baptized. That even if she has been baptized, she should not receive communion during menstruation."
[12]Canon 5 of St Timothy of Alexandria: "That couples who have just slept together should not receive communion."
[13]Canon of St John the Faster on sodomy: "A child who has once been perverted cannot proceed to the priesthood. For even though he himself did not sin, because of his youth, yet his vessel has been broken and become useless for the divine ministry."
[14]Canon 36 of St Nicephorus of Constantinople.

on the revelatory function of bodily love as "a type of our desire for God,"[15] and on the manifestation of God as the bridegroom and lover of our souls. In the same way, such a dismissive attitude cannot coexist with the glorification of the body in the Church's iconography, or with the position of the Virgin Mother of God in the theology, liturgical life and piety of the Church.

In order to understand the Church's canons, we have to regain and stand firm on the presuppositions and the spiritual level of their age, and the theology which formed them. In the texts of the fathers and the theological decisions of the councils which laid down the canons relating to sex, and in the liturgical life and art of the period, one problem alone is paramount: how to manifest and safeguard the fact of salvation, of man's salvation from death—the possibility for man to participate in the true life of incorruption and immortality in his entirety, in his own flesh and the flesh of the world.

This absolute and radical priority given to participation in existence "according to truth," to bringing about the personal distinctiveness and freedom which constitutes life, leaves no room for conventional evaluations and romantic embellishments of man's mortal biological hypostasis and the way it is composed. The composition of man's biological hypostasis is inevitably subject to two implacable *passions* of nature: to the existential need and impulse for nature to become absolute as an individual, autonomous entity, and to the identification of this impulse with corruption and death. At each natural birth the inevitable fragmentation of nature into individual entities is put into effect, and with it the "condemnation" of human existence to confine its life to individual survival and to be subject to corruption.[16]

---

[15]John of Sinai, *Ladder*, step 26, PG 88, 1024B.

[16]"The biological constitution of man's hypostasis suffers radically from two 'passions' which destroy precisely that towards which the human hypostasis is thrusting, namely, the person. The first 'passion' is what we may call 'ontological necessity.' Constitutionally the hypostasis is inevitably tied to the natural instinct, to an impulse which is 'necessary' and not subject to the control of freedom. Thus the person as a being 'subsists' not as freedom but as necessity . . . The second 'passion' . . . may be called the 'passion' of *individualism*, of the *separation* of the hypostasis. Finally, however, it is identified with the last and greatest passion of man, with the disintegration of the

The cause of this subjection is neither the fact that the body is material, nor sexual love, nor the natural process of motherhood. On the contrary, sexual love is the ecstatic power in existence, the potentiality for self-transcendence and loving communion.[17] In the same way, motherhood is an ontological fact of relationship, a real transcendence of the ego which is shared out and passes on existence, removing the exclusiveness and self-sufficiency of the biological hypostasis. But sexual love and motherhood alike are existential possibilities subject ultimately to the rebellious self-sufficiency and autonomy of nature. They express, effect and serve the subjection of hypostatic distinctiveness to corruptible and mortal bodily individuality, to the necessity for nature to perpetuate itself in the succession of mortal individual entities.[18] Thus sexual love and the physiological process of motherhood tragically fail to achieve the existential end to which they are directed. They do not perpetuate personal distinctiveness and freedom: they perpetuate nature through a succession of mortal individuals, and they perpetuate the subjection of nature to corruption and death. They are functions of existential failure, in other words of sin—functions of death.[19] And as such they are dealt with by the canons of the Church with absolute realism.

The canons' role is to distinguish and separate life from

hypostasis, which is death": John Zizioulas, "From Prosopeion to Prosopon," pp. 308-309.

[17]"Every man who comes into the world bears his hypostasis, which is not entirely unrelated to love: he is the product of a communion between two people. Erotic love, even when expressed coldly without emotional involvement, is an astounding mystery of existence, concealing in the deepest act of communion a tendency towards an ecstatic transcendence through creation": ibid., p. 308.

[18]"Man as a biological hypostasis is intrinsically a tragic figure. He is born as a result of an ecstatic fact—erotic love—but this fact is interwoven with a natural necessity and therefore lacks ontological freedom. He is born as a hypostatic fact, as a body, but this fact is interwoven with individuality and with death. By the same erotic act with which he tries to attain ecstasy he is led to individualism. His body is the tragic instrument which leads to communion with others ... But at the same time it is the 'mask' of hypocrisy, the fortress of individualism, the vehicle of the final separation, death": ibid., p. 310.

[19]"The tragedy of the biological constitution of man's hypostasis does not lie in his not being a person because of it; it lies in his tending towards

death; to distinguish the possibilities of the true life free from space, time, corruption and death, from the illusions of life which serve as a cover for death. And the realization of life "according to truth" is the trinitarian mode of existence found in the body of the eucharist; it is celebration of the eucharist and participation in it. This is why the canons also have to make a clear distinction between the process of natural perpetuation which is subject to death and the process of eucharistic life. The two processes are not compatible. They are not opposites: one does not cancel out the other. It is simply that the first must be transcended for the second to come about.[20] In order to celebrate the eucharist or take part in it, you have to be "conformed" to the mode of composition proper to the ecclesial, eschatological hypostasis of one who belongs to the communion of saints; you must distance yourself existentially, in manner and in time, from the autonomous impulse of natural perpetuation expressed by the reproductive process. This distancing is what the canons lay down. In the same way, they mark out the only possibility of freeing sexual love from subjection to natural necessity: that of the mystery of

becoming a person through it and failing. Sin is precisely this failure. And sin is the tragic prerogative of the person alone . . . The body tends towards the person, but ultimately leads to the individual . . . [Death], the 'failure' of the survival of the biological hypostasis, is not the result of some acquired fault of a moral kind (a transgression), but of the very *constitutional make-up* of the hypostasis, that is, of the biological act of the perpetuation of the species": *ibid.*, pp. 309-310.

[20]"For salvation to become possible, for the unsuccessful hypostasis to succeed, it is necessary that eros and the body, as expressions of ecstasy and of the hypostasis of the person, should cease to be the bearers of death. Two things therefore appear to be indispensible: (a) that the two basic components of the biological hypostasis, eros and the body, should *not* be destroyed (a flight from these elements would entail for man a privation of those means by which he expresses himself equally as ecstasy and as hypostasis, that is, as person); and (b) that the *constitutional make-up* (or 'mode') *of the hypostasis* should be changed—not that a moral change or improvement should be found, but a kind of new birth for man. This means that although neither eros nor the body are abandoned, they nevertheless change their activity, adapt themselves to the new 'mode of existence' of the hypostasis, reject from this activity of theirs which is constitutive of the human hypostasis whatever creates the tragic element in man, and retain whatever makes the person to be love, freedom and life. This is precisely what constitutes that which I have called the 'hypostasis of ecclesial existence' ": *ibid.*, pp. 310-311.

THE FREEDOM OF MORALITY

marriage, in which the death of nature is taken up as a cross and transformed into an event of kenotic self-offering and loving communion, according to the prototype of Christ's obedience.

In other words, the canons do not express a system of law. They express one thing only: the ontology of the Church, the mode of existence within the church body. Nor do they do this with theoretical formulations; they delimit the practice and realization of life in relation to the individual survival which is subject to death. With this ontological criterion, all the canons relating to sex take on meaning and can be correctly interpreted; they can also interpret the Gospel message of salvation. The only thing is that this ontological interpretation of the canons cannot be accepted and lived without an absolute and radical inner insistence upon the distinction between death and life, without an insatiable thirst for existential fulness and eternal life. And it seems that this demand cannot easily be fulfilled on the level of the "liberal," "humanistic" affirmation and embellishment of illusions of life.

5. The legalistic interpretation of the canons

It would nevertheless be mistaken and one-sided to attribute modern man's inability to understand and accept the Church's canons, particularly those relating to sexual matters, exclusively to the "humanistic" and "liberal" mentality of recent centuries. We must also note a second, more important factor: the fact that the ontological content of the canons, and indeed of salvation, is underestimated, neglected or even totally ignored in the Christian world itself. Faith and piety have widely taken on a legalistic character, a process which began in western church life and was later transplanted to pietistic and academic environments in the Orthodox East. This strips the canons of their soteriological character and meaning, transforming them into neutral, formal stipulations to torment man. It subjugates life to a "system" of law which is devoid of existential justification, and consequently dead.

In a climate of legalism and moralism, the canons no longer distinguish life from death: their function ceases to be one of revelation and liberation, of healing and care. They operate as a ruthless code of moral legislation which evaluates individual transgressions and metes out exemplary punishments.

The legalistic and moralistic interpretation of the canons introduces into liturgical life the criteria of individual justification, and so a mentality completely opposite to the truth of salvation. It therefore has consequences diametrically opposed to those intended by the life of the Church. Instead of caring for sinners and healing them, instead of comforting man, wounded and degraded as he is by sin, it leads to fear of guilt, the threat of condemnation and the shadow of death. Those who "faithfully observe the canons," the "pure," are usually people who need a framework of law to give them security as individuals. Thus they come to inflict merciless punishment on all those "insignificant" people who constitute a provocation to objective moralistic standards by their very presence, their tragic struggle between falling and repentance. The parable of the Pharisee and the Publican is fulfilled in history once again, with the Law and the observance of regulations always at its root.

6. The codification of the canons

There has been much talk in recent years about the need to "codify" the canons of the Orthodox Church.[21] The paradigm for codification is a western one: the *Corpus iuris canonici* of the Roman Catholic Church.[22] The aim would be to "systematize" the canons in accordance with modern

[21]For the history of the attempts at codification, the arguments and relevant bibliography, see the study by Archimandrite Bartholomaios Archontonis (now Metropolitan of Philadelphia), *On the Codification of the Holy Canons and Canonical Regulations in the Orthodox Church.*

[22]See B. Archontonis, *op. cit.*, especially pp. 7 and 114ff. The author is entirely correct in connecting the attempts to codify canon law with the spirit of enlightenment and positivism in the eighteenth and nineteenth centuries.

"scientific" requirements,[23] so as to give the Orthodox churches
a unified canon law, efficient and easy to use,[24] and cleared of
"contingent" provisions and canons which have fallen into
disuse. "Similar" canonical provisions would be amalgamated,
while canons which "contradicted" each other or provided
for penalties considered excessive for our own times would
be revised. Finally, such new canons would be created as were
thought necessary to make the code "systematic."[25]

The idea of codifying the canons has been put forward
by theologians who sought with genuine fervor to serve the
truth of the Church and nothing else; and it has had widespread and positive repercussions in the Orthodox churches.
It is equally, however, an idea which came to birth in the
theological climate of the early years of our century, when
the western mentality which looks for "objective" criteria, in
the differentiation between "confessions" as much as in the
organization of church life, had been accepted without question by Orthodox theologians. Thus, it seems, some fundamental questions arising out of the idea of codification were
overlooked.

To begin with, one might wonder if it is really fortuitous
and meaningless that many canons are contingent and consequently relative in character, that there are inconsistencies
between them, or that parallel regulations similar in scope
are retained, along with canons which have been in disuse
for some centuries of church life. In other words, is it fortuitous and accidental that for centuries the Church has refused
in practice to turn the canons into a convenient and efficient
body of "legislation" for her life? Can it be that the reason
the canons were made and the way they operated in the

[23]"The usefulness and positive results of the codification, when it
happens, will be felt in many spheres. In the first place, one must take
serious account of the great impetus this will give to a wider development
and cultivation of Orthodox ecclesiastical law, both during its preparation
and afterwards, as was shown with the codification of Latin canon law,
which led to a real flowering in the science of canon law in the western
Church": Archontonis, p. 59.

[24]". . . a code which goes beyond the mere collections, being more systematic and scientific, more official and authoritative and therefore more
useful": Archontonis, p. 59.

[25]Archontonis, p. 69ff.

Church is very far from the modern "science" of law with its need for codification, if not diametrically opposed to it? Can a codification of this sort be brought about without distorting or even destroying the ontological content of the "semantics" of the canons, the distinction between death and life?

If the purpose of the canons is to mark the limits of life, and if life, as promised by the Church, means *love* or freedom from any predetermination, then how can the canons be identified with a codified body of legislation? Legislation goes no further than defining and punishing transgression, whereas the canons distinguish sin only to mark the starting-point for repentance, while the penance defines how repentance is to be put into practice. But repentance is a gift of life, which can come into existence, grow to maturity and be measured only where there is freedom and measureless love. The contingent character of many of the canons, the inconsistencies between them, the repetitions and the cases of disuse manifest the primacy and the indeterminancy of life, which cannot be codified. A code by definition seeks to systematize and clarify legislation, and above all to make it definitive—to make life subject to a "system" of regulations which is complete and efficient. The canons, on the other hand, are subordinated to the life of the Church which is love, in order to manifest her healing character. They cannot be restricted to defining transgression, like a legal code, because they provide for the transfiguration of transgression into repentance and life.

Again, one might wonder whether what precludes the codification of the canons according to modern "scientific" criteria is not their outward formulation, but primarily the miracle of their antinomy: they are regulations, and yet they do not constitute "law." They mark the limits of morality, but without making it subject to the logistics of individual evaluations. They impose penances, yet these are not penalties to atone for guilt but means of healing. They protect good order in the church organization, without subjecting the working of the eucharistic body to a "totalitarian" uniformity. They provide for and mark out sin and failure in

administrative structures or in personal life, while at the
same time respecting man's freedom, and creating possibilities
for contrition and an atmosphere of repentance.

This saving antinomy is embodied and expressed above
all in the way the canons are subject to the bishop's gift of
spiritual fatherhood. As the bishop is charged with keeping
the canons, so he is equally charged with setting them aside.
He has been given the grace "to bind and to loose." It is he
who interprets the canons, applies them, and supplements them
or sets them aside, because in the practice and life of the
Church he holds the position of Christ. The formulation of
the sixth canon of the Fourth Ecumenical Council expresses
by far the most general attitude and practice in the Orthodox
tradition: "We have decreed that the local bishop shall have
authority to exercise clemency." Can this authority to exercise
clemency, which resides in the bishop and by extension in the
confessor who is his deputy, be reconciled with the idea of a
code, which requires that the regulations be made definitive
and accepted, observed and imposed by all?

The great comfort and the great hope that the canons
give us is that they confirm the truth and fulness of life as a
personal conquest and achievement of freedom. In the
struggle to attain this feat, we are always going to be judged
by the canons. And the more severe we are on conventional
ways of making the struggle easier, the more profoundly
mistrustful of the illusions which mirror our existential demands as if they were truth, the sweeter the fruit of authentic
life in our souls.

Additional Note: The body of the Church has no other hypostasis,
whether legal or administrative, apart from the eucharistic assembly. The
eucharistic synaxis constitutes, realizes and manifests the Church. The
ability to represent the eucharistic body cannot be invested in an impersonal
administrative structure or organizational mechanism, or in some founding
charter or constitution made up of canons; it cannot constitute a "legal
person." The only possible way in which the eucharistic body can be
represented is through a natural person, the person of the *father* of the
synaxis who is the bishop, "as type and in place of Christ." For the Church
is a reality of life, and life has only a personal existence and hypostasis.
The bishop embodies and sums up the life of the Church, her personal
mode of existence, the fact of personal communion and relationship which
constitutes the Church. This again is why the bishop is above the canons,

since he embodies and sums up all that the canons simply indicate and delimit. And at the same time, because the canons delimit the life of the Church, it is they that indicate also whether the bishop is representing her truth genuinely or unworthily; but again, not as a code which constitutes and exhausts the identity of the Church body, but as limits and pointers to life, which has solely a personal existence and hypostasis. Furthermore, the canons which "define" and judge the integrity or unworthiness of the bishop are themselves defined by the synod of bishops, since the bishops represent and express the feeling and experience of each local Church. Not even an ecumenical council is an autonomous structure or a legal person with impersonal jurisdiction over that of the bishop. The way the life of the Church is represented and summed up in the person of the bishop follows from the truth of the personal mode of existence which the Church embodies. It is therefore also the ultimate hazard for the Church, her historical adventure. How much the body of the Church has suffered from bishops who were unworthy or had no understanding of their office is well known, from history and present-day experience alike. Holy bishops are as rare as holy lay people. For this is our truth, the truth of our human nature which does not cease to be sinful even when embodied in the persons of bishops. Yet the sins of bishops do not remove the possibility of salvation, any more than do the sins of lay people—on the contrary, they underline the marvelous paradox of salvation celebrated in the eucharistic body. When the Church is subject to impersonal structures and legal codes, however, and to charters and constitutions of canons unrelated to the personal adventure of freedom and repentance, then that does distort the truth of the Church; it destroys the possibility of salvation and removes man's hope of life.

CHAPTER ELEVEN

The Historical and Social Dimensions of the Church's Ethos

1. The problem of moral "efficacity"

We are trying to demonstrate the *ontological* content of the Church's ethos or morality, and how it relates directly to the salvation of life from passions, corruption and death, not to illusions and conventional projects for "improving" corporate life. But the transcendence of any corporate expediency or utility, the refusal to connect morality with improvement in the objective conditions of human life, gives rise to the reasonable question: do not the ethics of the Orthodox Church result merely in an abstract idealism or mysticism, a subjective experience unrelated to the immediate reality of life, to its social and historical realization? Is there not a danger that the freedom from any individual, objective predetermination, the way the person is distinguished and affirmed within the eucharistic community, and the transcendence of all theories of values and obligations, end in a vague quest for imaginary goals which leave unanswered the concrete problems of human relations, those relationships which determine and shape the reality of life?

This question arises in a particularly acute form today, when the great movements for securing human rights and for the improvement of living conditions seem to have achieved in a few decades objective results far beyond anything that Christian ethics have achieved in twenty centuries. What can

the Christians' ethic mean, then, when it lacks the capacity
to change and transfigure historical reality? What meaning
has the ethos of the eucharistic community, the ethos of the
person, in a world of individuals suffering oppression and
injustice, a world which continues to be dominated by impersonal power structures and which is crushed in the relentless circuit of autonomous economics and militarism, when
it cannot even heal the open wounds of naked aggression,
hunger and disease? There seems to be a very acute moral
dilemma between the Church's eschatological vision or existential aims, and the immediacy of social, and more particularly
political, action. Is it not incomparably more "moral" to play
an active part in the political and social movements which,
with varying amounts of realism, offer the immediate possibility of action to improve the objective conditions of life
and bring relief to men? And the struggle against social
injustice, against the fossilized structures of oligarchy and its
vested interests, with the self-denial and sacrifices this requires
—is this not incomparably more "moral" than participation in
a mystical experience of a "communion of saints"?

These questions certainly oppose the morality constructed
by the Church to the immediate needs of society as a whole—
to the claim that all should have an equal share in the good
things of life. We must examine in a serious and coherent
fashion how far this opposition is a real one, and how far it
is artificial. The problem posed by the above questions is
specific and practical, a problem of discriminating between
truth and utopia, between a real possibility and a romantic
illusion. In the way these questions are put, they have the
clarity of "common sense." They are, nevertheless, based on
two premises which are taken as self-evident, without necessarily being so. One such premise is that organized effort,
where individuals enlist in struggles against other individuals
or structures which maintain social injustice, is capable of
bearing fruit and restoring the life of society as a whole to
its correct functioning. The other premise is the conviction
that correct functioning of life in society as a whole can be
secured by an objective, ultimately rationalistic, control of

the individual's rights and duties, and by the dynamic, political imposition of this control.

A whole culture, the western European culture which now extends world-wide, is founded almost exclusively on these two premises. Western man's moral concern seems not to go beyond the framework that these premises define: an ethic of individual behavior and socio-political efficacity, an ethic of "improvement" both in character and in the organizational structure of society as a whole.[1] What, then, does this moral concern have to do with the truth and the ethos or morality of the Church? Is it possible for the churches of the Orthodox apostolic and patristic tradition ever to accord with this level of moral concern which presupposes an understanding of man, the world and history diametrically opposite to their own truth and life? In the milieu of the ecumenical movement, we often hear it imputed to the Orthodox as as a shortcoming that they have no social ethic to put forward. Could it be, however, that this shortcoming means quite simply that the Orthodox are incapable of subjugating themselves to the level of moral concern imposed as self-evident and obligatory by the western way of life? And if this way of life is today taken as a *fait accompli* with world-wide possibilities, is the inability of Orthodoxy to fall in with it simply a historical embarassment or a mere absence of theological vigilance?

2. The moral inadequacy of individual virtue

Why, however, do we say with such certainty that the moral concern of modern man is diametrically opposite to the Orthodox view of man, the world and history? It seems as if, in our day, the ethic of socio-political efficacity and of improving the structures of social life provides the supreme

[1]"What should hold our attention is the historical conjunction of an ethical asceticism and an economic development, as part of a progressive rationalization of life. This conjunction has a significance not only on the historical level ... but is of worldwide importance since it has determined the very destiny of the world": Julien Freund, "L'éthique économique des réligions mondiales selon Max Weber," *Archives de sociologie des religions* 13 (26) 1968, p. 13.

possibility for man to realize his "social" nature and justify his existence by extending it into the realm of "public concerns." Socio-political claims do not necessarily stop at utilitarian immediacy; they do not end with the satisfaction of sectional or class demands. One might say that the inner motivation with which modern man takes up the struggle for these claims is almost metaphysical; consciously or unconsciously, it looks to the vision of the Kingdom of justice, reflecting, perhaps, some sort of corporate archetype of the lost paradise.

Even beyond this existential justification for western man's socio-political ethic, there is no mistaking its concrete historical results. The declarations of human rights and the popular struggles to have them applied, the progressive political movements and their efforts to extricate power from its subjection to the interests of an economic oligarchy, trade unionism and the organized struggle for the rights of the unprotected working man—all these forms of "moral" mobilization may not have transformed the world into paradise, but they have achieved, chiefly in western societies, a significant improvement in the objective conditions under which human beings are living, a definite moderation in the high-handedness of autonomous structures, and a fairer distribution of the good things of life.

The magnitude of these achievements in western societies far exceeds the dreams of the nineteenth-century European. Indeed, it has surpassed the expectations of even the most optimistic visionaries. And these are achievements of a sociopolitical ethic which seeks as a rule to be not merely unrelated to Christian ethics, but actually opposed to them—at least on one westerner's view of Christian ethics.[2] Being a Christian, as the average western man understands it, means that you transfer the immediate problems of social prosperity and historical progress to an abstract "transcendence," or that

[2]"Insofar as economic, political and cultural reasoning long ago won its own freedom, the claim of faith functions all the more as a subsequent justification of that which has been reached without it. The Church's claim to free worldly systems from their worldliness ... today has become ineffectual": Jürgen Moltmann, *Kirche in der Kraft des Geistes* (Munich, 1975), p. 190.

you confront them with the passivity of an individual virtue which, however rationally justified, is never sufficient to influence the march of history as a whole.[3] In the eyes of modern western man, the truth of the Church is no longer a teaching with the power to transfigure the world, as opposed to merely interpreting it. It is not a truth which can have a vital influence on social development, or give meaning and purpose to human history and man's relationship with the material reality of life. The western alienation of Christianity has turned the truth of the Church into an "ideology of decline," a soothing moralism powerless to free man from the various alienations into which modern social groupings lead him, restricted as it is to the sorry utilitarianism of "improving" individual character.

Today, certainly, it often seems as if western Christianity has a sense of moral inadequacy. This is the only way to explain the manifest crisis of historical inferiority expressed in the desperate effort on the part of Christians to conform to the standards and requirements of the ethics of the irreligious European, which have proved so efficacious.[4] It is above all the so-called "political theology," that synthetic neo-leftism which is neither politics nor theology, which seems to bear the brunt of western Christianity's historical inferiority complex and to serve as a psychological over-compensation for it. It looks for the roots of the revolutionary socio-political movements in the Bible itself: the Bible serves as a treatise on political ethics, a theory of revolution whose aim is the

[3]"The impression was given that Christianity had nothing more to say than 'love and do what you will,' and that it now had nothing definite or peremptory to declare about the norms of good conduct that make for the good life and the common good": A. Vidler, *The Church in an Age of Revolution* (Penguin Books, 1976), p. 279.

[4]"The Church cannot remain neutral, but must engage itself strongly in favor of social justice. Without judging our predecessors—popes, bishops and priests—it is necessary to admit that preoccupation with affirming authority and maintaining the social order has hindered us from recognizing that this so-called order was a stratification of injustice, with our passivity vis-à-vis oppression. We have justified Marx when he said, 'Religion is the opium of the people.' We have offered to all the oppressed—those from poor countries as well as those from rich countries—an opium for the peoples": Don Helder Camara, *Au Synode des Évêques*, October 1974. Dorothée Sölle, *Atheistisch an Gottglauben* (Olten, 1969).

paradise of a classless society. In consequence, being a Christian today means that you take an active part in the dynamic uprising against social injustice and political oppression. A mass-meeting is an act of "worship," a revolutionary slogan is a creed, and unity in political action is the new form of ecclesial communion.[5]

The question very naturally arises: why is it not enough just to be politically committed or to be a revolutionary? Why does one need to be a Christian as well? But this is precisely the question that brings us to the psychological motives behind "political theology."

3. The totalitarian dimension of objective ethics

"Political theology" seems to have accepted the two premises which are taken for granted by socio-political movements in the West. One of these is the feasibility of determining solutions to social problems objectively, in terms of concrete proposals, schemes and demands. The other is the feasibility of imposing these solutions dynamically, politically. The attitude or approach represented by these two premises is summed up in the demand for objectivity: the solutions should be objectively determined and objectively imposed. And objectivity means opposition to the subjective factor: it means precluding personal differentiation, and making the theory which introduces the solutions and the policy which imposes them independent of any actual human being's wish or capacity to put the proposed solutions into practice. Political theories and the corresponding political action which

---

[5]From the extensive bibliography on the subject, see for example: Francois Biot, *Théologie du politique. Foi et politique. Eléments de réflexion* (Paris, 1972). Alan Booth, *Christians and Power Politics* (London, 1961). René Coste, *Les dimensions politiques de la foi* (Paris, 1972). André Dumas, *Théologies politiques et vie de l'église* (Lyon, 1977). Alfredo Fiarro, *The Militant Gospel: An Analysis of Contemporary Political Theologies* (London, 1977). Joseph Hromadka, *Der Geschichte ins Gesicht sehen. Evangelische und politische Interpretationen der Wirklichkeit* (Munich, 1977). Juan Luis Secundo, *Liberation of Theology* (New York, 1976). Gustavo Gutierrez, *Théologie de la liberation—Perspectives* (Brussels, 1974). Siegfried Widenhofer, *Politische Theologie* (Stuttgart, 1976).

accompanies them take precedence over the human being they want to help, and whose life they want to "improve." The intellectual forms of the solutions, the structures of the organization which applies them, and the "ethics" of obedience to the ideological "line" subjugate individuals and make them all alike; and the same happens also to thought and judgment, and to the dynamic differentiation in approaches to solving the problems of life. Theoretically it is the majority or the faceless and mythical "people," but in practice it is a tiny minority which decides and imposes the solutions which are to "save" everyone, whether they like it or not.

Totalitarianism is another word we can use to express quite candidly the meaning and content of that "objectivity" which is taken as a self-evident premise for the "moral" concern of socio-political systems in the West—or at least of the extreme consequences of that objectivity. Totalitarianism is not the exclusive characteristic of certain political regimes, parties or organizations which manifest it more or less undisguisedly. It is not an exceptional phenomenon, detached from the fabric of western civilization; it is an organic symptom, a product of that civilization which is entirely in character. The basis on which the historical and cultural life of the West has been built is the objectification of truth, the identification of truth with a particular function of human logic, a function which restricts knowledge to the conventionally "consistent" and therefore commonly accepted use of concepts, or, even more positively, of mathematical relationships.[6]

"Objective" truth presupposes "rationality" as the one and only possible way of interpreting and ordering natural and historical reality. Truth is no longer something achieved by a personal approach and personal experience, but a complete, closed "system" of concepts and intellectual relation-

[6]"In the West for several centuries, this peculiar imaginary notion has been created according to which everything is 'rational' (and in particular mathematizable), that is to say, it is essentially exhaustible; and the goal of knowledge is mastery and possession of nature": Cornelius Castoriadis, *L'institution imaginaire de la société* (Paris, 1975), p. 369. See also M.-D. Chenu, *La théologie comme science au XIIIe siècle* (Paris, 1969). H.-X. Arquillière, *L'augustinisme politique. Essai sur la formation des theories politiques du Moyen-Age* (Paris, 1972²). Gerald Cragg, *The Church and the Age of Reason* (Penguin Books, 1976⁶), pp. 159 and 280.

ships which interprets natural and historical reality definitively and with authority, with the "axioms," "principles"
and "laws" of "scientific" positivism. Thus truth becomes a
useful means and an instrument in man's hands for subjugating the world and history to the rationalism of need and
desire. Those who possess "objective" truth with the help of
the "laws," "principles" and "axioms" of "scientific" positivism, and who represent and interpret it with authority, are
also the people who determine the "objective" needs and
desires of the whole society which the truth is meant to serve.

When truth becomes "objective," this leads to the "infallibility" of its representatives and interpreters,[7] of the bureaucratic structures which ensure its "objective" implementation.
It is thus justifiable even to subjugate by force people who
disagree with the visible authority of dogma. The institution
of the Holy Inquisition and torture as a method of interrogation in the trials of heretics, the concentration camps, the
psychiatric hospitals for "reforming" dissidents, the emasculation of conscience by the party line, one-dimensional trade
unionism and the organized brain-washing of the masses—
all these are consequences which come inevitably with every
use of rationalism in the service of religious, political or any
other "sacred" ends—with every demand for the objectification of the truth. It was the Christian theology of the West
which first taught the "objectivity" of truth,[8] so that without
reference to Thomas Aquinas and Calvin it is impossible to
interpret the totalitarian manner in which even advertizing
works today: we remain unaware of the foundation of the
West's cultural and historical life, which is the objective

[7]For the first formulation and defence of the principle of "infallibility,"
see Thomas Aquinas, *Summa Theologiae* II, 2, 1, art. 10.

[8]Cf. Thomas Aquinas' definitions of the objectivity of knowledge: *De
anima* II, 12 and III, 8: *Summa Theologiae* I, 87, 3 and I, 88, 2 ad. 2:
De veritate, qu. I, art. 9 and qu. III, art. 2: *Summa contra gentiles*, I, 53;
De potentia, qu. XI, art. 5. See also M.-D. Roland-Gosselin, "La théorie
thomiste de l'erreur," *Mélanges thomistes* (=Bibliotheque thomiste 3,
1923), pp. 253-274. *Idem*, "Sur la théorie thomiste de la verite," *Revue des
sciences philosophiques et théologiques* 10 (1921), pp. 223-234. C. Van Riet,
L'épistémologie thomiste (Louvain, 1946). Étienne Gilson, *Le Thomisme*
(Paris, 1972⁶), especially p. 281 ff. *Idem, Réalisme thomiste et critique
de la connaissance* (Paris, 1938).

proof and imposition of the usefulness of God, or Capital, or the Proletariat, or the Revolution.

The objectivity and efficacy of social ethics in the western world seems to begin by doing away with the very goal at which it aims: the possibility of *communion* or *society*, of the corporate functioning of life. Communion or society— personal relationships which go to make up a community of life—cannot possibly exist when truth is an objective datum, when there are no distinct personal approaches to the truth which permit the distinctiveness and freedom of persons—the potential for relationship—to become apparent. In an age when the rights and duties of the individual are rationalistically regulated there is no "society," despite the multiplicity of "social" systems. In the same way, the truth of the city, the *polis*, is gradually being lost, even though individuals are becoming generally more politicized. Our life together is being neutralized into the coexistence of anonymous individuals, living in parallel and without contact; and these individuals are prisoners, packed away in the spaces created by modern, "efficient" housing, mobilized *en masse* in the party or in class factions pursuing individual rights to prosperity (meaning total solitude). They are "one-dimensional" individuals whose judgment and thought have been formalized by the mass media—by the propaganda of consumerism or of the party. Every aspect of the lives of the anonymous masses— their margins for consumption, the educational possibilities open to them, and the range of ideological influences on them—is regulated by rationalistic means; it is the technocrats, embodying the doctrines of cybernetics or some other special "applied" science, who achieve this regulation best, which is to say most efficiently.

It requires a degree of short sight not to perceive that the need for rationalistic and "efficient" regulation, a basic premise of western man's social ethics, inevitably puts the management of public affairs, in other words politics, in the hands of the technocrats. They are the people who have the specialized knowledge required for such regulation, especially in the highly-developed and complicated mechanisms of the economy, the balance of armaments, and the control of those who manipulate armed force. To be sure, while preserving impersonal, "efficient" structures the technocratic bureaucracy does not neglect to preserve also the need felt by the "masses" for idealism; and this it does with romantic catchwords from the pretechnological era, such as democracy, parliamentary government, freedom of thought and expression, and the like. Or alternatively, they make use of analogous but more modern idealistic inventions, like anti-imperialism, the new economic order, world peace, or power for the people. And the masses give vent to their emotions, applauding those who mouth these catchwords and making legends of them—or alternatively demanding a greater show of democracy and "freedoms," intoxicated with the utopianism of political mobilization, of "man's direct power to shape his historical destiny and his future with his own hands," a utopia which again is made possible through rationalistic regulation. One respects and sometimes admires the pure heroism and self-sacrifice that may accompany this political commitment, but one is also pained by the tragic senselessness: by the way man is alienated and estranged from the essentials of his existential truth without suspecting his own alienation, so that he is unequivocally "antimetaphysical" and yet subject to childish myths and medieval expectations. Today, politics is plainly the opium which drugs the masses, and more particularly the intellectual masses, against metaphysics.

4. Visions of "general happiness" and their cost

The achievements of western socio-political "efficacity" are greater than the nineteenth-century European could have dreamed of. But then neither could he have contemplated how great would be the cost of bringing them about. This cost alone accounts for the fact that, in countries where the ideals of western man's social ethics—material comfort for all and a distribution of good things which is not provocatively inequitable—have been implemented with satisfying completeness, it has not ceased to be taken for granted that people should join ever more radical politico-social movements in pursuit of basic demands concerned with the *quality* of human life, with how to save man from the mechanistic, leveling organization of his "happiness" as a prosperous consumer.

The two rival systems which vie with one another to put into effect the vision of "general happiness," capitalism and marxism, are almost on a level in the price they have demanded for putting their principles into practice. And it is precisely this virtually equivalent cost which reveals in practice how the two systems are essentially identical: they have common starting-points and premises, a common descent from western metaphysics, and common roots in a rationalism which necessarily produces infallible authority and totalitarianism.[9]

This revelation to which the cost has led us is perhaps more painful than the magnitude of that cost itself. Against the nightmare of the totalitarian and imperialistic structures of capitalism, nineteenth-century man could at least set the concrete hope and dynamic of the marxist movement: marxism made its appearance as a message of radical change in human society. It was a philosophy which aspired to transcend abstract theorizing and become a daily dynamic act, giving man the capacity to shape history with his own hands. He would be able to shatter the structures of his oppression and alienation, liberate work from enslavement to the interests of an oligarchy, and show the value of the material side of life, transforming the world, its natural resources and its good things into a gift offered equally to all.

Twentieth-century man has seen marxism reach the great moment of putting its principles and ambitions into practice— he has seen the popular uprising of 1917 in Russia, which enabled the marxist vision of social change to become a possibility. But the price exacted in the name of this change has

[9]Cf. Lukacs' apophthegm: "Historical materialism is the self-consciousness of capitalist society," in Maurice Clavel, *Ce que je crois* (Paris, 1975), p. 156. See also the similar conclusion reached by Julien Freund: "Capitalism and all the economic systems born of it, socialism included, have developed the rule of the *impersonal* and have elicited, at this point, a break with the old economic mentality, dominated by personal relations": "L'éthique économique et les religions mondiales selon Max Weber," *Archives de sociologie des religions* 13 (1968), pp. 24-25.

made it clear that by the very nature of its theoretical origins, marxism is subject to the laws and premises of the capitalist system. In order to become political action and a social order, marxism, proved bound to submit to the capitalist methodology of "efficiency," which means that the centralized, bureaucratic structures of the system of production become autonomous. It had to submit to the deterministic relationship between capital and labor which degrades the human "material" into a neutral, secondary factor subordinated to the needs of capital production—with the trifling difference that, in the case of marxism, the capital is state-owned rather than private.[10]

Russia had to go through the most inhuman atrocities history has ever known: the "Gulag archipelago" with its tens of millions of victims, the nightmare of the police state, compulsory submission by the people to religious worship of those in power, and the destruction of all forms of individual freedoms and rights.[11] The ruthless force of military occupation was required to subjugate the countries now known as the "eastern block" to the marxist ideal, and uprisings by the workers and people in East Germany, Hungary and Czechoslovakia had to be drowned in blood. This enormous and agonizing price had to be paid, not to realize the marxist vision of

[10]"Never did Marx or the marxist movement think otherwise than of 'placing technique (capitalist) at the service of socialism,' of shifting the 'profits of production' (rapidly identified, moreover—and not by chance—with legal forms of ownership)": C. Castoriadis, *L'institution imaginaire* . . . , p. 479.

[11]Amidst a host of now well-known historical indications and personal testimonies, as well as critical analyses and political theories, I should like to single out the violent and bitter commentary on the collapse of the marxist vision in Russia represented by André Glucksmann's book, *La cuisiniere et le mangeur d'hommes, essai sur l'Etat, le marxisme, les camps de concentration* (Paris, 1975). Glucksmann asks, "But what about this Marxist-Leninist doctrine which, in claiming to be the 'science of government' of the twentieth century, has undertaken the second campaign for the westernization of Russia—after that of Peter the Great—injecting it with those European values which have always governed the relations of master/slave, despot/plebian, or State/People? Is not the 'Gulag Archipelago' the cutting edge of the West? What blindness or calculation could oppose radically challenging this theory and this practice of 'revolution from above,' the modern version of tyranny, which claims to end in having the State governed by the simple Russian 'stew pot' and has done nothing but deliver it to the cold monster of the Gulag, to statist barbarism, to the law of 'eating men'?"

social change, but to destroy it once and for all; to transform the "great soviet fatherland" of the proletariat into a typically capitalist, imperialist superpower. The internationalist ideal of marxism has been swallowed up by the Russian party oligarchy's greed for military and economic strength. The messianic aspirations to produce a classless society have been betrayed, since centralized bureaucracy inevitably creates its own rigid aristocracy. And the Russian model has been copied universally and with perfect faithfulness, so that today there is no longer any marxist group or movement over which the grass roots have any real control. The idea of obedience to the party and of infallible leadership, the rationalistic conception of unity and the bureaucratic way it is institutionalized, are the basic characteristics of marxism in the second half of the twentieth century—organic consequences of positivism and objectivity, those basic premises for every form of western social ethics.[12]

In terms of theoretical interest, the most important modern survival of this ethic is the critique of marxist theory and practice "from the left," the search for dynamic forms of liberation to free man from the tyranny of the autonomous structures of technocratic bureaucracy, capitalist and marxist alike. This search found a striking and unexpected embodiment in the spontaneous student uprisings of 1968, in America, Germany, France, Italy and Japan. This was the first time that violent and radical questioning of the objectified, oppressive structures of social life in the West had broken out on such a scale.

The most representative of these uprisings was undoubtedly the "French May '68"; this above all embodied the peculiar complexion and the uniqueness of these student disturbances. It was also the most general of the uprisings, uniting workers and peasants alongside the students and producing the most impressive mobilization of the people and general strike in the history of Europe. Within a few hours, it had paralyzed the whole "system" of social organization,

[12]"The essential point is that [Marxism] is a rationalist philosophy, and like all rationalist philosophies, it gives in advance the solution to all the problems that it poses": Castoriadis, *Institution imaginaires . . . .*, p. 57.

bringing the mechanisms for its functioning to a standstill. And all this took place in an atmosphere of spontaneity and improvisation with no predetermined purpose or rationalistic organization. With unpremeditated "occupations" of their places of work or study, people were laying claim to the places and material facilities which made up their daily lives— claiming them from the neutralized structures and impersonal intermediaries who managed them by default.[13]

This claim had such an unfounded romanticism and was expressed in such anti-rationalist slogans[14] that it seemed more like the uproar caused by a festival or a popular fair—though this is not to say that the revolt was not daily paid for in blood. And it was typical that the institutionalized, bureaucratic representatives of the "people," the communist party and the trade unions alike, denounced the revolt and ultimately betrayed it: the revolt was stifled with the first rationalistic manoeuvrings of political strategy, and also by the ruthless force of the inevitable state intervention to safeguard "order" and "security."

The lesson of May '68 was a traumatic one; it gave western societies a severe shock and left its mark on their life. For the first time, the wave of questioning went beyond utilitarian demands and the institutionalized representatives of such demands, bringing to light an "ethical" understanding of life which was not confined to consumer prosperity or to the utopianism of totalitarian "paradises." And it is this taste of a life freed from mechanistic rationalization which the theorists of the "meta-marxist" quest continue to cultivate.[15]

[13]See Jacques Baynac, *Mai retrouvé* (Paris, 1978). Alain Delale and Gilles Ragache, *La France de 68* (Paris, 1978). Jean-Marx Salmon, *Hôtel de l'avenir* (Paris, 1978). Patrick Poivre d'Arvor, *Mai 68, Mai 78* (Paris, 1978).

[14]"Be realists: Demand the impossible!" "After the barricades (lit.: beneath the paving stones), the beach." "Life (*vie*) against survival (*survie*)." "Get out of sight, thing (i.e., world of objectivity)!" "Imagination takes power." "Action shouldn't be a reaction but a creation." "A storm is brewing: We must try to live." "Creativity, spontaneity, life." "The revolution leads nowhere. It is free. It is the dance of Dionysus." "Shit to prosperity. Live!"

[15]See C. Castoriadis, *L'institution imaginaire de la société* (Paris, 1975). *Idem, Les carrefours du labyrinthe* (Paris, 1978). Claude Lefort, *Eléments d'une critique de la bureaucratie* (Geneva, 1971). *Idem, Un homme en*

Among the representatives of this quest, it is the Greek Cornelius Castoriadis who has taken his questioning right to the basis of the ontology on which the western way of life and organization is founded. He was felt to have played an important part in preparing the theoretical climate which gave birth to the French May of '68.[16] In his book *L'institution imaginaire de la société,* Castoriadis outlines an interpretation of how the structures in the capitalist system have become autonomous, and of the bankruptcy of the marxist vision, with reference to their common "metaphysical" starting-point in the foundation underlying what he calls "Greco-western" civilization.[17] This ontology objectifies being into an intellectual datum, an inevitably entitative concept which correspondingly petrifies the historical and social realization of being— the functioning of knowledge, the development of science and the way life is organized—into definitive aspects of a simplified logical identity, and ultimately into institutionalized objective forms and rigid structures. In exceptionally ingenious arguments, drawing on virtually all areas of modern knowledge, Castoriadis indicates the arbitrary and conventional character of this "deterministic" ontology and the consequent objectification of being, setting against it all the data

trop, réflexions sur "L'Archipel du Goulag" (Paris, 1976). *Idem, Le travail de l'oeuvre, Machiavel* (Paris, 1972). *Idem, Les formes de l'histoire* (Paris, 1978). Edgar Morin, Claude Lefort, Jean-Marc Coudray, *Mai 68: la brèche* (Paris, 1968). Bernard-Henri Levy, *La barbarie à visage humain* (Paris, 1977). Andre Glucksmann, *La cuisinière et le mangeur d'hommes, essai sur l'Etat, le marxisme, les camps de concentration* (Paris, 1975). *Idem, Les maîtres penseurs* (Paris, 1977).

[16]Typical is the reference to Castoriadis by Daniel Cohn-Bendit—the student who came to symbolize the student uprising of '68 because of the leading role he played and his subsequent deportation from France—in an interview given on French television (TF3) on 7 May 1978.

[17]Castoriadis takes for granted the arrogant scheme of western historiography: western civilization is the only direct and organic continuation of the ancient Greek tradition. Western philosophy, though it started from nothing more than a few books of Aristotle, translated from the Arabic at that, likes to consider itself unique in its direct line of development from pre-Socratic and post-Socratic philosophy. The "Hellenic" reading of the ancient Greek philosophers by the Byzantine commentators, and the organic assimilation of their thought in the dynamic synthesis of the Greek fathers— the ontological premises of that other civilization, diametrically opposed to the utilitarian "objectivity" of the westerners and its inhuman consequences— remains a closed book to Castoriadis.

THE FREEDOM OF MORALITY

constantly arising from both scientific research and historical experience which point to the "essential" indeterminacy of natural, historical and social "becoming." He concludes with the proposition that the objectification of the concept of being into a logical and intellectual identity, the identification of the existent with its definitive meaning or essence, should be replaced by an understanding of *being* as *becoming*. It is the tendency and movement of dynamic realization which constitutes being and which cannot be limited to a defined entitative identity, and therefore cannot be made subject to *a priori* principles and laws of conventional logic, but can be interpreted only with reference to the *imaginary element*, which is shaped in an indeterminate way through social coexistence, and at the same time constitutes the dynamic for transforming social life.

The socio-political and therefore "moral" consequences of Castoriadis' ontological theories certainly require extensive study and need to be confronted—although his views probably will be illustrated and worked out more fully in works still to be published. The extremely summary indication of his position here serves simply to introduce the following question: Does an "objective" or "holistic" or "general" theory of the dynamic indeterminacy of being really amount to transcendence of the static "objectivity" of western metaphysics? A holistic theory inevitably makes life subject to its own general and consequently schematic limits, even if it presupposes the dynamic indeterminacy of life and the freedom and distinctiveness which give rise to it. And the theory of the dynamic indeterminacy of life *is* holistic when there is no *hypostatic* bearer of this freedom and distinctiveness; that is to say, when freedom and distinctiveness are not an achievement but an objective datum. As for replacing the "entitative identity" of the structures of historical and social life with the indeterminate dynamism of the "imaginary element" which gives shape to those structures, the interpretation of *being* as *becoming*, is there not perhaps a danger that this may lead to a neo-Hegelism which makes the indeterminate "becoming" into a metaphysical absolute, and may at the same time force us to defer to or even mythologize the impersonal "dynamism" of the masses? And within this given dynamic indeterminacy of social and historical "becoming," what room is there for man's failure and "sin," for the egocentric way in which he fortifies himself in the secure forms of conventional identity, in the efficiency of objectified structures or in the authority of oversimplified mechanistic theories?

These questions, however, lead on to the area of enquiry which principally concerns us here, and which arises out of the connection between social and political ethics and ontology —and that enquiry takes us back to our initial question about the social ethic of the Orthodox Church.

5. The ontological fact of communion and its existential realization

The ethos of the Church is a communal or "social" ethos, and the communal ethos of the Church is identified with the ontological content of her truth, the truth of life as communion. Communion constitutes life; existence is an event of communion. The "cause" of existence and the "source" of life is not being-in-itself—being does not represent an absolute category *per se* but it is the divine, trinitarian communion which hypostasizes being as a fact of life. For the Church, communion is an *ontological* fact: not the consequence of the ontological fact, but a fact essential to being. The historical fact that people live together in groups and the phenomenology of what is called "communal" or "social" life—the political, social, economic and governmental organization of human groups—is only one expression of this fact.

Communion constitutes life; it also constitutes the ethos of life, the dynamic of life, the impetus and movement towards the realization of life. The phenomenon of what is called "communal becoming"—the historical or "objective" dimension of communion—expresses and indicates the ontological fact of communion, certainly; but it does not exhaust the *ethos* of communion, the *manner* in which life is existentially realized as communion. If we make the ontological fact of communion definitively objective in its historical, phenomenological dimension, we then remain bound by the metaphysics of conventional intellectual identities; we are simply putting the idea of "communion" in the place of the concept of being-in-itself as an entity.

If communion is an ontological fact and not an entitative, intellectual concept which objectifies the phenomenology of history, then this presupposes that it has a dynamic, existential realization—that there must be a *hypostatic* bearer of the potential for communion, which is every member of the communion or society. And the potential for communion assumes also a potential for non-communion, which is to say that it presupposes freedom as a definition of the fact of communality. In the same way, it assumes a differentiation in the potentialities for communion; each will participate in communion, in society, in a distinctive way. The dynamic, existential realization of communion—communion as an existential achievement and not as an "objective" datum—brings out the distinctiveness of the hypostasis bearing the potential for communion.

Thus freedom and distinctiveness *define* the ontological fact of communion; there is no communion unless participation in it is free and distinctive. And this is an *ethical* definition of the fact of communality: the realization of life as communion has an ethical dynamic indeterminacy irreconcilable with any definitive relation of identity, any schematic or legal predetermination of communion, because the fact of communality is defined by the freedom and distinctiveness of the members who *achieve* communion.

The dynamic indeterminacy of communal life, and the fact that freedom and distinctiveness are *ethical* coordinates for the ontological fact of communion, are not conclusions drawn from syllogisms or abstract principles which enable us to form a logical, holistic view of the given reality of history and society. Freedom and distinctiveness are the hypostatic realization of life, the existential fact of the person. The person is the hypostasis of the existential potentiality for life, for the life which is communion and relationship; but it also represents the hypostatic possibility of refusing communion and alienating life. The freedom of the person hypostasizes life, the ontological fact of communion. But it is freedom, an existential event of self-realization for the person, because the person is able also to negate itself; to put into effect, existentially, the rejection of life, the replacement of communion with individual survival and egocentric self-sufficiency, and the alienation of life into a conventional coexistence. This is a coexistence which simply puts a cloak of rationalism over the threat to individual survival represented by the "other's" independent claim for individual survival, the existential *distantness* of the "other's" hypostasis when it is individual and no longer in communion.

Only when it is seen in this way is communion not an objective datum, but a personal existential achievement of authentic life. The dynamic indeterminacy of communal "becoming" may present freedom and distinctiveness as notional "objective" coordinates for human coexistence; but this "objectivity" is simply an intellectual conception making an abstract composition out of historical data, while the real sphere in which freedom and distinctiveness are realized existentially, as an event of communion or a failure to attain communion, is the human person alone.

It is consequently contradictory to talk about an objectively applicable "communal" or "social ethic," since the ethical dimension of the fact of communion or society, its dynamic realization, is judged exclusively within the framework of personal freedom. Whenever the possibilities for ethical, dynamic realization of communion are taken outside the sphere of the personal existence which is the hypostatic bearer of these possibilities, this inevitably creates types of communion with no substantial, hypostatic basis; imaginary and abstract forms of communion alien to life and its existential realization. And when we try to impose these forms, alien as they are to life, by convention or compulsion, and to "create" communion "from above," setting our programmatic limits and rationalistic laws or using unsubstantiated canons of freedom or justice or other objective "values," then we are crippling life itself and tormenting mankind.

If by the term "social ethics," then, we mean a theory, a

THE FREEDOM OF MORALITY

program or a code which aims at an "objective" improvement in people's corporate life, an "objective" change in the structures and preconditions for their coexistence, and better regulation of the "objective" relationships which form people into organized groups—if these aims are pursued independently of personal distinctiveness and freedom, the sphere in which they are dynamically and existentially realized—then certainly so long as the Church remains faithful to her ontological truth she has no such ethics to display, nor could she come to terms with such an ethic.

It is hardly necessary to stress that *personal* existential realization of life as an event of communion does not in the least mean taking refuge in an individual or subjective ethic, and identifying the ethos or morality of human coexistence with the sum total of "virtues" achieved by the individuals living together: the difference between the *individual* and the *person* has been set out repeatedly in the preceding pages. Indeed, the very concept of an "individual" precludes the ontological view of the fact of communion: it confines being to the "closed" entitative identity of the existent being and its character as a phenomenon. This is why an individual ethic is not substantially different from a holistic ethic, an ethic of general rules and principles for the organization of corporate life. What we usually mean by the term "individual ethics" is nonetheless an "objective" ethic, an objectification of life within the framework of given evaluations of behavior —categories of behavior made into entities in themselves. The idea that by achieving a moral "improvement" in individuals we shall have a resultant moral improvement in corporate life, and the idea that achieving a moral "improvement" in the organization, structures and principles of corporate life results in individuals being "happy" and "moral," both assume the same phenomenological interpretation of life and its reality as communion. Such an interpretation bears no relation to the existential adventure of human freedom, or to the existential achievement of life as communion.

6. The communal dynamics of repentance

The Church is a fact of communion and a dynamic realization of communion. The Church's truth is the only ontology of the fact of communion, the ontology which identifies being with the person, that is to say, with the existential realization of life as communion. This realization is a dynamic ethical event. Communion for the Church is an ethical existential achievement. The truth of communion is the ethos, the "morality" of the Church. The ethic of the Church is a communal ethic, a social ethic.

The ontological content of the Church's communal ethos leaves no room for compromise with religious, political or ideological systems of ethics and social organization which distinguish the fact and the ethos of communion from its precondition of personal freedom, from the dynamic existential realization of communion in the framework of personal distinctiveness. It is a matter of incompatible ontologies, not merely incompatible value-judgments. For the Church, to treat freedom as a precondition for realizing the fact of communion is not a "principle" in her system of values. It is a presupposition for remaining faithful to the existential truth of man, to his true mode of existence. Every vision or aspiration that overlooks or violates personal freedom, even the vision of a "paradise" of universal happiness, is a denial of existential truth and consequently a distortion of life, a cause of alienation and torment for man.

The Church respects and values freedom not only as the realization of communion, but also in the form of personal failure to attain communion. Respect for man's failure to realize life as communion is respect for his freedom; it affirms freedom, not as a "value" and a legal "right," but as man's existential truth. And this affirmation of freedom has practical significance, because the Church accepts the sinner, the person who has failed, and transforms his failure into an event of communion through repentance. The ethical "paradox" of the Church, which makes her radically different from any system of ethics or social organization, is the way she renounces any

objective, evaluative precondition for the individual's participation in the community. Only the personal dynamics of love
can save freedom and form a communion out of failure to
attain communion. The event which constitutes the Church is
the dynamic act of taking man up, in his failure, and "grafting" that failure into the communion of saints; it is the
freedom of love, the "absurdity" of love which rejects every
rationalistic criterion for participation in the life of communion: "It receives the last even as the first; it shows mercy
to the last, and cares for the first. To the one it gives, and
upon the other it bestows freely. It accepts the works and
welcomes the endeavor: it honors the deed, and commends
the intention."[18]

7. The eucharistic starting-point for transformations in society

The social ethic of the Church aims neither at an "improvement" in the objective conditions and structures of
corporate life, nor yet at an "improvement" in the character
of individuals. Its aim is to enable life to operate in the
limitless scope of personal freedom, the freedom which can
be existentially realized only as an event of communion. This
one, unique criterion for the Church's ethos means overturning the conventional canons of moral behavior in the most
radical and revolutionary way: it signifies the dynamic indeterminacy of life once it is freed from slavery to objectivity
and individualism. By this criterion it is possible, in the framework of organized coexistence, for the endurance of tyranny,
injustice and oppression to be an achievement of freedom
and a realization of communion. In the same way, an uprising
against tyranny and oppression can also be an achievement of
self-denial and an extreme risk taken by love; an event, once
again, of freedom and communion.[19] The right and wrong

[18]Paschal Homily attributed to St John Chrysostom.

[19]In contemporary "political theology," desperate efforts are made to
formulate and justify objectively a "theology of revolution" which will
allow Christians living under restrictive and totalitarian regimes, particularly
in the third world, to engage actively and with "theological" backing in

in each case, the good and the evil, can be judged only by the measure of the realization of freedom, which is sacrificial self-transcendence and a struggle to attain communion.

The measure and standard for the communal ethos of the Church is illumined and embodied in the event which constitutes ecclesial communion—in the eucharist. The eucharist is life as communion—not an abstract life, but the precondition for earthly life which is food, that object of contention which tears life apart. Within the eucharist, partaking of daily nourishment is to partake in Christ's sacrifice, to partake in that death of individual demands and claims which raises life up into the miracle of communion. The bread and wine of the eucharist are the body and blood of Christ, the reality of His theanthropic nature—a participation and communion in His mode of existence. It is the first-fruits or leaven of life, for the transfiguration of every facet, every activity in human life into an opportunity for communion and an event of communion. As people live the sacrificial ethos of the eucharist, it suffuses economics, politics, professional life, the

the revolutionary liberation movements usually monopolized by Marxists. This need for an *a priori*, objective theological safeguard in taking personal moral risks is a typical mark and consequence of any holistic ethics. As an example of a different ethical mentality, one may consider the way Orthodox clergy took part in armed struggles for the liberation of the Balkan peoples in the nineteenth century. These were mainly Greek bishops, but also some priests and deacons, who took up arms and rose up with the people in 1821, often fighting as leaders of corps of soldiers. They even resorted to the use of armed force without having first assured their individual moral justification with passages of Scripture or some "theology of revolution." They knew quite well that violence was diametrically opposed to the truth of the Church and the ethos of the Church, and that according to the Church canons they were endangering the grace of priesthood bestowed on them and risking excommunication, risking the salvation of their souls. Yet what was paramount in their eyes was not their individual salvation but the salvation of the people, the liberation of its life from enslavement to tyranny—it was "we" and not "I," as Makriyannis characteristically puts it. They therefore did not care if they themselves would be "condemned." Their struggle was a feat of ultimate self-denial, an extreme risk taken out of love, an act of freedom and communion. For further information on modern "theology of revolution," see: H. E. Tödt, *Theologie der Revolution, Analysen und Materialien* (Frankfurt, 1968). J. G. Davies, *Christians, Politics and Revolution* (London, n.d.). J. Miguez-Bonino, *Doing Theology in a Revolutionary Situation* (Philadelphia, 1974). E. Feil and R. Weth, ed., *Diskussion zur Theologie der Revolution* (Munich/Mainz, 1969). G. Gutiérrez, *Theologie der Befreiung* (Munich/Mainz, 1973).

family and the structures of public life in a mystical way—
it acts with a dynamic indeterminacy beyond the reach of
objective predetermination. And it transfigures them—it
changes their existential presuppositions, and does not simply
"improve" them.

To be even more exact, the eucharist sums up a mode of
existence which finds its social realization in the asceticism
of the Church. As we have seen in a previous chapter,
asceticism is not an individual exercise of the will, nor a
masochistic attitude towards human needs and desires, but
an opportunity for communion and an act of communion. The
Church's asceticism aims at the subjection of individual, biological desires to the absolute primacy of personal relationship and communion. Experience of true communion among
human beings, like the encounter with the personal reason
and meaning in natural reality and the discovery of the personal God in history, requires the ascetic self-transcendence
of individuality and the reality of personal relationship and
self-offering.

One might venture to maintain, then, that asceticism, as a
social manifestation and practical application of the Church's
truth, represents also a radical moral, social and ultimately
political stance and action. Radical, because it directly and
actively undermines the holistic systems of individualistic
utilitarianism and their totalitarian mechanisms. These systems are not endangered by the revolutionary movements and
ideas which are contained with painstaking contrivance in
the same "logic" of systems. Holistic systems are endangered
only by the existential stance, the existential action which
gives absolute priority to achieving the *personal* truth of
man. Not to the "development" of the individual nor to the
education and "cultivation" of the social unity, but to the
achievement of personal distinctiveness: that distinctiveness
realized dynamically on the frontier between freedom and sin,
in the trial of self-transcendence in love, in discovering and
bringing out the personal reason and meaning in the reality
of the world, and in encountering the personal God revealed
through history.

This existential stance and action is a radical denial of the hypnotic illusions of consumer prosperity. It refuses to restrict its concern with political problems to the capitalist-marxist polarization,[20] to the issue of whether consumer needs should in principle be satisfied through competition or through state control. It refuses to imprison politics in the inhuman mechanization of the autonomous economy, and rejects the debauchery of industry over the living body of the world for the sake of consumer greed.

This is the stance and the action of the Orthodox tradition and of Orthodox life. It is the dynamics of social transformation embodied in the eucharistic community, the diocese or parish. When the diocese and the parish form a true ecclesial communion, this leads dynamically and organically to the transformation of mass coexistence into a communion of persons. It provides a basis for social justice which is genuine and not merely rationalistic; it liberates work from slavery to need, transforming it into a personal relationship, and it brings out each human being's creative distinctiveness. Through the correct functioning of the eucharistic community there is created a form of politics which serves the existential truth and authenticity of man, a form of science which gives reason and meaning to man's relationship with the world, and a form of economics which serves life rather than subjugating it.

8. The communal ethos of the eucharist and its cultural expression

In today's technocratic society, the network of rivalries between the international holders of big capital is taken for granted; the needs of production and consumption are autonomous, the development of machines carries all before it, and political power is inevitably totalitarian. Within this framework, it seems at least like romantic utopianism or poetic nostalgia to talk about the social dynamism of the eucharistic community. Even if historically that dynamism was once real-

[20]See Ch. Yannaras, "Études de théologie politique," *Contacts* No. 95 (1976/3).

ized to some extent, it still belongs quite definitely to the past.

Historically, it is true, the widespread influence of the Church's communal ethos—the social dynamism of the eucharistic community—does indeed seem to have been bound up exclusively with the rural or early urban stages of communal life. As a historical example of such influence, we probably have only Byzantium. Medieval western societies, dominated by the feudal system[21] and with extremely sharp class distinctions,[22] make it impossible for us to speak of the eucharistic community as dynamically extended throughout social life and culture. They were certainly societies organized on a religious basis, but had little or nothing to do with the primacy of personal distinctiveness and freedom which constitutes the eucharistic ethos of communion.[23] In Byzantium, by contrast,

[21]The feudal system was a product and a hallmark of western European societies, unknown in the Greek (or "Byzantine") East. It was not until the end of the seventeenth century that feudalism made its appearance in the East, in the Ottoman Empire, as a sign that economic and social organization was becoming westernized. "The idea of *Byzantium* is strictly irreconcilable with that of feudalism . . . The interminable struggle of central government against the great landlords has left its mark on the whole of Byzantine history . . . The absence of any formal social distinctions gave Byzantine administration a popular character which made it radically different from the stratified societies of the West . . . The Byzantine and Ottoman worlds alike considered any procedure for concentrating land ownership as *anti-social*": K. Vergopoulos, *The Agrarian Question in Greece* (in Greek—Athens, 1975), pp. 20, 26, 27, where the relevant bibliography is given.

[22]Bibliography on class distinctions in western societies includes: George Duby, *Adolescence de la chrétienté occidentale* (Geneva, 1967), p. 57ff. Robert Fossier, *Histoire sociale de l'Occident médiéval* (Paris, 1973). Jacques de Goff, *La civilisation de l'Occident médiéval* (Paris, 1972), pp. 319-386.

[23]The totalitarian character of religious organization in western medieval societies and the way they undervalued human personality is attested generally and without dispute by western historiography itself. It would suffice to call to mind just a few institutional expressions of this religious totalitarianism: the famous *Dictatus* of Pope Gregory VII (1073-1085), the principle of papal infallibility (*De Romani Pontificis infallibili magisterio*) founded on Thomas Aquinas' *Summa Theologiae*, the bull of Pope Gregory IX (1233) which instituted the Holy Inquisition, the introduction of torture as a method of interrogation in heresy trials by Pope Innocent IV (1252), etc. Furthermore, this religious totalitarianism was the breeding ground for the many forms of religious rebellion in modern European man, and also gave rise to the capitalist system which led religion decisively to lose its

we have a popular culture which reveals in its every expression and manifestation the absolute priority of the truth of the person, and a way of life which is articulated liturgically, becoming an event of personal communion.

This is not the place to show how, in Byzantine civilization, art, economics, politics and legislation all expressed the attitude of life and the communal ethos of the Church; how they preserved the liturgical understanding of the world and history and the creative "word" or reason in man's relationship with things, a reason which follows from the subordination of individual arbitrariness to the harmony and wisdom in the world.[24]

We may simply state the conclusion that, for a thousand years, Byzantium put into action the dynamic operation of eucharistic communion in the dimensions of the inhabited earth, the *oikoumene*. In Byzantium, the *oikoumene* takes on the mystical depth and dynamic meaning of the word *proslemma*, "that which has been assumed," as this term is used in the Christology of Chalcedon. The conceptual center of the *oikoumene* is the Church, the supreme manifestation of the Wisdom of God which created the world, the fulfilment in history and dynamic continuation of the event of God's incarnation, where He assumes the irrationality of natural man so as to transform it into a rational principle of relationship and communion, into the archetypal city, the Kingdom of God.

Within this process, there is a hard and fast distinction

vigor in western societies. Specifically on the roots of capitalist ideology in Roman Catholic scholasticism and particularly in Thomas Aquinas, see Werner Sombart, *Le Bourgeois. Contribution à l'histoire morale et intellectuelle de l'homme économique moderne* (Paris, 1966²), p. 226ff.

[24]To substantiate this view of Byzantine civilization, the following books may be mentioned: Steven Runciman, *Byzantine Style and Civilization* (Penguin Books, 1975). A. Gervase Mathew, *Byzantine Aesthetics* (London, 1963). Philip Sherrard, *Constantinople, Iconography of a Sacred City* (London, 1965). Dimitri Obolensky, "The Principles and Methods of Byzantine Diplomacy," *Actes du XIIe Congrès International d'Etudes Byzantines*, I (Belgrade, 1963), pp. 45-61. Hélène Ahrweiler, *L'idéologie politique de l'empire byzantin* (Paris, 1975). Louis Brehier, *Les institutions de l'Empire byzantin* (Paris, 1970). J. M. Hussey, *Church and Learning in the Byzantine Empire* (London, 1937). P. Charanis, "On the Social Structure of the Later Roman Empire," *Byzantion* 17 (1944-45), pp. 38-57.

between the beauty of personal life and communion and the irrational impulses of natural barbarism. But at the same time its scope is unlimited in that the rudeness and disorder of the hordes who are outside this communion have to be assumed and grafted into the liturgy of life. In every aspect of its historical and cultural life, Byzantium brought about the assumption of whatever is natural, irrational or common, transfiguring it into communion and sacred history and God-manhood—into the Church.

With the fall of Byzantium, the social dynamism of the eucharistic community did not disappear; it simply contracted from the bounds of the inhabited world to those of the social and cultural life of *Romiosyne,* the Christian people under the Ottoman yoke. For four whole centuries, local government, local justice, business and credit, associations and guilds in the Greek East under Turkish rule, functioned in a way that revealed a liturgical structure in the community, the priority of personal relationships and the pursuit of communal virtue. The liturgical structure of the enslaved Greek community was expressed with equal clarity in hospitality, popular song, dance, folk costume, architecture and iconography. All these manifestations of life and art serve to reveal a cultural level and ethos unattainable in later times, a real paradigm of social organization, and a rare sensitivity among the people, despite the absence of formal education.

It is the ethos of *personal* life and relationship, the total exclusion of any impersonal, rationalistic organization, which provides the basis for all aspects of social life. Nowadays we need to be exceptionally cultivated, and perhaps even to undertake special studies, in order to appreciate or even just to follow the amazing level of culture in that humiliated Hellenism. Yet we know that, at that time, this was not the level of a few experts but a general manifestation of popular sensitivity, down to the last village and monastery. The way community life operated during the Turkish occupation was born of the people's need and their virtue. It was the product of the people's ethos, not of theoretical, cerebral principles and axioms. Equally a product of the people's ethos was their completely original and genuine art, their song, their dancing, their costume and their festivals.[25]

The free ethos of enslaved *Romiosyne* remains ultimately a model for a social realization which respects personal uniqueness and manifests the liturgical unity of human co-existence. The high point of this unity is the festival. The life of the community becomes part of the eucharistic cycle of feasts in the Church's life, the daily triumph of the Church over the irrationality of time and corruption. The traditional Greek festival always centered on the Church's commemoration of a saint; it was always a feast-day. Round this ecclesial event, the people joined in fellowship, singing and dancing and eating together. Differences and misunderstandings melted away; people declared their love, and the foundations were laid for new families. To this day, no form of socialism nor any rationalistically organized popular movement has been able to restore this genuine dimension of the popular festival, or to respond fully to man's deep-seated need for festivals.

9. The sole program—reconstruction of the parish

Today, however, that social and cultural realization of the liturgical ethos of the Orthodox Church seems just a nostalgic memory. Yet before we conclude with certainty that the social dimension of the eucharistic community is in our day pure utopianism, there is one question which needs to be confronted. In modern times, we have seen a change in the structures and premises of social life; we have passed from the limited community of personal relationships to impersonal, mass coexistence, from creative work to automated production, and from personal need to artificially contrived consumer greed. Now does this radical alteration in man's

---

[25]See John Campbell and Philip Sherrard, *Modern Greece* (London, 1968), especially pp. 189-213. Steven Runciman, *The Great Church in Captivity* (Cambridge, 1968). Manouel Gedeon, *The Cultural Progress of the Nation in the Eighteenth and Nineteenth Centuries* (in Greek—Athens, 1976). Angeliki Chatzimichali, *The Guilds—the isnafia* (in Greek—Athens, 1950). *Eadem, Greek Folk Costume* (in Greek—Athens, ed. T. Yannaras, 1978). Dimitris Pikionis, "Our Popular Art and Ourselves" (in Greek) in *Filiki Etaireia* 4 (1925), p. 145ff.

way of life distort even the reality of the eucharistic synaxis of the faithful? Does it alienate or destroy the existential fact of personal communion in the body of the Church? Does it neutralize the dynamic extension of the eucharist into all other aspects of social life?

The appearance of the symptoms leaves no alternative but to answer in the affirmative. Yes; the consumer culture—the culture of mass media for news and entertainment, mass production systems, housing complexes for people to live together *en masse* and organized mass demands—has proved incomparably stronger than the culture and ethos of eucharistic communion. All the immediate evidence suggests that, at least in today's big cities, the eucharistic community too has been distorted into an impersonal, mass religious grouping. A parish contains thousands of people, often tens of thousands, and there is no personal communion or sense of being a body. People do not gather in the churches to constitute the body of the Church, to manifest and realize the true life of the communion of persons; they come to satisfy their individual religious needs and to pray as individuals, in parallel with the rest of the congregation, more alone perhaps than on the sportsground or at the cinema.

At the same time, it seems as if the axis and aim of the liturgy has been transfered away from participation in Christ's body and the approach to the cup of the unity of the faithful, and now consists in listening to a moralistic sermon offering prescriptions for social behavior. The sense of mystical unity, that unity which constitutes the Church's mode of existence and the salvation of man, is often so atrophied, even non-existent, that one wonders how far the eucharistic synaxis today still preserves the truth of the universal Church, the full possibility of life beyond corruption and death. Where the parish has been distorted, or substantially abolished and replaced by an organizational, impersonal understanding of the Church (or "Christianity") as a "religious" institution analogous to other conventional expedients of corporate life, this means that the Church loses her identity; there is a dangerous confusion in the preconditions for salvation, and the Church's communal ethos is deprived of its strength.

It is hard to imagine the possible cultural developments and the dynamic transformations in technologically advanced society if there were living liturgical communities present at its heart, if the leaven for social transformation—the eucharistic realization of the Church's communal ethos in the parish —had been preserved. The social and historical dimension of the Church's ethos is not a dimension of moral or ideological influence over the masses, rationalistically planned; it is a change in the way people live together, a change that is real and existential, and therefore defies objective definition. This change has its starting-point and its axis in the eucharistic body of the parish. The truth of the Church, the reality of salvation, the abolition of sin and death, the contradiction of the absurdity in life and in history, the dynamic adaptation of the organizational   structures of corporate life to personal distinctiveness and freedom—all these are the eucharist incarnate in the body of the parish. The liturgical unity of the faithful, under whatever conditions and in whatever institutions, networks and structures, is the starting-point for the transformation of mass coexistence into a communion of persons, a society; for the achievement of social justice and not merely a program for it; and for liberating work from slavery to mechanized necessity and transforming it into a personal relationship, an event of communion. Only the life of the eucharistic body of the parish can give flesh to the formal idea of the "priestly" character of politics, the prophetic character of science, the philanthropic character of economics and the mystical character of the family. Without the parish, all this is theory, naive idealism and a romantic utopia. Within the parish it becomes a historical reality, an immediate possibility and a concrete experience.

It seems today that institutionalized church organizations are totally subject to the culture of "externals," the culture of utilitarianism and efficiency, of individual logic and individual ethics; but this does not mean that the ethos of eucharistic communion is impracticable within the framework of modern social life, any more than the alienation of sexual love in the same society means that people are quite incapable of being truly in love. The eucharistic ethos is not being put into practice and manifested in society today, but it would be arbitrary to infer from this that such an ethos cannot possibly achieve existential realization. Precisely by virtue of the existential dynamism of the eucharistic ethos, we are enabled to discern the personal weakness of those who represent it today, and their failure to realize and manifest its social consequences.

It is not an "objective" factor, then—the passage from a rural society to a technological one or the particular way in which modern "developed" societies are structured—which prevents the eucharistic ethos from being realized in society. No objective fact can cancel out the existential possibility for life to be realized in personal ways. Only a deliberate betrayal of these possibilities—man's *sin,* his failure to realize his personal distinctiveness and freedom—can explain why the Christian churches today are historically mute in the realm of social affairs. This does not mean that we should overlook the great personal trial faced by each Christian within the framework of our modern consumer way of life, in a culture which corresponds almost exclusively to man's impersonal, instinctive nature—to his autonomous need to possess, to find sensual enjoyment and to forget his mortality.

If, even in isolated cases, some bishops decided to return to the eucharistic truth and identity of the Church, which would mean restructuring the parish as a body with organic unity, then the historical and social dimension of the Church's ethos would not be slow to make its appearance in culture, being realized in quite specific ways. These would be living realizations, and consequently could not be determined objectively or *a priori;* and they would come about even amidst the all-powerful economic and political networks which dominate modern life. Restructuring of the parish means in the first instance local eucharistic communities of strictly limited size, so that communion and relationship amongst the faithful and between them and their pastor is a real possibility. But this is not all. The eucharistic community is not simply an arithmetical unit of a size which permits direct personal acquaintance and contact. It is first and foremost a community of life; it involves a dynamic sense of being a body, and a certain faith in the truth of the "true life" which is communion in love and self-offering, a realization of the trinitarian prototype of life. Concealed behind the present destruction of the parish through its enlargement is the individualism of the cultural framework of our life, the pietistic concept of individualized salvation.

Ultimately, however, even a mere reduction in the size of parishes could be a first step towards awareness of the eucharistic truth of the Church, and the starting-point from which we could eventually reach a practical theological consciousness of ourselves as a eucharistic community. All it would need is for some bishops to take the risk, and realize that without eucharistic communities gathered into a body of communion, they themselves hold merely the title and not the position of bishop. They are then mere administrative officials, however exalted, in a conventional institution which has no essential justification, despite the many "charitable foundations" that they may organize.

Having eucharistic communities of limited size inevitably means that parishes multiply, and may mean the gradual disappearance of the professional priesthood. A suitable member of the eucharistic community can receive the grace of priesthood and take on the duties of pastor, while continuing to make his living from his private profession. Undoubtedly the professional priesthood has certain advantages for church life; but especially in today's social environment of secularism, the departure from it might help us significantly in extricating ourselves from the idea of the Church as a conventional institution with a professional hierarchy "to serve the religious needs of the people." The loss of a professional clergy, so far from hindering a return to the eucharistic basis of church life, is actually of primary importance for the social dynamism of the Church today. It would help to free the church organization from the mentality and the restrictions of an "institution" subject to relations of economic dependence and canons of professional behavior. Once the presbyter of the eucharistic synaxis ceases to make his living from serving as a priest, then he expresses nothing other than the truth and experience of his liturgical community; he is not the professional representative of an institutionalized organization which gives him financial support. Priesthood rediscovers its charismatic character, and the eucharistic community its missionary dynamism.[26]

There is always, of course, a host of ready objections based on the practical difficulties of returning to the eucharistic hypostasis of the Church and reconstituting the small parish. But our attempt to deal with the problem cannot stop at the difficulties, whatever they may be, since this is a question of the truth of the Church, of man's salvation from the tyranny of the irrational and from death. Restoration of the eucharistic community as the central axis of the Church's life undoubtedly means repudiating the centralized institutionalization of the Church as an organization which today is taken for granted, and this is no easy task: it means that we really have to abrogate the facilities afforded by the "Vaticanization" of the Church.[27] The reconstitution of the eucharistic community, however, is not just one of the many problems facing the Church, albeit the most serious. Prior to any problem, it is the very precondition for the true existence of the Church; it is faithfulness to the gospel of salvation, the practical

[26]This experiment has begun to be carried out under pressure of immediate necessity in some parishes of the Orthodox diaspora, mainly in Europe where the small number of parishioners cannot maintain a priest financially so that he is not distracted by the cares of earning a living. Thus people qualified in widely differing fields carry on their personal professions in order to maintain their families, and look after their parishes at the same time. The results of this experiment have been exceptionally positive, especially when the break with professional priesthood is accompanied by a lively theological awareness of the priest's duty. Nevertheless, all we have said here about restricting or abolishing the professional priesthood is only one aspect of the problem: undoubtedly, a real priest and father of his parish who does not have some other occupation in order to maintain his family has less distraction and is more dedicated to God than a real priest who does.

[27]"Vaticanization" of the Church means that the center of her life is transfered from the eucharistic synaxis to the institutional dimension of her organization. The symptoms of this transference are a supreme "staff" of titular bishops, archbishops and metropolitans deprived of episcopal functions in the church body, staff officers with "specialist" clergy, successive celebrations of the eucharist in the same church on the same day, or celebration of the eucharist for certain social classes or organizations only, etc. See John Zizioulas, "La continuité avec les origines apostoliques dans la conscience théologique des Eglises Orthodoxes," Istina 1/1974, pp. 85-87.

proclamation of the truth of salvation. Once it is understood that the eucharistic theological self-awareness of the Church and its incarnation in the parish community are thus absolutely primary, then no difficulty can prevent the problem being faced and solved.

The communal ethos of the Church is not an abstract ethical theory, nor a system of values codified into command-mends. It is the fact of the eucharist and its extension to the universal dimensions of life, the dynamic realization of personal distinctiveness and freedom in the context of the encounter between human effort and divine grace.

CHAPTER TWELVE

The Ethos of Liturgical Art

1. Worship, art and technology

When the eucharistic community becomes once again the axis of the Church's life, this leads to a rediscovery of the communal character and ethos of liturgical art. The ontological content of the eucharist—eucharistic communion as a mode of existence—assumes that the communal reality of life has a cosmological dimension: it presupposes matter and the use of matter, which is to say *art*, as the creative transformation of matter into a fact of relationship and communion.[1] Man's art, the way he takes up the world and uses it, is a basic element in life, whether it brings about the alienation of life, or makes it incorruptible and raises it to an existential fulness of personal distinctiveness and freedom.

An idealistic ethic, unrelated to matter and art, is incapable

[1]The Greek word τέχνη, "art," is "the science of fashioning anything," "the fashioning of the work" and "concerned with making, involving a true course of reasoning," according to Aristotle (*Nicomachean Ethics* 6, 4). It comes from the word τεύχω which means to build, to be the builder of a work, to create, to give "reason" to matter. See Pierre Chantraine, *Dictionnaire Étymologique de la langue grecque*, vol. IV, part 1 (Paris, 1877), p. 1111. Cornelius Castoriadis, *Les carrefours du labyrinthe* (Paris, 1978), pp. 222-223: "The Greek word τέχνη goes back to a very ancient verb, τεύχω (attested exclusively but innumerable times by the poets . . .) whose central meaning in Homer is "to make," "to produce," "to construct"; τεῦχος—"tool," "implement"—is also the implement *par excellence*: arms. Already in Homer the shift was accomplished from this meaning to that of causing, of making something to be, of bringing into existence, often detached from the idea of material fabrication, but never from that of the suitable and effective act."

of expressing the ontological ethos of ecclesial communion. We understand this when we look at the organic identification of art with worship in the context of the eucharist. The worship of the Church is art: it is the work of a *communal* use of material reality, building and shaping the earth's material so as to render it capable of serving life, that existential fulness of life which is communion and relationship. And the Church's art is worship; it is not merely decorative, but manifests and highlights the "rational" potentialities of matter, the harmony of praise formed by the "words" or inner principles of created things when they are serving the eucharistic event of communion. The "true life" of the eucharist operates and is celebrated within the given realities of nature. The Church's liturgical time—the daily, weekly and annual festive cycles—and her liturgical space—the way the church as a dimensional entity is articulated through architecture and painting—are elements as essential for the operation of the eucharist as the bread and wine of the mystery; they are the direct link between the salvation of life and the function of eating and drinking.

For the man of the modern technological age, however, use of the world, that is to say, life as art and the construction of the personal event of communion, has altogether lost the immediacy of a relationship. Technology now comes between man and the world, replacing the personal attainment of art with the impersonal product of the machine. Of course, the organic cord connecting man with the world, the function of eating and drinking, has not been lost. But food has ceased to sum up man's participation in the life of the world, to sum up man's art or skill, his direct relationship with the materials of life and the way he creatively transforms them into a potential for life. In a rural society, the craftsman and tradesman as well as the peasant would earn their living by their art or skill, by the way in which they encountered the natural or social potentialities of life, the potentialities for serving life in natural matter itself. In that society, man knew the demands, the resistances, the behavior of the material; and to say that he knew nature means that he *respected* it. His life and his art were a study of the world, an expression of respect for the world. With his body and his art he studied the life of the world, not doing it violence but taking part in it, in harmony with the natural rhythm of life—birth, growth, fruition, decay and death, the changing seasons and the whole working of creation.

Today the majority of people in "developed" societies partake only indirectly in the life of the world. In a large modern city life is organically severed from the reality of nature, completely isolated in a rhythm of its own which is unrelated, even contrary to the natural flow of life and subject to the conditions imposed on it by the rationalistic organization of corporate life. Man knowns how to use machines but not how to use the world; he earns his bread by technology, not by his art. This is why it is impossible for bread and wine to represent for urban man the summing up of life, the life and work of a whole year with four seasons, a year of sowing and harvest, subject to weather and winds. The church texts bring him images from a different experience of life: "And as this bread was scattered over the mountains, and was gathered together and became one, so let Thy Church be gathered together from the ends of the earth into Thy Kingdom." For modern man these are all beautiful poetic images, but they are not his life. His own bread is hygenically packaged and displayed in the supermarket windows beside the jams and the packets of frozen vegetables. Bread is no longer of central importance for his life; other foods have taken first place. And the consumption of food connects man's life not with the productive *principle* in nature as it is revealed within the relationship created by an art or craft, but with the way in which the "relations of production" become a matter of purely human rival claims. Consumption makes life subject to impersonal networks of economic, trade union or political mechanisms, autonomous and unrelated to any reverence for the principle or reason in natural reality.

2. **The asceticism of art and the art of *ascesis***

In the realm of worship, then, the crucial problem of

modern life is summed up. How can life operate once again
in the dynamic dimension of a communal use of the world?
How can technology rediscover the ethos of art and serve the
authenticity of life, the communal realization of man's personal distinctiveness and freedom through his use of the
world? How can the eucharistic mode of existence even
today reconcile the rationalism of technology with a reverence
for the inner principle or reason in created things, and do
away with the pollution and rape of nature, the debauchery
of industry over the living body of the world?

There are certainly no answers to these questions which
could serve as objective rules or formulae laying down how
life should be organized. If there are answers, they will
emerge organically once our life is worked out in the right
way, and to this end eucharistic liturgy and art can guide us
in a dynamic fashion. What must be made clear first and
foremost is that the eucharist of the Church loses any ontological content and turns into a conventional outlet for religious feelings once the bread and wine of the mystery are
turned into abstract symbols, and cease to sum up the cosmic
dimensions of life as a communal event.

If we accept that man's relationship with God is not simply
intellectual, nor in a legalistic sense "moral," but necessarily
involves his use of the world, then the Gospel truth of salvation is being undermined by the way modern man is cut off
from *ascesis,* from the practical study of natural reality and
respect for it, and is isolated in the autonomous self-sufficiency
of technology. Even from the earliest years, the Church has
used every means to defend her truth against the danger of
being turned into an abstract, intellectual system of metaphysics or a legal code of utilitarian deontology. In every
heresy, she has perceived above all the primacy of an individual, intellectual understanding of her truth, and ignorance
or neglect of the experiential immediacy with which the
Church lives the event of salvation. The Christ of the heresies
is a moral paradigm of the perfect man, or else an abstract
idea of a disincarnate God. In both cases, man's life is not
substantially changed in any way: his existence is condemned
either to annihilation along with his body in the earth, or

else to an immortality necessary *by nature,* while individual or collective "improvements" in human life turn out to be fraudulent and senseless, or else a naked deception.

In the period of the ecumenical councils, the Church stood out against the intellectual forms of the heresies in order to preserve the cosmic universality of her eucharistic hypostasis, the salvation embodied in the bread and wine of the eucharist. She stood for the salvation of man's body, not merely his "spirit," from the absurdity of death; she stood for the belief that it is possible for the humble material of the world—the flesh of the earth and of man—to be united with the divine life, and, corruptible though it is, to put on incorruption. It took centuries of striving before language was able to subdue the arbitrariness of individual logic and to express the dynamics of life as revealed by the incarnation of the Word. And, side by side with the language, there was the artist's struggle to speak the same truth with his brush, not schematically or allegorically, but imprinting in design and color the glory of man's flesh and the flesh of the world made incorruptible. Then there was also the formative song of the architect who makes stone and clay into "word," giving them reason and meaning; and in his building the One who is uncontainable is contained, He who is without flesh is made flesh, and the entire creation and the beauty of creation are justified. And, besides these, there was the hymn of the poet and the melody of the musician, an art which subjugates the senses instead of being subjugated by them, revealing in this subjection the secret of life which conquers death.

Thus man's separation from the asceticism of art and the art of *ascesis*—the practical encounter with the potentialities for salvation in the flesh of man and of the world—and his isolation in the individualistic self-sufficiency provided by technology leads to a "religious" alienation of the Church's truth, to the Christ of the heresies—a moral paradigm of perfect man, or an abstract idea of disincarnate God.

A eucharistic use of the world certainly does not preclude technology, the use of technical means; on the contrary, any form of ascetic art always requires highly developed technical skill. However much technology develops it does not

altogether cease to be a "rational" use of the world, a use
with reason and meaning. But the problem begins as soon as
this "rationality" is restricted to man's individual intellectual
capacity and ignores or violates the principle of the intrinsic
beauty of the natural material; as soon as man's use of the
world serves exclusively to make him existentially autonomous, and proudly to cut him off from the rhythm of the
life of the world. What we now call technocracy is technology
made absolute, or, better, the ethos which accompanies a
certain technological use of the world. It does not aim to
serve life as communion and personal relationship, and therefore ignores also the *personal* dimension of the world, the
manifestation of God's personal energy in the world. It is
geared towards man's greed as a consumer, his instinctive need
to acquire possessions and to enjoy himself.[2]

If the autonomous operation of capital—of absolute individual or corporate interests—did not make human beings
subject to the mechanized necessity for production, and if
machines served the communal reality of life, the personal,
responsible and creative participation of every worker in

[2]The ethos expressed by modern technocracy does not cease to be a
derivative of human nature, of the existential adventure of man's freedom.
So the ascetic knowledge of man, the empirical exploration of the mysterious
depths of man's rebellion by the saints and wise men of the desert, has
also described the ethos of technocracy with astounding clarity, at a time
when the problem of that ethos could be posed only on a very small
scale. St Isaac the Syrian writes, characteristically: "When knowledge follows the desire of the flesh, it brings with it these tendencies: wealth,
vanity, adornment, rest for the body, and eagerness for the wisdom of that
logic which is suitable for the administration of this world; it is constantly making new discoveries both in skills and in knowledge, and abounds
also in everything else that is the crown of the body in this visible world.
As a result of this, it comes to oppose faith ... for it is stripped of any
concern for God, and makes the mind irrational and powerless, because it
is dominated by the body. Its concern is wholly confined to this world ...
It thinks that everything is in its own care, following those who say that
the visible world is not subject to any direction. Yet it is unable to
escape from continuing concern and fear for the body. So faintheartedness
and sorrow and despair take hold of it ... and worry about illnesses, and
concerns about wants and lack of necessities, and fear of death ... For it
does not know how to cast its care onto God, in the assurance of faith
in Him. It therefore engages in contrivances and trickery in all its affairs.
When its contrivances are ineffectual for some reason, it does not see the
secret providence, and fights the people who are obstructing and opposing
it": *Mystic Treatises* 6, pp. 256-257.

production, then their use could perhaps be as much a liturgical and eucharistic act as sowing, harvesting or gathering grapes. But anything of that kind requires a particular ethos in man, a definite attitude on man's part towards the material world and its use. The eucharistic use of the world and its relationship with man's technical accomplishments find a complete *communal* model in the case of ecclesial or liturgical art. So perhaps the most substantial contribution that theological ethics can make to solving the problems created by modern technocracy should be to study the ethos of church art—or, more precisely, to study how the problem of technology is posed, and what ethos is expressed by the technology, the technique of liturgical art.

3. The ethos of ancient Greek and Gothic architecture

Architecture is probably the art which gives us the most opportunities to approach our theme. The reader must forgive us for inevitably confining ourselves to general observations and preliminary explanations.[3]

The first characteristic one might note in the architecture of the "Byzantine" church, as we now call it, is respect for the building materials; an attempt to manifest the inner principle of the material, the "rational" potentialities of matter, and to bring about a "dialogue" between the architect and his material. But what do these statements mean in terms of the actual technique of church construction? To find the

---

[3]There are to my knowledge no works on the theological view and interpretation of Orthodox church architecture. Perhaps unique of its kind is Gervase Mathew's *Byzantine Aesthetics* (London, 1963). For this chapter, I have made use of the following limited bibliography: P. A. Michelis, *An Aesthetic Approach to Byzantine Art* (Athens, 1946; Eng. trans. London, 1955); Marinos Kalligas, *The Aesthetics of Space in the Medieval Greek Church* (Athens, 1946); Erwin Panofsky, *Gothic Architecture and Scholasticism* (Latrobe, 1951); Olivier Clément, *Dialogues avec le Patriarche Athénagoras* (Paris, 1969), pp. 278-283. Ch. Yannaras, "Teologia apofatica e architettura byzantina," in *Symposio Cristiano* (Milan, 1971), pp. 104-112; idem, "Scholasticism and Technology," *Eastern Churches Review* 6.2 (1974), pp. 162-169.

answer, we shall inevitably have to resort to comparisons, setting the Byzantine building side by side with ancient Greek classical architecture and medieval Gothic.

In ancient Greek architecture, the building material is subjugated to a given "principle" or "reason" which the craftsman wishes to serve and manifest. Matter *per se* is non-rational; it is formlessness and disorder until reason forms it into being and life. Reason gives form to matter; it brings everything together and leads it to the harmony and unity of the "cosmos," because the reason or principle of a being means that it takes its place in the universal unity of the world, and becomes subject to the laws of cosmic harmony and order which differentiate life and existence from disorder and chaos.[4] These are given laws; they are the logical and ethical necessity of life. The architect's task is to decode them, to reveal them through the reason or principle in his construction. It is to demonstrate the "rational" relationships which ensure harmony and unity, in other words the ethical potential of life; and ultimately to teach how the initial formlessness can be turned into a world, a "cosmos," "beautiful indeed," and the initial group of people living together can be turned into a city under the same laws of cosmic harmony and the ethical potentialities of life.[5]

[4] "This ontological monism which characterizes Greek philosophy from its inception leads Greek thought to the concept of the 'cosmos,' that is, of the harmonious relationship of existent things among themselves ... Greek thought creates a wonderful concept of the world, that is, of unity and harmony, a world full of interior dynamism and aesthetic plenitude, a world truly 'beautiful' and 'divine.' However, in such a world it is impossible for the unforeseen to happen or for freedom to operate: whatever threatens cosmic harmony and is not explained by 'reason' (*logos*) which draws all things together and leads them to this harmony and unity, is rejected and condemned": J. Zizioulas, "From Prosopeion to Prosopon," pp. 289-290.

[5] "Against the world of chaos and fate, Doric thought opposes order and the victory of the intellect ... The Parthenon is not merely a joy to the eye, it is also ethical beauty. With the strict calculation of its architecture and the harmonious equilibrium of its masses, its inner ethical system receives tangible expression. Its meaning is that life is subject to the aims set forth by a soldier mind. It is a chart of all the values in the Greek world: a heroic symphony of athletic virtues, an ethical ascesis. The severe outward form is nothing other than the tangible expression of inner obedience": Markos Augeris, "Mysticism in Greek art" (in Greek), in *Greek Critical Thought—A Selection*, ed. Z. Lorentzatos (Athens, 1976), pp. 120-121.

Ancient Greek architecture succeeds in imprinting the
laws of cosmic harmony on a building by making its construction technique obey the "principle" of proportion in size.
The parts of the ancient Greek temple are measured mainly
by the "rule of proportions." The architect uses his material
in order to form perfect proportions, and thus achieve a
flawless rationalistic harmony which reveals and teaches the
beautiful as symmetrical perfection. Typical of the absolute
priority of the given proportions is the fact that when an
ancient Greek temple is doubled in size, all its dimensions are
doubled accordingly. The dimensions of its door and steps
and all its parts are doubled so that the basic proportions
remain the same, even though the door then becomes excessive
and need only be half the size for a man to pass through it
comfortably, and the steps become so large that they are
almost impossible to climb. The over-riding priority is to
preserve the harmony of proportions *per se,* regardless of
what sizes are necessary. The point of reference is the mind
of the observer; it is this that the craftsman wishes to delight
and instruct by the harmony of the proportional relationships
in his work.[6]

The same subjection of the material to an *a priori* logical
conception is again expressed with remarkable technical competence by Gothic medieval architecture. In a Gothic building,
the craftsman is not concerned with the inner principle of the
building material; his aim is not to study this inner principle,
to coordinate and reconcile it with the inner principle of his
own creative will, bringing out the material's potentiality to
embody the personal activation of the principle in created
things. On the contrary, he subjugates the material to given
forms, squaring off the stone and doing violence to its static
balance, so as to fulfil the ideological aim envisaged by the
construction. This ideological aim is externally and arbitrarily
set; it bears no relation to the study of the material and the
struggle of construction. It is an objectified knowledge which
the craftsman simply takes up in his work in order to analyse
it into particular notions.[7]

[6]See Michelis, *An Aesthetic Approach . . .*, pp. 35-36.
[7]"Like the High Scholastic *Summa,* the High Gothic Cathedral . . .

The ideological aim of Gothic architecture is to create an impression of the authority of the visible body of the Church, an authority which exerts influence and imposes itself not only through its absolute monopoly in handling God's wishes and revelations, but also through the palpable and immense majesty of the way it is articulated as an organization. Organizational structure creates both the principle of the western Church's unity and the rationalistically secured static balance of Gothic architecture. This is not an organic unity of distinctiveness in principles, the unity which brings about communion as an achievement and a gift of personal distinctiveness and freedom. Instead, it is a uniform submission to given rules and preconditions for salvation or for static balance. It is the theanthropic nature or essence of the Church embodied in the authority of the church organization, which is treated as prior to the personal event of salvation, to the personal gifts of the life conferred by the Holy Spirit, and to the transfiguration of man, the world and history in the person of God the Word incarnate and the persons of the faithful.

In his study on Gothic architecture and scholastic thought, Erwin Panofsky[8] has pointed to the common attitude and the attempt to explore truth intellectually which characterizes both scholastic thought and Gothic architecture,[9] and to the exact chronological correspondence between the evolution of the two:[10] "It is a connection . . . more concrete than a mere

sought to embody the whole of Christian knowledge, theological, moral, natural and historical . . . In structural design, it similarly sought to synthesize all major motifs handed down by separate channels and finally achieved an unparalleled balance": Panofsky, *Gothic Architecture . . .*, pp. 44-45. Cf. Auguste Choisy, *Histoire de l'architecture*, vol. II (Paris, 1899), pp. 260 and 265. Also Georges Duby, *L'Europe des Cathédrales* (Geneva, 1966), p. 40: "The calculation of the mathematicians secured the means of giving reality to these rational constructions . . . The universe ceases to be an ensemble of signs where the imagination gets lost; it is the clothing of a logical form which it is the cathedral's mission to restore by putting in their place all visible creatures."

[8]See above, n. 3.

[9]P. 27f. See also Duby, *L'Europe des Cathédrales*, p. 106: "The new cathedral appears . . . more concerned about a dialectical analysis of structures. It aims at the rational clarity of scholastic demonstrations."

[10]". . . this astonishingly synchronous development . . . ," p. 20; cf. p. 3ff. Also M.-D. Chenu, *Introduction à l'étude de Saint Thomas d'Aquin*

'parallelism' and yet more general than those individual 'influences' which are inevitably exerted on painters, sculptors or architects by erudite advisors: it is a real relationship of cause and effect."[11] Gothic architecture is the first technological application of scholastic thought, following it directly both in time and in substance: it is the technique which sets out in visible form the scholastic attempt to subject truth to the individual intellect, the new structure for a logical organization of truth introduced by scholastic theology. In the thirteenth century, for the first time in the history of human learning, the formulation and development of a truth is arranged systematically, with a variety of divisions. A complete work is divided into books, the books into chapters, the chapters into paragraphs and the paragraphs into articles. Each assertion is established by systematic refutation of the objections, and progressively, phrase by phrase, the reader is propelled towards a full intellectual clarification of a given truth.[12] It is "a veritable orgy of logic," as Panofsky says of Thomas Aquinas' *Summa Theologiae*.[13]

Correspondingly, the technique of Gothic architecture is based on a structure of small chiselled stones of uniform shape. The stones form columns, and the columns are divided into ribbed composite piers, with the same number of ribs as those in the vaulting which receives them.[14] The arrangement of the columns and the division of the ribs create an absolutely fixed "skeleton plan" which neutralizes the weight

(Paris, 1974), pp. 51-60, where he concludes: "Theology is the first great technique of the Christian world . . . The men who built the cathedrals [also] constructed *summae*." This is affirmed also by Jacques Maritain, *Les degrés du savoir* (Paris, 1932), p. 583.

[11]P. 20. See also Duby, *L' Europe des Cathédrales*, p. 105: "These monuments inscribed in inert matter the thought of the professors, their dialectical ramblings. They demonstrated Catholic theology."

[12]". . . the construction of a knowledge within the faith. From this theology is established as a science": M.-D. Chenu, *La théologie comme science au XIIIe siècle*, p. 70. "The first preoccupation of every bishop in his cathedral . . . was to place the Christian faith beyond uncertainty and the obscurity of prelogical thought, to construct a spacious doctrinal edifice, varied but firmly ordered, to show to the people convincing deductions in it": Duby, *L' Europe des Cathédrales*, p. 9.

[13]*Op. cit.*, p. 34.

[14]See Michelis, *An Aesthetic Approach . . .* pp. 89-90.

of the material by balancing the thrusts of the walls. Here again, the thesis is reinforced by systematic refutation of the antithesis, "the supports prevail over the weights placed on them," and the weight of the material is neutralized by the rationalistically arranged static balance.

This technique conceals "a profoundly analytic spirit, relentlessly dominating the construction. This spirit considers the forces, analyzes them into diagrams of statics and petrifies them in space,"[15] forming a unity which is not organic but mechanical, a monolithic framework. "Our sense of stability is satisfied but amazed, because the parts are no longer connected organically but mechanically: they look like a human frame naked of flesh."[16] It is technology, human will and logic, which subdues matter. The structure manifests the intellectual conception and will of the craftsman rather than the potentialities of the material—the moral obedience of matter to spirit, not the "glory" of matter, the revelation of God's energies in the inner principle of material things.[17]

Finally, Gothic architecture and the structure of scholastic thought alike restrict the possibility of experiencing truth exclusively to the intellectual faculty, logical analysis and emotional suggestion. This is why both these instances of "technique" leave us with the feeling of an inability to transcend the bounds of individual existence; we remain predetermined by the capacities of our individual nature, with no *personal* room left for the unforeseen, for freedom—a feeling that there is no escape. "In the Gothic form, excess and immensity are characteristic," says Worringer; "and this is due to the passion for seeking deliverance, a passion which finds an outlet in intoxication, vertigo and emotional ecstasy."[18] The endeavor of Gothic architecture is to elicit an emotional response by demonstrating intellectually the antithesis of

[15]Michelis, p. 90.

[16]Michelis, p. 90. Michelis refers also to Worringer, *Formprobleme der Gotik* (Munich, 1910), p. 73.

[17]On the particular relationship between Gothic architecture and the cosmology evolved by the theologians of the medieval West, and the relationship between this cosmology and modern technocracy, see *The Person and Eros* §§ 34, 35.

[18]*Formprobleme der Gotik*, pp. 113 and 50; quoted in Michelis, p. 40.

natural and supernatural, human smallness and the transcendent authority, the power from on high.[19]

"Gothic art," observes Choisy,[20] "operates with antitheses, contrasting with the plains the elevation of its perpendicular lines and enormous spires." What we have here is not simply an aesthetic or proportional contrast, however, but an anthropocentric tendency, a demand for the earthly to be elevated to the transcendent. The union of created and uncreated is not here regarded as a *personal* event, as the transformation of man, the world and history in the person of God the Word incarnate. It is an encounter between two *natures,* with human nature clothed in the dignity and transcendent majesty of the divine nature—which is exactly what happens with papal primacy and infallibility, and with the totalitarian centralization of the Roman Catholic Church. "The vaulted construction of a Gothic church desires, and tends, to give the impression of a monolithic framework"[21]—it is the image that the Roman Catholic West has of the Church. Approaching the divine presupposes in this context a comparison between human smallness and the grandeur of divine authority, an authority tangibly expressed by its monolithic, unified and majestic organization and its administrative structure. The Church is not the world in the dimension of the Kingdom, the harmonization of the inner principles of created things with the affirmation of human freedom in Christ's assumption of worldly flesh; but it is the visible, concrete potentiality for the individual to submit to divine authority. This is why in a Gothic church the material is not "saved," it is not "made

[19]"It was nevertheless the art of the Gothic cathedrals which, in the whole of Christendom, then became the instrument—perhaps the most effective one—of Catholic repression": Duby, *L'Europe des Cathédrales*, p. 72. Direct experience alone can justify and verify these conclusions. In the cathedrals of Cologne, Milan or Ulm, and other European cities, anyone with experience of the theology and art of the Eastern Church can see the justification for the "rebellion" of the Reformation and for the various ways in which man revolts against this transcendent authority which is expressed with such genius in architecture: it is an authority which humiliates and degrades human personhood and even ultimately destroys it. Revolt is inevitable against such a God, who consents to encounter man on a scale of such crushing difference in size.
[20]*Histoire de l'architecture*, vol. II, p. 414.
[21]Michelis, pp. 52-53.

word" and it is not "transfigured": it is subdued by a superior
force. To use specialized terminology once again: "The supports prevail over the weight placed on them . . . the vaulting
with its supple formation clearly shows that it concentrates
there all the action in the forces, and compels matter to rise
up to the heights."[22] This *compulsion* of matter in Gothic
architecture represents a technology which leads straight to
contemporary technocracy.[23]

4. The ethos of technology in Byzantine building

We have referred at such length to Gothic architecture
in order to elucidate by comparison a prime characteristic of
"Byzantine" architecture which we mentioned at the start: its
respect for the construction material and its endeavor to bring
out the "inner principle" in the material, "rational" potentialities of matter—to effect a "dialogue" between the architect
and his material.

Contrary to what we have said about Gothic art, the
Byzantine architect seems free and untrammelled by any *a priori*
ideological aim. This does not mean that he is unclear in his
purpose: he too is trying to build the "Church," to manifest
her truth, the space in which she lives, and not merely to
house the gathering of the faithful. For the Byzantine, however, the point is precisely this: the truth of the Church is
neither a set ideological system whereby we ascend by analogy
to the transcendent—the excessive or the immense—nor a
majestic organization with an authoritatively established administrative structure which mediates between man and God.
The Church for the Byzantine is the event of the eucharist,
the participation of what is created in the true life, the
trinitarian mode of communion and relationship. And this
mode is the body of the Church, the flesh of the world which
has been assumed by Christ: it is the whole of creation in the
dimensions of the Kingdom.

[22]Michelis, p. 50.
[23]See Ch. Yannaras, "Pollution of the Earth," *Christian*, vol. 3, no. 4
(1976), pp. 317-321. *Idem*, "Scholasticism and Technology," pp. 166-169.

Byzantine architecture studies and reveals this reality of
the worldly flesh of the Word, the fact of God's *kenosis* and
the "deification" of created things, the way in which by taking on our material nature, God hypostasizes our existence in
the divine life of incorruption and immortality. Like the
ascetic in his direct encounter with his body, the architect
encounters his material with the same freedom of humility
and self-abnegation; and he studies the points of resistance
and also the potentialities of nature. He looks for the inner
principle, the "reason" in matter which was in abeyance before
the incarnation but is now dynamic; that reason which connects the baseness and resistances of the natural material with
the amazing potential in that same matter to contain the
Uncontainable and give flesh to Him who is without flesh,
to be exalted into the flesh of God the Word—into the
Church.

Each Byzantine building is a eucharistic event; it is a
dynamic act whereby each individual entity joins in the
universal reality of ecclesial communion. This is a realization
of personal distinctiveness, but a realization within the framework of communion, which means the rejection of individual
emotions, individual intellectual certainty and individual
aesthetics. Every Byzantine building embodies this ascetic
rejection and self-abnegation on the part of the architect, and
consequently manifests both his personal distinctiveness and
at the same time the universal truth of the Church. As a
technical construction, each work has a revelatory personal
distinctiveness, and in this personal distinctiveness the universal truth of the Church is manifested. As Michelis writes
in a technical description which unconsciously discerns the
theological truth, Byzantine churches "are the dynamic compositions of a subjective sense, rather than the static arrange-
ments of an objective theory . . . No work of Byzantine architecture is a pure type, a model which can be repeated . . .
Each Byzantine church is an individuality, an act of emanci-
pation from the model . . . It is not really important how
precisely it fits together or how regularly it is laid out. The
walls are not always at right angles, the roofs often have
different inclines . . . the ground plans are not rectangular,

the domes are not always absolutely circular at their base, the facades are irregular and the bricks fit together haphazardly. From the point of view of our very strict requirements, a Byzantine plan is always a mistake, but an acceptable mistake—one that works . . . The whole structure is a piece of music which the virtuoso craftsman has sung in a different way each time, and always so successfully that repetition is out of the question."[24]

The character of objective asymmetry and dissimilarity in each Byzantine building is the element which above all manifests the craftsman's respect for the peculiar "reason" in the natural material. It reveals his *ascesis* and his endeavor to fit the "rational qualities" of matter into an organic unity and a harmony of reasons—to "church" matter, which means leading it to the "end" or goal of its existence, which is to constitute the flesh of God the Word.[25] The objective asymmetry and dissimilarity of each Byzantine building is simply the visible manifestation of the architect's *love* for his natural material; that love which respects and studies creation and reveals it as a means to salvation,[26] an organic factor in the communion of created and uncreated, the recapitulation of all in the loving relationship between the Father and the incarnate Word.[27]

The ancient Greek temple expresses the Greek view of the world as a given harmony and order, and consequently it

[24]Pp. 45-46.

[25]St Maximus the Confessor sees all creation, from the angels down to inanimate matter, as a unified and continuing event of *eros*, a dynamically structured "erotic" relationship, and a universal "erotic" movement which forms creation—personal and impersonal, animate and inanimate—into a "communal" sequence with an impulse turned back towards God. Inanimate matter partakes in this universal "erotic" event "according to its customary role, which is its quality." See *Scholia on the Divine Names*, PG 4, 268C-269A.

[26]Cf. John Damascene, *First Homily in Defence of the Holy Icons*, PG 94, 1245AB; critical edition by B. Kotter, vol. III, p. 89: "I shall never cease to venerate matter, through which my salvation was brought about."

[27]"The mystery of the person as an ontological 'principle' and 'cause' consists in the fact that love is able to make something unique, to give it an absolute identity and name. This is precisely what is meant by the term 'eternal life,' which, for precisely this reason, means that the person is able to raise even inanimate objects to a personal dignity and life; it requires only that they be an organic part of a relationship of love. Thus, for example,

gives reason and meaning to the actual natural environment by reducing it to relationships of proportional harmony.[28] By the same token, the Byzantine church expresses the Church's view of the world, of the world's participation in the dimensions of the life of the Kingdom. It therefore recapitulates the personal distinctiveness of both the site and the building material, summing up the mode of created order and beauty as the *locus* for the relationship between created and uncreated—as the Church. Material creation is given form: it takes the form of the flesh of the Word. The building of a Byzantine church is the body of the incarnate Word, the earthward movement of the "bowed heavens"; it shapes the incarnation into the form of a cross.

It is the Byzantine technique of constructing domes, apses and arches which provides the supreme possibility for personal and free study of the "reason" in matter. On the levels of appearance and symbolism alike, the first impression is that the domes, apses and arches enable the Byzantine architect to express tangibly the movement of the incarnation, of God's descent into the world, the movement of the "bowed heavens" ("He bowed the heavens and came down," Ps. 17:9). It is a movement which expresses the apophatic principle in the theory of theological knowledge, the principle that God's energy is the prime factor in man's knowledge of God: ". . . having known God, or rather being known of God" (Gal 4:9).[29] As Michelis writes, "In the Byzantine building, we could say that the composition begins from the top and works downwards, rather than *vice versa*.[30]

Apart from the appearance of the building and its symbolic

the whole of creation can be saved through being 'recapitulated' in the loving relationship between the Father and the Son": J. Zizioulas, "From Prosopeion to Prosopon," p. 307, n. 35.

[28]Purely by way of parenthesis, we may note here that our admiration for the monuments of ancient Greek architecture is extremely superficial if we ignore the cosmic truth they embody and isolate them from the natural environment which they seek to interpret. The beauty of the buildings on the Acropolis, for instance, is essentially impossible to understand now that modern development has destroyed its natural surroundings and changed the lines and appearance of the Attic landscape.

[29]See N. Nisiotis, *Preface to the Theory of Theological Knowledge* (Athens, 1965).

[30]P. 50.

interpretation, the technology of the domes, apses and arches is a striking study in the potentialities of the natural material, the potentialities for transforming *static* balance into a *dynamic* composition. The weight of matter is not counterpoised statically, with rationalistically calculated mechanical supports; it is transferred dynamically in the form of thrusts which are shared out, combined and annihilated reciprocally, as the apses succeed the domes and continue organically to the curved triangular tympana, the arches and the cross-vaults, to end in the decorated capitals, in a manner that is entirely imperceptible because the feeling of weight has flowed away, and the whole construction simply presents an image of a living body.

All this construction is done freely, without a mould. The Byzantines built their domes without using a form, building freely, in the void.[31] Thus the natural material loses all weight, all artificial support; the weight of matter is transformed into relationship, into a connection and communion of "reasons." The material is no longer a neutral object: it is *the product of an action,* a personal operation. We may recall here the words of St Gregory of Nyssa: "None of the things we consider attributes of the body is in itself the body; neither shape, nor color, nor weight, nor height, nor size, nor anything else that we consider as a quality; but each of these is a 'reason,' and it is the combination and union of these which becomes a body."[32]

So the body of the faithful which comes together in the church building to constitute and manifest the Church, the Kingdom of God and the new creation of grace, is not simply housed in this architectural construction, but forms *with it* a unified space of life and an event of life. The building joins the people in "celebrating" the eucharist of creation, the *anaphora* of the gifts of life to the Giver of life, forming an image of the new heavens and new earth through a dynamic "passage to the archetype." The building and the people together, the "reason" of matter harmonized with the hymn of glory which affirms human freedom, compose the universal

[31]Michelis, p. 50.
[32]*On the Soul and the Resurrection,* PG 46, 124C.

liturgy of the Church, the manifestation of Christ's body. By His incarnation Christ enthroned the whole of material creation on the throne of God: creation became the flesh of the Word, and all the world became the Church.

This reality of God who has become man, and of the world which has become the Church, is expressed in Byzantine architecture by yet another technical concept of striking genius: the introduction of the human scale into the dimensions of the building. All parts of the church are measured according to man's dimensions. The doors, windows, railings and columns are to the measure of man, and retain the same measurements regardless of the size of the building. The measurements are multiplied but not increased. Thus in Haghia Sophia, for example, the lines of arches have five openings at ground level and seven on the upper level, and the windows in the tympana of the arches multiply in successive rows so that the smallest openings correspond with largest; the space increases the higher we look, broadening out and finally breaking into infinity amidst the forty windows in the crown of the dome.[33]

In this way, the Byzantine architect succeeds in preserving as the measure of his building the "great world in miniature" of the human body, creating the living unity of a body with organic members, the reality of a whole which does not do away with the part but makes it stand out, and the reality of the part which is not lost in the whole but defines it. This organic relationship between the part and the whole, the elevation of the human measure to the dimensions of the building as a whole, is the most thrilling tangible formulation of the truth of the Church, of the relationship between the person and the totality of nature. Nature is defined by the person; it does not define the person. The Church, as a new nature of grace, is not a monolithic organization which imposes itself in an authoritative manner upon the separate individuals; it is an organic unity of persons who go to make up life as communion, and communion as a unified, living body, without vanishing in the totality of that body. The image of the Church incarnate in the Byzantine building is an image

250 THE FREEDOM OF MORALITY

of the body of the incarnate Word; it is also the space within which we see manifested the personal gifts and energies of the Comforter, and the personal, free submission of the Son to the Father's will, His participation in it, in the free "dialectic" of death and resurrection.

Byzantine architecture succeeded in conveying the image of Pentecost, the creative work of the Holy Spirit who builds the Church as flesh of the Word, which is also the flesh of the Virgin, an incarnate affirmation by man's personal freedom of the Father's pre-eternal will for the "deification" of the world. The Father "foreknows," the Word "effects," and the Spirit "perfects" the body of the Church—the created universe is "filled with the light" of the divine energy of the Trinity. In the Byzantine church building the light plays an organic role in forming the liturgical space. The brilliant natural light of the East is tamed by the position of the windows, their relatively small size and their large number. It enters the space at a slant, indirectly; it falls on the domes and apses, and "turns back on itself" to be diffused everywhere. It penetrates the marble slabs of the walls and becomes one with the colors in the icons, and folds back within the space to become "inner" light, "light of the heart," the light of the transfiguration of the created world.

It would be an immense subject to study the use of light in Byzantine architecture, the way it is totally transformed into a real "architecture of light,"[34] a tangible expression of the space in which the Holy Spirit is personally present and personally received. Gothic architecture expresses an absolute Christological interpretation of the Church as a strictly constructed body, centralized in its organization; it makes use of a unified and concrete space which leads us progressively through the aisles to the high altar. By contrast Byzantine architecture, with its interpretation of the Church as the trinitarian mode of existence, marks out a space which is concrete and yet without bounds, a space continually divided up which yet has its center everywhere. The eucharist is accomplished everywhere, in the place where each Christian is present, bearing in himself Christ and the Spirit.

[34]Olivier Clément, *Dialogues avec le Patriarche Athénagoras*, pp. 278-283.

We have attempted briefly to demonstrate the ethos expressed in both the Gothic and the Byzantine edifice—the ontological, cosmological and theological premises for the human attitude to natural material expressed in the art of these two cultures. Because of its brevity, this account inevitably presents the subject schematically, in a way that may be arbitrary and is certainly incomplete. Any attempt to draw theoretical conclusions from a work of art runs some risk of being arbitrary, since art expresses experiences and not theorems, and "understanding" it requires participation in the same experiences, not the intellectual interpretation of them.

It is certain that neither in Byzantine nor in Gothic architecture did the craftsmen set out with the intention of expressing ontological, cosmological or theological dogmas and "principles" and imprinting them on the building. But inevitably—and this is where their artistic skill lies —they do express the living experience of those "principles" and dogmas, which in their time were not abstract ideas but the life and practical spirituality of their Church, the *ethos* of their culture. If we insist here on the spiritual and cultural differences expressed by art, this is to give a few hints as to the differentiation in the ethos of technology between East and West. Today the consquences of this differentiation can no longer be exploited for sterile theological polemic or for the sake of confessional self-satisfaction, for technology has created a problem common to East and West, an insoluble crisis for our entire civilization.

The techniques of Gothic architecture on the one hand and Byzantine on the other reveal two different attitudes towards the world, two different ways of using the world. Not only do both have specific starting-points in theology and living experience, but both find specific historical realization outside the realm of art—they express an entire ethos and influence the whole life of a society. As we have said above, we discern an organic link between Gothic architecture and the progressive development of technology, its growth into an absolute, and the alienation of man in industrial societies. And we discover the technique of Byzantine architecture behind the historical realization of the social and cultural ethos of Byzantium and the Greek people under Turkish domination —a realization which never had time properly to confront the technocratic ethos of the West, but was rapidly assimilated by it.

The same differentiation in attitude towards the world, in ways of using the world and natural material, which is expressed in architectural constructions can also be studied in the technique of icon-painting—but with a much greater risk of becoming theoretical and schematic.

5. Religious "naturalism"

In recent decades, Russian theology in the European diaspora has produced some interesting examples of how the symbolism of Eastern Orthodox icons can be interpreted, indicating also how they differ from western religious painting.[35] Here we need only underline the fact that these differences are not confined to style, choice of theme or allegorical

[35]See L. Ouspensky and Vl. Lossky, *The Meaning of Icons*, tr. G. E. H. Palmer and E. Kadloubovsky (Boston, 1969; rev. ed. Crestwood, N.Y., 1982). L. Ouspensky, *Essai sur la théologie de l'icône dans l'Église Orthodoxe* (Paris, 1960; Eng. trans. Crestwood, N.Y., 1980). Paul Evdokimov, *L'art de l'icône—théologie de la beauté* (Paris, 1970). Idem, *L'Orthodoxie* (Neuchatel, 1965), pp. 216-238. G. P. Fedotov, *The Russian Religious Mind* (Cambridge, Mass., 1946). N. P. Kondakov, *The Russian Icon*, trans. G. H. Minns (Oxford, 1927). P. P. Muratov, *Les icônes russes* (Paris, 1927). One may observe that these examples represent a peculiar and probably typically Russian mentality in interpreting icons, as impressionistic as Russian iconography itself. The themes of the icon are analyzed into detailed aesthetic impressions, usually by means of reduction to geometric patterns; the aesthetic impressions are translated into ideas, and the ideas are used to express in concrete form the symbolism of the thematics, the design and the coloring. A typical example of this way of interpreting icons is the analysis of Rublev's Trinity in Paul Evdokimov's book *L'Orthodoxie*, pp. 233-238. This is a method which certainly expresses a wealth of poetic sensitivity, but often leads to schematic interpretations which fail to do justice to the immediacy and universality of the "semantics" of iconography. It is certainly characteristic that the examples used for these interpretative analyses are taken almost exclusively from the Russian iconographic tradition. The Greek icon (or "Byzantine," as we say today) displays a strenuous resistance to any intellectual approach. This is probably why the particular interest recently shown by Westerners in Orthodox iconography is confined almost entirely to Russian icons, ignoring their Greek prototypes.

symbolism; they mark a radical distinction and contrast between two views of truth and knowldge, of existence and the
world, of the incarnation of God and the salvation of man—
in short, they sum up two incompatible ontologies.

Even from the thirteenth century—a key point for our
understanding of all subsequent religious and cultural developments in the West—we can no longer speak of ecclesial
iconography in Europe, but only of religious painting. And
this means that in the western Church artistic expression ceases
to be a study and a manifestation of the Church's theology—
at least on the preconditions for theology in visual art formulated by the Seventh Ecumenical Council.

Religious art in Europe is dominated by the "naturalistic"
or, better, "photographic" representation of "sacred" persons,
places or objects. The "sacredness" of what is depicted lies
exclusively in the theme, the given meaning of the subject
matter, and the allegorical or analogical way the viewer will
interpret it. The persons, objects or places depicted are themselves those of everyday experience in dimensional space and
measurable time; they have nothing to do with the space and
time of the Kingdom, the change in mode of existence which
constitutes true life and salvation. Western religious painting
does not aspire to transcend the time-bound and ephemeral
character of the individual entity as a phenomenon, its subjection to the laws of corruption and death. In consequence,
any young woman can serve as a model for a painting of the
Mother of God, any young man can represent Christ or a
saint, and any landscape can take the place of the scene of
biblical revelation.

In western religious art, from the thirteenth century it
seems that the fundamentals of the ecclesial truth and hope
of the faithful were already definitively lost. Visual art no
longer seeks out the truth about personal existence beyond
dimensional individuality, the possibility of transforming
space and time into the immediacy of a relationship or the
realization of incorruption and immortality in the communion
of saints. The function of painting is purely decorative and
didactic—it does not serve as a revelation. It represents the
fallen world and tries to give it "religious" meaning, which

is to say emotive content, without concerning itself about the possibilities of existence and life beyond entitative individuality. The style—the use of colors, positions, figures and background—is subject to the requirements of "naturalism" and "objectivity." It seeks to convince us of the "reality" of what is depicted, and reality is understood simply as obedience to the laws of dimensional space and measurable time. And it seeks to evoke emotion "objectively"; hence the perspective, the suppleness, the background and the optical illusion become the artist's means to arouse emotion, to shock our nervous system and "uplift the soul."[36]

The purely artistic reaction to the "photographic" naturalism of the emotional religious style which began in the West with the Renaissance certainly has greater "theological" interest. It is incomparably more consistent with the existential bewilderment of western man, with the tragic *impasse* created when the truth of the person is lost. In modern western painting, there are heights of creativity which express with striking clarity the hopeless search for possibilities of form beyond "entity," the revolt against idols which refuses to make the ephemeral identification of "forms" with "essences." Ultimately they express the dissolution of forms in abstraction, the artist's attempt to spell out the truth of the world from the beginning, through completely primitive color and shape experiences.

6. The "passage" to the hypostasis of
   the person through iconography

The problem which Byzantine iconography had to face was the same as that confronting church architecture: How is it possible for natural material to manifest its "rational"

---

[36]Characteristic is the line of argument used by Calvin in rejecting images and symbols and precluding their presence in churches—even the sign of the cross. Given the premises of the western religious painting he had in mind, a painted church is nothing but "a banner erected to draw men to idolatry." Oblivious of the iconographic tradition of the undivided Church, he ridiculed the Seventh Ecumenical Council and its decrees: see *Institution de la Réligion chrétienne*, Book One, XI, §§ 12, 13, 14, 15.

potentialities, to be transfigured into flesh of the Word, of the word of life beyond space, time, corruption and death? And more specifically: How can design and color be used to depict not *nature,* the corruptible and mortal individual entities, but the *hypostasis* of persons and things,[37] that mode of existence which makes being into hypostasis in true life? Certainly, the Byzantine icon is not a creation *ex nihilo.* As in the formulation of theological truth, so also in the manifestations of her art the Church has assumed the actual historical flesh of her time, transfiguring what she has assumed into a revelation of the event of salvation, a revelation ever present and immediate "yesterday and today and forever."

The historical flesh of the Byzantine icon is the Roman art of the first centuries of the Church, or strictly speaking its Greek roots. This ancient Greek art had evolved a technique which permitted the *abstraction* of the individual and circumstantial characteristics of the person or object depicted, so as to reduce the concrete object to a direct vision of its "reason," inner principle or *essence.* The ancient Greek artist did not aim at a faithful representation of the natural prototype— an artificial reproduction of it—but at that form of depiction which makes possible a dynamic and personal view, a *conscious vision* of things.[38] Thus "the artifact, the statue, serves as a measure for the beauty of the natural prototype, and not *vice versa.*"[39] The artifact is called ἄγαλμα, a statue, because it offers the gladness and rejoicing (ἀγαλλίαση) of the true way of looking at the world; it sets out the way to look at the object *with reason,* and relates physical objects to their *rational* reality which, for the Greek, is more real than the incidental impression they create; art offers a way of seeing which interprets the world.

Ancient Greek art thus prepares the way for Byzantine

[37] Cf. the definition given by St Theodore the Studite: "When anything is depicted, it is not the nature but the hypostasis which is depicted": *Antirrheticus* 3, 34, PG 99, 405A.

[38] This observation arises out of the study by Christos Karouzos, "The Principles of Aesthetic Vision in the Fifth Century B.C.," in his book *Ancient Art* (in Greek—Athens, 1972), p. 43ff., where he defines the *conscious vision* which characterizes fifth century art, as opposed to the *subconscious vision* which has left its mark on archaic art.

[39] Karouzos, *op. cit.,* p. 51.

iconography. The Roman painting which comes between them historically is a forerunner of Byzantine icons to the extent that it preserves, albeit in decadent form, elements of continuity from ancient Greek artistic expression, while at the same time making progress in technical skill, especially in fresco painting. But although Byzantine iconography is an organic continuation of the Greek vision and interpretation of the world through artistic representation, it also represents a radical transcendence and transmutation of the fundamental characteristics of Greek art. This is because the Byzantine icon represents a cosmology and an ontology totally different from that of the ancient Greeks.

It is certainly through Greek tradition and technique that the Byzantine iconographer reaches the point of transcending the individual and incidental characteristics of the person or object depicted. This transcendence, however, does not aim to manifest the *idea* of the entity, to reduce the actual existent object to an ideal "universal." For the Byzantine iconographer, the only existential reality beyond corruption and death is the person, the dynamic transcendence of individuality which constitutes a transformation in the mode of existence. It is no longer a matter of reducing the concrete to the abstract universality of an idea which is a "metaphysical" datum, accessible to the intellect alone. At issue is the potential existing in concrete reality, in man's individual flesh and the flesh of the world, to participate in the true life of personal distinctiveness, of freedom from any natural predetermination. In the icon, the iconographer sets out the personal mode of existence which is love, communion and relationship, the only mode which forms existential distinctiveness and freedom into a fact of life and a hypostasis of life.

How is it possible, then, to use the material means of artistic expression to represent a mode of existence which does not do away with material individuality, but merely removes its existential autonomy, that is to say, the dimensional space of individual contrasts and distances, and measurable time with its progression from earlier to later? This achievement is not unrelated to the artistic talent of the great Byzantine masters. The technique of the icon—the restriction to two dimensions, the rejection of dimensional "depth" and of temporal sequence in events depicted, the use of colors, attitudes, figures and background—leads Greek "abstraction" to a remarkable level of expressiveness, in which the concrete reality operates as a *symbol* of the universal dimension of life. It is a *symbol* in the sense that it *puts together* (συμ-βάλλει) or co-ordinates and reconnects the particular experiences of personal participation in the one, universal mode of existence which is the distinctiveness of the person as dynamically fulfilled in the framework of communion and relationship.

The Byzantine icon, however, is not merely an artistic proposition, an individual achievement by the artist which is put forward as his personal participation and "symbolic" elevation to the universal. It is, properly speaking, the expression of a common attitude of life, an operation of life which the artist undertakes to depict by abstracting as far as possible the elements of his individual intervention. The Byzantines were conscious of the fact that it is the Church which paints the icon "by the hand" of the painter. Thus the technique of abstraction is not an exercise in individual skill aimed at going beyond what is concrete and contingent; it is an exercise in subjecting arbitrary individual judgment to a set iconographic type, formed from the ascetic experience of earlier teachers of the art, in harmony with the universal experience of the Church.

The subjection of the individual view to a set iconographic type applies not only to the artist, but also to the person looking at the icon. The icon does not put forward a "logically" perfected and ideal view of an entity, but *summons* us to a direct communion and relationship with what is depicted, a dynamic passage to the archetype,[40] to the hypostasis of what is depicted. And this passage requires the subjugation of individual resistances—of the sentiments, aesthetic emotions and intellectual elevation of the individual—so as to liberate the potential for *personal* relationship and participation. The set form of iconography works precisely as a starting point,

[40]"For the honor paid to the icon passes to the prototype": St Basil the Great, *On the Holy Spirit*, 18, 45, PG 32, 149C.

helping us to go beyond individual ways of looking at things and to accomplish a personal passage to the hypostasis of the things depicted, as opposed to the way they appear. This is why we say that Byzantine iconography does not "decorate" the church but has an organic, liturgical function in the polyphony of the eucharistic event, existentially elevating us to the hypostatic realization of life.

The technique of icons is incomprehensible apart from the liturgical experience of icons, the practical acceptance of their *calling* or *beauty*[41]—apart from a personal affirmation of their visual witness to the immediate presence of the whole body of the Church, living and departed, militant and triumphant, in the oneness of eucharistic life. In other words, the technique of "abstraction" in Byzantine iconography is much more than a style: it expresses and puts into practice the *ascesis* of the Church. The artist and the person looking at the icon alike are restricted by the canons of asceticism, and totally liberated by the possibilities for abstraction which this same form provides. Through these possibilities we are enabled to attain a dynamic renunciation of the individual way of seeing things and an elevation into harmony with the universal view of persons and things, that of the whole Church.

There are objective rules as to how the iconographer is to make the "background" for the icon, how he is to add the "flesh," how to achieve the highlights while keeping the background color for the "shadows," how to do the mouth and eyes and how to add the "lights" at the end. These rules are unwritten and yet absolutely precise, and are not taught theoretically but handed on from master to pupil as an experience of life and *ascesis*. As he studies his art, the pupil is guided by the teacher in the life of the Church and her truth; he fasts and practices self-abnegation, in order for his icon to be the work of the Church, not his individual contrivance— for the Church to recognize in his work the archetype of her truth. The objective rules and the established form of the icon

[41]"... as it *calls* all things to itself; hence it is also called *kallos* ('beauty') ..." Dionysius the Areopagite, *On Divine Names* IV, 7, PG 3, 701C.

subject the painter's individual view of iconographic truth, his individual idea or conception, to a view which is an event of communion. He represents reality, not as he sees it with his natural eyes, but with the aid of symbols which are models common to the Church's consciousness. "For the making of icons is not an invention of painters," says the decree of the Seventh Ecumenical Council, "but an ordinance and tradition approved by the universal Church . . . It therefore expresses the conception of the holy fathers and their tradition, not that of the painter. Only the art belongs to the painter. The regulations clearly are those of the venerable holy fathers."[42]

The paradox, from the viewpoint of anyone without experience of the Church, is that subjecting the artist to set forms of iconography does not restrict his creative inspiration and initiative; it is not a kind of "censorship" or intellectual emasculation imposed on the artist's talent and ability. On the contrary, the more he is freed from his individual aesthetic impulses, the more clearly is revealed the personal distinctiveness of his work, and the whole Church recognizes her own universal truth in what he personally has made. It is extraordinary what artistic progress there has been in Byzantine iconography, what boldness of innovation purely in terms of painting, and what a level of artistic sensitivity has distinguished the various schools and trends in iconography.

Here we should perhaps add that it is essential for the artist to have at the outset a full and detailed knowledge of and competence in "worldly" painting. It is well known that those who were trained in iconography went through long and arduous "studies" in landscape compositions and portraits before coming on to the icon. They knew very well the secrets of the art of painting, and had practiced this art with exceptional assiduity before submitting themselves to the rule of iconography. Here, as in every aspect of the Church's life, the transcendence of nature takes place not in the abstract and intellectually, but with complete faithfulness to what is natural, with real knowledge and study of the

---

[42]Acts of the Seventh Ecumenical Council, Mansi XIII, 252C; in the edition of J. Karmiris, *The Dogmatic and Symbolic Monuments of the Orthodox Catholic Church*, vol. I (Athens, 1960), p. 238f.

resistances and possibilities of nature. The transfigured creation of the Church does not represent an ontological transformation, dematerializing or spiritualizing nature, but an
existential transformation. Nature remains the same, but its
mode of existence changes. The dematerializing and spiritualizing of nature is simply an intellectual concept, existentially
realized as the "moral" imitation of an ideal prototype, and
represented in art as a schematic allegory which works by
analogy. The existential transformation of nature, however,
can only be approached in life and art through the exercise of
freedom, through the way of repentance. The achievement of
Byzantine iconography is that it avoids the danger of "conceptual idols" and remains faithful to the "identity" of
nature and the "distinctiveness" of its existential transformation: "It represents distinctiveness, but distinctiveness as likeness."[43]

The ascetic study of nature and faithfulness to it, designed
to lead us up to its existential transfiguration, appears more
clearly in the comparison between Greek (or "Byzantine")
iconography and Russian iconography—a delicate and sensitive
issue.[44]

We have mentioned the existence of a rule in Orthodox
iconography. The use of this rule defines the scope of the
artist's obedience, the distinction between his personal approach and the experience of the Church; and while it subjugates the individual view, it brings out personal universality
without ending in impersonal formalism.

Russian iconography does not always escape the temptation
to theoretical formalism, to schematic "style." Looking at a
Russian Orthodox icon, what one finds very often is not proof
of the existential transfiguration of nature but rather the
idea of transfiguration, presented in a schematic and orna-
mental way. Formalization replaces faithfulness to nature,
and tends to aid the *impression* that nature is spiritualized
and dematerialized. The folds of the clothing do not corre-

[43]See Epiphanius, *Against Heresies* 72, 10, PG 42, 396C.
[44]This distinction was first drawn to my attention by the artist Andreas
Fokas. I am also indebted to him for other valuable observations which have
improved my attempts at interpretation.

spond to a real body underneath, and the positions and movements of the bodies are not natural but geometrically formal;[45] the lighting is diffused, almost blending in with the color, so as to give the *impression* once again that matter has its own light. It is hard to describe these real differences in words, but they become apparent when we compare a Russian and a Greek icon.

This distinction makes Russian iconography more easily accessible to modern western man; it corresponds to the way the European, through his own tradition, understands abstraction as a way of making things spiritual and non-material. Nor is this attitude unrelated to other peculiar features of Russian church life and theology, such as the baroque style which prevailed in Russian church architecture, the way liturgical music was taken over wholesale by the anthropocentric sentimentality of western "harmony," or the "sophiological" tendencies Russian theology, so akin to western mysticism.

7. The last hope

We started with the question: How does the problem of technical skill, of technology, present itself, and what ethos is expressed by technique or technology in the field of liturgical art? And we have tried to seek in church architecture and iconography the particular attitude of life or ethos which is capable of transforming the application of technology into a liturgical and eucharistic action, of making our relationship with matter once again a communion and a personal fulfilment. We cannot go further than a semantic description of the conditions of this attitude, this specific ethos, without a danger of producing a formal deontology.

There is no one theory to specify how the application of technology is to be transfigured into a communal event and a potential for man's existential fulfilment. There is, however, a dynamic starting-point for this transformation of life and use of the world. This is the eucharistic synaxis, the com-

[45]See Paul Evdokimov, *L'art de l'icône—théologie de la beauté*, pp. 188-189, 210. *Idem, L'Orthodoxie*, pp. 227-228.

munal realization of life and art in the parish and the diocese. No political program, however "efficient," no social ethic however radical, and no method of organizing the populace into "nuclei" for revolutionary change, would ever be able to bring about that transformation of life which is dynamically accomplished by the eucharistic community, or to lead us to a solution of the extreme existential problems which technocracy today has created.

The danger of nuclear annihilation, the lunacy of armaments, the international growth of systems and mechanisms for oppressing and alienating man, the exhaustion of the planet's natural resources, pollution of the sea and the atmosphere, the attempt to repress or forget the thought of death in a hysteria of consumer greed and trade in pleasure—all these, and a host of other nightmarish syndromes, form the world which today greets every infant who becomes a godchild of the Church through holy baptism. And in the face of this world, all we Christians seem like complete infants, feeble and powerless to exert the slightest influence over the course of human history and the fate of our planet. This is perhaps because, through the historical vicissitudes of heretical distortions of our truth—distortions which lie at the root of the present cultural impasse—we seem to have lost our understanding of the manner in which our weakness and powerlessness "perfects" the transfiguring power of the Church. Our power is "hidden" in the grain of wheat and the tiny mustard seed, in the mysterious dynamism of the leaven lost in the dead lump of the world—in the eucharistic hypostasis of our communal body.

The eucharistic community, the resuscitation of our eucharistic self-awareness and identity, the nucleus of the parish and the diocese—these are our "revolutionary" organization, our radical "policy," our ethic of "overthrowing the establishment": these are our hope, the message of good tidings which we bring. And this hope will "overcome the world": it will move the mountains of technocracy which stifle us. The fact that the world is being stifled by technocracy today is the fated outcome of the great historical adventure of western Christianity, of the divisions, the heresies and the distortions of the Church's truth. So equally the way out of the impasse of technocracy is not unconnected with a return to the dynamic truth of the one and only Church. Men's thirst for life has its concrete historical answer in the incarnation of Christ, in the one catholic eucharist. And the one catholic eucharist means giving absolute priority to the ontological truth of the person, freeing life from the centralized totalitarianism of objective authority, and spelling out the truth of the world through the language and art of the icon. Even just these three triumphs over heresy are enough to move the stifling mountains of technocracy. The field in which this triumph takes place is the local eucharistic community, the parish or diocese; only there can we do battle with the impasse of technocracy. And the more sincere our search for life while the idols of life collapse around us, the more certain it is that we shall meet the incarnate answer to man's thirst—the eucharistic fulfilment of true life.

It has taken about nine centuries to move from the *filioque*, "primacy," "infallibility," and loss of the truth of the person to the present unconcealed and general impasse created by the western way of life. Time is very relative, and no one can say when and through what kinds of historical and cultural development people will perhaps realize that escape from this impasse is a possibility. When the words of these pages are wiped from human memory and all of us have disappeared under the earth, the succession of generations, "all the generations" who make up the Church, will still be continuing to bring about the coming of the Kingdom of God within the eucharistic "leaven." However far off in time, the escape from heresy is a contemporary event—not because the historical scope of western civilization in its impasse is even now limited, but because such is the present, eschatological truth of the Church, hidden within the eucharistic "leaven."

In a new age yet to come, the eucharistic realization of the Kingdom will be embodied once again in dynamic forms of social and cultural life, without doing away with the adventure of freedom and sin, because this communal dynamism is the *nature* of the Church, the organic consequence of her life.

THE FREEDOM OF MORALITY

This new age will spell out once again, in humility, the truth of the world, the reason in things and the meaning of history: it will once again fashion in the icon the transfigured face of man.

Additional note: Given the limited possibilities of conceptual distinctions, it is difficult to give a clear explanation of the difference between the "transfiguration" of natural material and its "dematerialization." By the word "transfiguration" we are attempting to express the result of *ascesis*, of man's struggle to reveal the truth of matter, the potentiality in the created world for participaion in true life—the possibility for the human body, and man's construction material and tools, to form a communion; to serve and manifest the "common reason" in ascetic experience, the experience of personal distinctiveness and freedom. On the other hand, by the term "dematerialization" we mean the impression matter gives us when it is tamed by the power of the mind and will; when the hypostatic reality of matter goes almost unnoticed, since the natural matter has been absolutely subjugated to the inspiration of the craftsman, to the meaning he wants the work to serve, and the impression it is meant to make on the spectator. Gothic architecture definitely gives a sense of dematerialized space, an impression of earth raised up to heaven. It is precisely the overpowering violence of the craftsman's frequently outstanding genius which takes the natural material and subjects it to the demands of the given aim and meaning. In a way that parallels this precisely, the whole of scholastic theology is a brilliant intellectual "dematerialization" of the truth of the Church; it subjugates the "common speech" of the experience of salvation to the interests of individual intellectual certainty and objective support for the truths of the Church. None of this is meant to belittle either the "scientific" genius of the scholastics or the artistic genius embodied in Gothic buildings. No one denies that creations such as Notre Dame in Paris and the Chartres Cathedral are supreme achievements of human art. But as we recognize the aesthetic feat, so we ought also to make a distinction between the ethos and attitude to the natural material expressed by this art on the one hand, and that expressed by other forms of art, which embody man's struggle for the truth of matter and the world, a struggle with the natural material in order to reveal its *personal* dimension— a struggle and an ascetic effort to bring about the *communal* event of personal freedom and distinctiveness.

EPILOGUE

The Morality of Freedom

The bounds of the Church's ethos, the Church's morality,
are those of personal freedom, concrete and yet unlimited;
they are the universal bounds of life in the only way it can
truly be realised, which is hypostatic and personal.

This truth, while being fundamental, is also the hardest
of all to understand. We humans persist in transfering the
bounds of life to unreal spheres. We make idols of life, and
also of the evil which threatens life; we give artificial substance to imaginary threats, and objectify sin outside the
sphere in which it is actually committed, that of personal
freedom. We keep looking for radical methods and more
effective ethical systems, in the belief that we are fighting
evil in its historical, social, cultural and political manifestations. We forget or ignore the fact that these manifestations
of evil reveal our existential adventure, and that the game
of living is played exclusively within the bounds of personal
life.

This does not mean to say that the resultant effects of our
personal sins cannot create "situations" of evil, gears in the
mechanism for tormenting man which are given autonomy by
our freedom. But the problem of morality is from beginning
to end a problem of discrimination between reality and
utopia, between true and artificial realization of life. For man
can spend his whole life fighting objective "situations" of
slavery while the gears of the subjugation and alienation of
life go on working inside him, constantly reproducing torture.
In the same way, he can shut himself up in the hardened shell

265

of an individual "moralism" which deprives him of life and alienates him from it just as much as do the autonomous mechanisms of oppression.

The Church's criteria for human morality preclude the familiar and insoluble dilemma whether to start from the moral improvement of the individual or from a moral improvement in the conditions of corporate life. The dilemma is misconceived because it is based on a purely phenomenological and polarized concept of life, with the individual as the unit of life and the social whole as an aggregate of the unit parts. The Church, by contrast, sees the universal realization of life in the framework of personal existence, and personal existence as a communal, not an individual event. For the same reason, when existential failure and sin are overcome in the personal life of just one man the result is always a communal event of remarkable breadth and indeterminable dynamism.[1] But this change from a quantitative to a qualitative evaluation of the possibilities of life is not simply a different way of viewing the problem of morality. It is a different attitude of life which presupposes the existential transformation of man, that is to say, *repentance,* the dynamic revision of our aims in life.

The truth of the person distinguishes the life of the Church and the ethos of the Church from any other concept of ethics. In contrast with every other code of ethics, the Church does not seek to safeguard the individual, either in isolation or collectively; she does not aim at individual security, either transient or eternal. She asks man to reject his individuality,

[1]In the language of art, so much clearer than that of conceptual definitions, Solzhenitsyn has shown in his story "Matriona's House" how the true man who preserves the authenticity of life as love and self-offering is a reality of salvation for all of us: he saves a village or a town or a whole country, or indeed the entire world. This is the truth of the human person as preserved by the Orthodox Church's tradition and life. The person means the possibility of summing up the whole, the salvation of all in the person of the one, the manifestation of our common truth in the existence of the prophet and the martyr. So the man who "dies" as an individual in order to live out total love and self-offering sums up in his person the universal truth of man, an all-powerful truth. Such a man is a "second government" for his country, as Solzhenitsyn said and proved. Living in Russia, he himself embodied the dynamic greatness of life which the Kremlin had to fear, after fifty years of persecution and brainwashing.

to "lose" his soul. For this loss is the salvation of man, the existential realization of true life, of personal distinctiveness and freedom. It is a language of paradox. What, then, is the "social ethic" of the Church, the concrete result towards which she tries to lead mankind, the "program" she promises? It is the total responsibility of each human being for the universal realization of life within the unlimited scope of personal existence and freedom. Ecclesial man *saves* in his own person the universal possibilities of life, in the same way as a gifted poet saves in his own person the universal potentialities of poetry. And through what "plan of action" does the Church lead us to this attainment? Certainly not with abstract theories and intellectual analyses, but by a road equally accessible to the profound thinker and the illiterate: by physical acts of asceticism, practical rejection of individuality, fasting, continence, freedom from the cares of the consumer, participation of the body in prayer and the labor of serving others. From this path begins the ascent to freedom, to true communion. Outside this bodily, practical realization of life, no theory or ideology can free man from his subservience to natural necessity, his confinement in existential individuality. Any ethical or social theory which is not translated into practice and does not involve bodily renunciation of the "soul" or ego, produces nothing but shame.[2]

"When you enter upon the path of righteousness, then you will cleave to freedom in everything," says St Isaac the Syrian.[3] The way of righteousness means works of righteousness:[4] man's practical refusal to *wrong* his nature, endowed as it is with the potential for personal distinctiveness and freedom, and equally to *be wronged* by the "unnatural," impersonal demands of his nature in its rebellion. There is a double challenge, a double trial. "This flesh which is mine and yet not mine, my dear enemy," as St John of the Ladder

---

[2]"The word which comes from action is a fund of hope; and wisdom which is idle is a deposit of shame...Whatever virtue does not bring with it bodily toil, consider it a soulless abortion." St Isaac the Syrian, *Mystic Treatises* 1, p. 7, and 56, p. 229.

[3]*Logos* 23, p. 91.

[4]"These are the works of righteousness: fasting, charity, vigils, sanctification and the other works performed by the body": *Logos* 62, p. 254.

says.[5] When man gains empirical awareness of this reality, it means that he has already embarked on the great adventure to win unbounded freedom "in everything."

Such a level of existential requirements is surely irreconcilable with utilitarian moralizing. Over the centuries we have acquired a great facility for turning ethics and religion to the convenience of individual living. Social *mores* and the character of individuals must be "improved"—this is usually where ethics ends, and often religion also. And yet for the sake of a political dream, a dangerous exploration on earth or in space or a new conquest of science, we take virtually for granted people's readiness to sacrifice even individual survival. Ultimate self-denial for ends such as these has, to our eyes, a more direct connection with the realization and the service of life than does the moral security of the individual. We have to wrench ourselves free of the individual character of ethics, which seems so obvious, in order to understand that universal realization of the possibilities of life, in the limitless bounds of personal existence, presupposes the same readiness for self-denial, the voluntary loss of the "soul" or ego.

The ethos of freedom promised by the Church cannot be reconciled with hopes of existential self-sufficiency, security or improvements in the life of the individual. It is an ethos of hopelessness and *despair* as far as concerns the life offered by personal survival. And yet this despair constitutes the greatest possible dynamism in personal life, the power of freedom "in everything." St Isaac's words, though paradoxical, are very true: "There is nothing more potent than despair. Despair does not know how to be defeated by anything . . . When man in his own intellect cuts hope out of his life, nothing can be more courageous." What binds the man who has renounced individual survival, and what can threaten him? "Every sorrow that occurs is less than death. And he has of himself bowed down to accept death."[6] From then on, this "nonexistent" man starts to accept the gifts of existence "in amazement." "And striving, fear, trouble and toil in all

[5]*Ladder,* step 15, PG 88, 885D.
[6]*Logos* 19, p. 73.

things pass from him. And he is exalted above nature, and attains love."[7]

But who are we talking about?—our practical, "statistical" mentality counters once again. About a few "mystics," the anchorites of the desert? No: we are talking about the ethos of freedom attainable by every man, about the possibility of a culture which serves man's personal distinctiveness, not his subjection to the tyranny of impersonal recipes for "happiness." It is simply that such an ethos and such a culture are achieved primarily through the body, through the natural hypostasis of life, and not through the intellect—they presuppose "crucifixion of the body," not a utopian "exaltation of the mind." Through physical self-denial, the mind has to submit to the contest of love. The arrogance of the intellect has to submit to freedom from the ego—"the intellect, swift-flying bird and most impudent."[8] Why is the intellect a bird? Because of the swiftness, ease and impudence with which it transfers life to unreal spheres. "For its habitual attitude and its thoughts and all its subtlety and its tortuous methods become a great restraint."[9]

The most direct language for describing the ethos of ecclesial life is that of physical action. What is perfect love? "Abba Agathon said, I wanted to find a leper, and give him my own body and take his. That is perfect love."[10] We live in a world where planned living is increasingly replacing the immediacy of life, where freedom is sought among the objective premises of corporate existence; a world where the individual intellect is the strongest weapon for survival, and individual preference the only criterion for happiness. In such a world, the witness of the ecclesial ethos looks like a kind of "anarchist theory" to overthrow established customs, in the way it concentrates the universality of life once again in the sphere of personal freedom, and personal freedom in the asceticism of bodily self-denial. Yet this "anarchic" transference of the axis of life to the sphere of the truth of the

---

[7]*Logos* 18, p. 66.
[8]*Logos* 31, p. 134.
[9]*Logos* 19, p. 69.
[10]*Letter* 4, p. 374; cf. PG 65, 116C.

person is the only humane, reassuring response to our insatiable thirst for the immediacy of life and freedom, although it certainly does overthrow "efficient" and rigid structures, and also programs for "general happiness." So in the physical action of asceticism, we are spelling out in the language of the desert our resistance to the individualistic society of technocracy and consumerism which alienates our existence.

The message of the desert is not physical asceticism as an individual exercise for the will; it is a practical way of relating natural, mortal life to Christ's mode of existence, which is man's only real and substantial possibility of life. Physical works of asceticism are a crucifixion with Christ, a submission to the Father's will, and a resurrection with Christ into life-giving, filial communion with the Father. Through Christ our asceticism is brought to the Father, and thus every stage and every moment of asceticism is an invocation of the name of Christ. In the tradition of the desert this invocation is not an intellectual recourse, unconnected with man's body, but an uninterrupted recollection of the name of Christ, a "single-phrased prayer" blended with the rhythm of the body's breathing. To reach such ceaseless universal communion, the road of asceticism is long and arduous. But the invocation of the name of Christ, the repetition of the "prayer" bequeathed to us by the experience of the desert, at any moment of the day or night, is a seed of life in man's heart; it waters the desert in which we live with the springs of true life.

This invocation is able to water and bring to life the cosmopolitan desert of modern living, to give an immediate *taste* of God amidst the ignorance on which our prosperity is grounded. The prerequisite for prayer of the heart, beseeching Christ's mercy, is that man should be humbled, even involuntarily. And today—more or less involuntarily—this humiliation is seared on our bodies and our souls: it is the bankruptcy of our civilization, the tragedy of man's rebellious and unsatisfied thirst for existential self-sufficiency and autonomous pleasure. If we can discern and recognize the deprivation of life in our individual lives, honestly and without compromises that gloss it over, then this is the first and crucial step towards letting the invocation of Christ's name work within us, as an event of life and a potential for existential gifts. Certainly man has to pass through many falls and crushing defeats, through humiliations and suffering and repeated despair, in order to reach that ethos of "innocence" which characterizes the mature, and which permits the vision of things unseen.

This book has nothing more to offer on the large subject of the freedom of morality. I would only ask of the reader who has had the love and patience to journey with me thus far that we might end by reading together some excerpts from the wisdom of the desert, a few words from St Isaac the Syrian; that together we might feel our way into another language which may bring us onto the true road that leads to the freedom of morality:

To him who knows himself, knowledge of all things is given. For knowing oneself is the fulfilment of the knowledge of all things.

Forsake small things to find what is precious.

Let him who appears wise in this world become a fool, that he may become wise.

This is love of wisdom: that even in the most insignificant and trivial things that happen to a man, he is always vigilant.

It is better for you to free yourself from the bond of sin than to free slaves from slavery.

It is better to make peace with your own soul than to pacify those who are at variance by your teaching.

It is better for a man to purify himself for God than to speak of God as a theologian.

It is better for you to be slow of tongue, yet full of knowledge and experienced, rather than to pour forth a flood of teaching because you are sharp of mind.

Love stillness more than filling the hungry in the world, or bringing many nations to the worship of God.

It is better for you to be anxious about raising up your soul from the passions than to raise the dead. He who perceives his own sins is greater than he who raises the dead by his prayer.

He who sighs over his soul for one hour is greater than he who benefits the whole world by his contemplation.

He who is accounted worthy to see himself is greater than he who is accounted worthy to see angels.

Love sinners, and do not despise them for their faults. Remember that you partake in an earthly nature, and do good to all. Let your manner be always courteous and respectful to all. For love does not know how to be angry or lose its temper or to find fault with anyone out of passion.

Do not reprove anyone for any transgression, but in all things consider yourself responsible and the cause of the sin.

Avoid laying down the law, as you would flee from an untamed lion. Do not join in this with the children of the Church, nor with outsiders.

Shun impudence in speech as you would death; and beware of idle talk, but speak only what is necessary; and content yourself with poor clothing for the needs of the body. Partake of everything in small quantities, and do not despise some things while choosing others and desiring to fill your belly with them. For discretion is the greatest of all the virtues.

Be subject to all in every good work, except to those who love possessions or money.

Do not resist anyone on any matter; do not fight, do not lie, do not swear. Be despised, and do not despise. Be wronged, and do not do wrong. It is better to endure the destruction of bodily things together with the body itself, than to suffer harm in anything that concerns the soul.

When you approach God in prayer, become in your thoughts as an ant, as the creeping things on the earth or as a lisping child. And do not speak anything in knowledge before God, but draw near to Him with the mind of an infant, that you may be accounted worthy of His fatherly providence. For it has been said, "The Lord preserveth infants."

Do not distinguish rich from poor, and do not try to find out who is worthy and who is unworthy. Let all men stand before you equal in good.

There is no way that divine love can be stirred in the soul, if the passions are not conquered. If someone says that he has not conquered the passions and yet loves to love God, then I do not know what he means.

When does a man know that his heart has attained purity? When he considers all men good, and no man seems to him impure or profane, then he is truly pure in heart.

If you do not have stillness in your heart, at least be still in your tongue. And if you cannot keep your thought disciplined, then at least discipline your senses. And if you are not alone in your mind, then at least be alone in your body. And if you can do nothing with your body, at least be grieved in your mind. And if you cannot fast for two days on end, at least fast till evening. And if you cannot wait till evening, at least take care not to eat your fill. If you cannot show mercy, speak as a sinner. You are not a peacemaker; do not be a troublemaker. You are not zealous; be at least resolute in your mind.

Strive to enter the treasury within you, and you will see the heavenly treasury; for the two are one and the same. By entering one, you will see both. The ladder to that kingdom is within you, hidden in your soul.

It is like a mother teaching her little son to walk, moving away and calling him; and when he comes towards his mother and starts to shake, and to fall over because his feet and legs are soft and tender, his mother runs and picks him up in her arms. This is how God's grace carries and teaches men, those who have given themselves with purity and simplicity into the hands of their Maker, and those who with all their heart have renounced the world and come after Him.

Lord my God, You will lighten my darkness.

Christ, fulness of truth, let Your truth rise in our hearts. And according to Your will, may we know how to walk in Your way.

Lord, fill my heart with eternal life.

You are mighty, Lord, and Yours is the contest. Fight and prevail in it, Lord, for our sake.

According to Your will, Lord, so let it be with me.

Grant me, Lord, to hate my life for the sake of the life which is in You.

In truth, Lord, if we are not humbled, You do not cease to humble us.

Grant Lord, that I may be truly dead to all contact with this age.

Grant me to know You and love You, Lord, not with the knowledge that lies in dispersal of the mind and that comes of study; but count me worthy of that knowledge in which the mind contemplates You, and glorifies Your nature in the contemplation which steals perception of the world from the intellect. Place in me an increase of Your love, that drawn by my desire for You I may depart from this world. Stir within me an understanding of Your humility with which You went about in the world, in the tabernacle which You put on from our members through the mediation of the holy Virgin: that in this constant and ever-present remembrance, I may accept with pleasure the humiliation of my nature.

Index

275